The Politics of Housing in (Post)colonial Africa

The Politics of Housing in (Post)colonial Africa

Accommodating Workers and Urban Residents

Edited by
Martina Barker-Ciganikova, Kirsten Rüther,
Daniela Waldburger, Carl-Philipp Bodenstein

This publication was funded by the Austrian Science Fund (FWF), project number P29566-G28, and will be put into open access under Creative Commons License 4.0 CC-BY-NC.

Der Wissenschaftsfonds.

ISBN 978-3-11-077702-4
e-ISBN (PDF) 978-3-11-060118-3
e-ISBN (EPUP) 978-3-11-059873-5
DOI https://doi.org/10.1515/9783110601183

This work is licensed under a Creative Commons Attribution-NonCommercial 4.0 International License. For details go to: https://creativecommons.org/licenses/by-nc/4.0/.

Library of Congress Control Number: 2020930397

Bibliographic information published by the Deutsche Nationalbibliothek
The Deutsche Nationalbibliothek lists this publication in the Deutsche Nationalbibliografie; detailed bibliographic data are available in the Internet at http://dnb.dnb.de.

© 2021 Walter de Gruyter GmbH, Berlin/Boston
This volume is text- and page-identical with the hardback published in 2020.
Cover Image: Carl-Philipp Bodenstein
Typesetting: Integra Software Services Pvt. Ltd.
Printing and binding: CPI books GmbH, Leck

www.degruyter.com
www.africanminds.org.za

Contents

List of Illustrations —— VII

Martina Barker-Ciganikova
1　Introduction —— 1

Kirsten Rüther
2　The Rule of Rent: The State, Employers and the Becoming Urban Dweller in Northern Rhodesia Acting Across a Societal Field of Force, c. 1948–1962 —— 31

Sofie Boonen and Johan Lagae
3　Ruashi, a Pessac in Congo? On the Design, Inhabitation, and Transformation of a 1950s Neighborhood in Lubumbashi, Democratic Republic of the Congo —— 66

Martina Kopf
4　At Home with Nairobi's Working Poor: Reading Meja Mwangi's Urban Novels —— 98

Donatien Dibwe dia Mwembu
5　La problématique de l'habitat dans la ville de Lubumbashi (Elisabethville), province du Katanga, 1910–1960 —— 121

Daniela Waldburger
6　House, Home, Health and Hygiene – Social Engineering of Workers in Elisabethville/ Lubumbashi (1940s to 1960s) Through the Lens of Language Usage —— 141

Ambe Njoh and Liora Bigon
7　Spatio-physical Power and Social Control Strategies of the Colonial State in Africa: The Case of CDC Workers' Camps in Cameroon —— 167

Nicholas Sungura and Marlene Wagner in discussion with Martina Barker-Ciganikova and Kirsten Rüther
8 Concrete Does not Cry: Interdisciplinary Reflections on and Beyond Housing —— 185

Contributors —— 217

Index —— 221

List of Illustrations

Figure 3.1	Cover of a theme issue of the Belgian architectural journal *Rythme*, devoted to the work of the *Office des Cités Africaines*, issue #30, 1960 —— 71
Figure 3.2	"Elisabethville. Emplacement des cites indigènes." Map showing the spatial organization of Lubumbashi with: in the middle the "European city," to the south, the two "native town" of Kamalondo and Kenya (the third one, Katuba, not existing then), to the west, along the road to Kipushi, the mining camp of the Union Minière (here indicated as a "cité indigène") and, to the north-east, the OCA neighborhood of Ruashi —— 73
Figure 3.3	Building with the *Système Grévisse* in Lubumbashi —— 74
Figure 3.4a	"Ruashi/Elisabethville. Plan general d'aménagement." Overall masterplan for the Ruashi-neighborhood, Office des Cités Africaines, 1959 —— 77
Figure 3.4b	Scheme of the division of the Ruashi neighborhood, designed for around 32,000 inhabitants, distributed into five sections of about 6,000 inhabitants each —— 78
Figure 3.5	Fragment of the plan of the Ruashi neighborhood, indicating the public facilities and the main road infrastructure with the characteristic dead end streets —— 78
Figure 3.6	The central market of Ruashi, designed by OCA architect J. Castel-Branco, ca. 1959 —— 79
Figure 3.7	Aerial photograph of the Ruashi neighborhood anno 2010, with an overlay of those fragments of the original masterplan, indicating those parts which were executed according to the initial design —— 81
Figure 3.8a	Plan of the ground floor of the *maison extensible*-type, with living unit, kitchen, one bedroom and sanitary facilities —— 83
Figure 3.8b	Plan of the first floor of the *maison extensible*-type with two double bedrooms and two single bedrooms —— 83
Figure 3.9	Two-story OCA houses erected in the "experimental site" in the *Kamalondo* neighborhood, situation anno 2010 —— 84
Figure 3.10	Architectural drawing of a single-story OCA house for Elisabethville/Lubumbashi, type B, 1954 —— 86
Figure 3.11a	Two-story housing with shops for commercial activities on the ground floor. Notice the informal infrastructure for selling food in the front, situation late 1950s —— 87
Figure 3.11b	Two-story housing with shops for commercial activities on the ground floor and some storage facilities in the back. Notice the graffiti-like inscription *fantôme* ("ghost") on the side façade on the right, situation late 1950s —— 87
Figure 3.12	Enclosures in various materials in front of two-story houses with commercial shops on the ground floor, situation anno 2006 —— 88
Figure 3.13	Transformation of an OCA house with an extra room added to the front, situation anno 2010 —— 90

Open Access. © 2020 Martina Barker-Ciganikova et al., published by De Gruyter. This work is licensed under a Creative Commons Attribution-NonCommercial 4.0 International License.
https://doi.org/10.1515/9783110601183-203

Figure 3.14	Transformation of an OCA house with an additional facility added to the back side —— 90
Figure 5.1	Carte de la ville d'Elisabethville (Lubumbashi) en 1960 —— 122
Figure 7.1	A new CDC camp under construction: laborer camps. Notice the well-aligned buildings. —— 174
Figure 7.2	Typical housing unit for a ranking low-income employee, Moliwe —— 174
Figure 7.3	Intermediate Staff Quarters, Moliwe —— 175
Figure 7.4	Typical house for a senior level employee at CDC —— 175
Figure 7.5	Communal bucket toilet, CDC Camp, Moliwe (notice the bucket-holding compartments at the base of the building) —— 176
Figure 7.6	CDC Manager's House atop a hill, Moliwe —— 177
Figure 7.7	Moliwe Camp exemplifies spatial isolation —— 178

Martina Barker-Ciganikova
1 Introduction

Housing matters. That, however, is not the only – although the simplest – answer to the question of why a volume of collected contributions on housing in colonial and postcolonial Africa is of imminent importance. Housing matters because, as a multifaceted process in itself, it helps us understand and analyze more complex developments and transformation processes that make societies reflect about themselves. Using housing as a lens, an endeavor we undertake in this volume, means achieving insights into how seemingly insignificant everyday struggles and experiences influenced and shaped such large questions as the reformulation of policies and ideologies. Housing initiatives and shifts in housing programs have always been embedded in broader colonial and postcolonial approaches to labor, health, and urban planning, which themselves have been entrenched in the all-embracing (post)colonial ideology of trusteeship and later modernity.

We, the editors of this volume, conceive of housing not only as a physical space but also as a network of social, cultural, and legal relationships, a series of interactions and activities between various players each of whom cultivates their respective interests. Housing is construed of as an arena of contestation, used by all involved players as a means to put forward their particular views and have them challenge each other. The outcomes of these confrontations vary and encompass transfigurations, adaptations, hybridizations, appropriations or the re-imagining of proposed plans and policies.[1] After the Second World War, the colonial state, wished to legitimate its rule by showing that it would stress aspects of welfare and development, and controlled "emancipation" and involvement of colonial subjects in the exercise of rule. For urban settings, this entailed specific consequences. Employers – a crucial group of players in housing provision – in many countries wished to discipline laborers and their families and to tie an emerging "labor aristocracy" to paternalistically structured capitalism. Workers, in turn, had to decide whether they preferred to live in an environment where access to the infrastructures and commodities of modernity was offered through housing or whether they wished to take up residence in less circumscribed but materially disadvantaged township settings.

Housing thus unfolds in its multiplicity. It refers to a complex living environment encompassing a series of varying aspects, such as kinship and community

---

[1] See, for instance, Jennifer Robinson, "Global and World Cities: A View from off the Map," *International Journal of Urban and Regional Research* 26 (2002).

networking, provision of social services amongst neighbors, a site of production of informal sector goods, services, and income-generation activities more generally.[2] Housing, in some instances, incorporates a service (in creating a shelter) while in others it amounts to a socioeconomic asset generating wealth and improved livelihoods.[3] What housing means and how one conceives of housing is highly context-specific and changes not only within a given time and space setting but also depending on composition and on the set of involved players. As a result, the (metropolitan) planners' ideas and intentions of regulating people's lives often clashed with residents' preferences and understandings of housing as a place of belonging, community cohesion and identity or as a space that provides social benefits.[4] On some occasions, everyday realities determined how housing policies were reshaped; on others, policies changed but realities remained the same.[5] Housing as an everyday practice often collided not only with the imposed policies but also with the lack of financial means at the disposal of those who resided and dwelled and those who searched for houses, homes, and accommodation.

The provision of housing is an ambiguous matter full of friction as it reflects the constantly changing relations between the metropolis, the colonial state, local administration, employers, and society. As a result, it sheds light on how colonial policies, social service delivery, migration, economic growth and other issues of societal transformation intersected over a prolonged period of time. The intersections are also expressed via multiple interactions and changing relations between the involved players at different levels including metropolitan and central governments, local administration, municipalities, government and private employers, experts of architecture, planning and construction, landlords, and tenants. The relationships within the networks were by far not bipolar; they were rather multifaceted as conflicts among actors played out according to their individual interests, motivations, strategies, and goals. As Rüther suggests in her contribution in this volume, in order to better grasp the heterogeneous and intersecting perspectives of different players as

---

[2] Alan Gilbert, "Home Enterprises in Poor Urban Settlements: Constraints, Potentials, and Policy Options," *Regional Development Dialogue* 9 (1988). Abdi Kusow, "The Role of Shelter in Generating Income Opportunities for Poor Women in the Third World," in *Shelter, Women and Development*, ed. Hemalata C. Dandekar (Michigan: George Wahr, 1993). Graham Tipple, "The Need for New Urban Housing in Sub-Saharan Africa: Problem or Opportunity," *African Affairs* 93 (1994).
[3] Robinson, "Global and World Cities."
[4] Karol Boudreaux, "Urbanization and Informality in Africa's Housing Markets," *Institute of Economic Affairs* 28 (2008): 21.
[5] Richard Harris, "From Trusteeship to Development: How Class and Gender Complicated Kenya's Housing Policy, 1939–1963," *Journal of Historical Geography* 34 (2008).

well as the processes of contestation, it is useful to imagine all actors positioned in a so-called "societal field of force." This socio-spatial understanding of housing, its politics, and its provision enables us to explore how power and rule were enacted and shifted over time. It reminds us that the equilibrium of forces had to be rebalanced carefully after each perturbation, as none of the actors was able to make any move in isolation.

Conception of the Idea

The present volume was born out of the workshop "Studying Housing in Interdisciplinary Perspectives," which we organized in November 2017 at the Department of African Studies of the University of Vienna within the framework of our three-year research project on employment-tied housing in (post)colonial Africa.[6] Some of the chapters are revised papers presented during the workshop, while others, in particular those written by members of our research team, are based on a first sway of field research conducted in the United Kingdom, Belgium, Lubumbashi (Democratic Republic of Congo), Livingstone and Lusaka (Zambia), Thika and Nairobi (Kenya). The contributors to this volume draw on a rich variety of primary and archival sources including official colonial reports and dispatches, manifold correspondence and records such as minutes and memoranda, statistical surveys, company-owned propaganda publications, newspapers clippings, and many others. The multitude and heterogeneity of these materials reveal friction and are not easily woven into an all-too-cozy master narrative. The analyses benefit from that friction and help us keep in mind that there are always multiple ways of assessing housing dynamics.

Housing has many more dimensions and facets than we originally imagined. The fruitful discussions during the workshop revealed how diverse our conception of housing was: a discourse, a constellation of social relations, a tool of self- and class-assertion, an attempt to counter established patterns of mobility and to exercise closer surveillance, a response designed by the metropolis, or local settler government to deal with the threat posed by social unrest, a promise, an unfulfilled

---

[6] The project "Employment-tied Housing in Post-Colonial Africa: Language, Agency and Governance in Three Housing Projects in Kenya, Zambia and the Democratic Republic of Congo, c. 1940s to 1970s" is financed by the Austrian Science Fund (FWF project no. P29566-G28). We are a team of four: Kirsten Rüther, our principal investigator; Martina Barker-Ciganikova, post-doc researcher; Daniela Waldburger, post-doc researcher; and Carl-Philipp Bodenstein, pre-doc researcher. For more information see housing.univie.ac.at.

dream, a negotiation process, and almost always a means to achieve other ends. Against this backdrop, Carole Rakodi offers one possible definition encompassing the multifacetedness of housing: "Houses are not merely physical artefacts with practical functions and economic value. They also provide people with a sense of their own worth, enhance their sense of belonging, and empower them to act."[7] Hence we wondered whether housing really was a "tool of empire"[8] to exercise absolute control over private, social, and sexual relations of inhabitants and dwellers. Frequently it turned out to be an instrument in the hands of the "contained" to "reframe"[9] the imposed policies and practices according to their own rules and systems of agency. The factual mismatch between theory (planning), practice (implementation and building), and the creation of time- and space-specific ways of talking about houses leaves us assuming that it is both the attempt to coerce and a sign of civil resistance – a mechanism to defend oneself or even to defy the imposition of order.

This volume brings together scholars from different disciplines, such as history, architecture, urban planning, African studies, linguistics, and literature. Firstly, the contributors apply a range of distinct methodological approaches to the study of housing. This made us opt for an open format, the beginning of a conversation rather than for driving a closed argument which can only be a sequel to this exposition. Secondly, we hint at parallels between British, Belgian, and French colonialisms, an endeavor only rarely (if at all) undertaken in academic discussions on housing. We do not intend to provide a systematic synopsis of housing policies and experiences made under all the various colonialisms and labor schemes which once occurred on the African continent. We intend to cover perspectives from a variety of developments emerging from local situations on the continent. It is from these varieties of policies and experiences that we attempt to delineate the field rather than from a systemic view that presupposes that different colonialisms set the structures of productively opening up space for future comparison. Again, we stress that housing is a lens. Hence, thirdly, we use individual housing projects in the Democratic Republic of Congo, Kenya, Zambia, Cameroon, and South Africa to add to the currently vibrant academic debate on urban practices and their significance for past, present, and emerging social change. We want

---

7 Carole Rakodi, "Addressing Gendered Inequalities in Housing," in *Gender, Asset Accumulation and Just Cities: Pathways to Transformation?*, ed. Caroline O. N. Moser (London: Routledge, 2015), 82.
8 Daniel Headrick, *The Tools of Empire: Technology and European Imperialism in the Nineteenth Century* (Oxford: Oxford University Press, 1981).
9 See here Garth Andrew Myers, *Verandahs of Power: Colonialism and Space in Urban Africa* (New York: Syracuse University Press, 2003).

to establish how dwellers in various settings were exposed to the disciplining measures in housing arrangements and to a very particular circulation of ideas, values, and norms about urban life. In addition, we are glad to see that the contributors link the housing practices, planning ideas, and strategies to their respective metropolitan centers from where they (assumedly) emerged. We fully recognize that the housing policies and practices did not unfold in isolation; they were "nested" within a larger frame of the colonial discourse of subordination and pacification. In that sense, the workshop was also marked by linguistic traditions in academic production. On the one hand, participants worked with archival resources in different languages that reflected the linguistic situation in the metropolis as well as in the former colonies. On the other hand, all participants proofed their willingness to listen to presentations in English and French and some Swahili (sometimes with spontaneous interpreting). This plurilingual working mode showed that different concepts and notions of theory were a highly productive topic of discussion. The choice of the language for each paper in this volume was thus intentionally left to the authors.

Only rarely have comparative studies of housing dynamics been undertaken.[10] This is due to the Eurocentric framework that has dominated urban analyses since the colonial era and which concentrated on African urban developments relative to the West rather than encouraged a focus on intra-African urban variation.[11] Again, we take the liberty to not particularly highlight the metropolitan experiences impacting on developments and transformation processes in African surroundings or taking on their independent parallel political and technical priorities. The Eurocentric framework for analysis has also been one of the reasons why, in colonial as well as postcolonial settings but equally so in other periods of transition, it is deemed necessary to focus on "the slum", the most prevalent "other", as opposed to European forms and norms of housing.[12] We, however, wish to tie in with research that no longer takes that perspective but, instead, pursues a variety of alternative views on the city.[13]

---

[10] See for instance Garth Andrew Myers, *African Cities: Alternative Visions of Urban Theory and Practice* (London & New York: Zed-Books, 2011); Robert Home, *Of Planting and Planning: The Making of British Colonial Cities* (New York: Routledge, 2013).

[11] Kefa Otiso and George Owusu, "Comparative Urbanization in Ghana and Kenya in Time and Space," *GeoJournal* 71 (2008).

[12] See, for instance, Marie Huchzermeyer, *Cities with 'Slums': From Informal Settlement Eradication to a Right to the City in Africa* (Cape Town: University of Cape Town Press, 2011).

[13] See, for instance, Edgar Pieterse and AbdouMaliq Simone, eds., *Rogue Urbanism: Emergent African Cities* (Johannesburg: Jacana Media, 2013).

While the volume points to these complexities, the respective case studies target specific aspects of housing, thus making the understanding of its multifacetedness possible and accessible. Although the social and political realities of the individual case studies presented in this volume are context-specific and locally bound, they share a number of common patterns such as the use of coercive state control, the regulation of labor, or the disciplining of colonial subjects in and outside their respective abodes.

In this volume, the chapters range from depicting the daily life and housing conditions of mine workers in the Katanga Province in the Democratic Republic of Congo to tracing the question of what housing meant for dwellers by an analysis of Kenyan urban novels. The time span covered takes us from the foundation of Elisabethville (now Lubumbashi) in 1910 up to independent Nairobi in the 1970s. Overcoming the more conventional colonial/postcolonial divide characteristic of numerous studies, the contributors intend to highlight underlying continuities and changes across crucial periods and at times even point towards contemporary housing and urban developments. The majority of contributions in the volume is dedicated to the period between the late 1930s and 1960s, when colonial housing policies and practices underwent dramatic changes. The following section sheds light on the reasons behind and consequences of these changes. The final part presents the structure and individual chapters of the book in more detail.

Housing Policies and Practices

In the decades immediately before and after independence, an unprecedented demand for housing impelled governments into thinking about the provision, planning, and building of houses. What used to be a question of welfare in late colonial thinking came to overlap with the sensitive issue of who should enjoy a legitimate existence in African urban areas and hubs of commercialization and industrialization, and of how that existence would be imagined from various perspectives. Ever since then, housing has remained a pressing issue of urbanization and a key theme of relevance in the history of colonial Africa and thereafter.

Before 1940, apart from physical infrastructure projects by both Britain and France, there was only sparing metropolitan investment in their African colonies. The wartime metropolitan centers used colonies mainly as a resource; they focused on the extraction of commodities and the exploitation of the workforce, primarily through coercion and forced labor. The effects of these severe pressures were complex and manifold. Reactions to them included strikes, unrest, protests or sabotage, varying throughout colonial Africa depending on the level of coercion and forbearance of the "subjects". On the one hand, the colonial state became ever more intrusive in people's everyday lives. On the other, once the expansion of development and welfare projects following the Second World War shaped the path for new opportunities, social and political changes were inevitable.[14]

Young male workers and farmers, in particular, made use of the benefits and promises that the cash economy and wage labor brought. What followed was increased industrial and infrastructure production, urbanization, the reformulation of gender and family relations, and the creation and redefinition of new urban bonds and identities. The escalating demand for political freedoms combined with the cost of social and economic development eventually put an end to colonial ambitions and the chaos they produced. The two major colonial powers, Britain and France, both attempted to modulate demands by promising reforms, welfare, and inclusion in decision-making. Trade unions and political organizations, albeit carefully selected and controlled from the top, were acknowledged and recognized. Legislative councils, with both nominated and elected members, and a huge variety of local advisory boards and committees, were created. The "subjects" were promised to become accepted players.

The essential task for the colonial powers was "to identify and to cultivate 'moderate' African partners in order to head off more radical alternatives"[15] posing a direct challenge to colonial control such as Mau Mau in Kenya from 1952 to 1960. The anticolonial struggle for emancipation assumed violent form, particularly in settler colonies where the intrusion of white settlers into both the economic and political realms was the strongest. Elsewhere, the emerging African elite – together with colonial officials and politicians in the metropolitan centers – discussed the imminent questions of modernization and liberalization of both state and social

---

14 For a more elaborate discussion of the political and societal changes following Second World War see for instance: John Parker and Richard Rathbone, *African History. A Very Short Introduction* (Oxford: Oxford University Press, 2007); Frederick Cooper, *Africa since 1940: The Past of the Present* (Cambridge: Cambridge University Press, 2002); Walter Schicho, "Das Scheitern von Demokratie und Staat," in *Afrika: Geschichte und Gesellschaft im 19. und 20. Jahrhundert*, ed. Ingeborg Grau et al. (Wien: Promedia, 2003); Roland Oliver and Anthony Atmore, *Africa since 1800*, 5th edition (Cambridge: Cambridge University Press, 2004), 211–303; John Illife, *Africans: The History of a Continent*, 2nd edition (Cambridge: Cambridge University Press, 2007), 219–273. Franz Ansprenger, *Geschichte Afrikas*, 2nd edition (Muenchen: C.H.Beck, 2004), 88–102.
15 Parker and Rathbone, *African History*, 118.

structures of the colonial state – to different avail.¹⁶ While Britain negotiated the road to independence with each colony individually, France opted for a holistic approach via the creation of the "*Union française*" in 1945. But only in isolated cases did independence mean severing all ties with the metropolitan centers. Particularly in the economic sphere, the links remained intact and were even further strengthened by connections to new world powers and international organizations. What implications did these developments have for the development of urban centers in general and housing in particular?

New demographic trends and a changing global situation gradually raised housing expectations and produced a climate of opinion in which – almost worldwide – housing deficiencies came to be regarded as unacceptable. Political, cultural and associational life, among Africans and within Africa, unfolded in multiple directions. So did commercial, cultural, and intellectual networks which reached out to the ("cosmopolitan") world. Social mobilization, the emergence of independence ideologies as well as a "modern" and "educated" African middle class, or improved healthcare were only a few of the major societal transformations at play.[17] Wage labor, urban-rural mobility, and consequently rapidly growing cities with the concurrent need for housing became key characteristics of African societies and posed a significant challenge to colonial powers and their control over their "subjects" and "becoming citizens".[18]

Before the Second World War, Africans were not conceived of as belonging to the urban social sphere by the colonial administration. In the late 1930s and 1940s, a wave of disaffection with living and working conditions swept many African ports, mines, railways, and commercial centers in different countries.[19] In Kenya, for instance, unrest, protests, and labor strikes were directly linked to low wages and poor living and housing conditions. The 1946 Housing of Africans in the Urban Areas of Kenya Report noted that: "It cannot be denied that slum conditions [...] produce the worst type of citizen. Discontent becomes rife and efficiency decreases. One of the prime causes of the Mombasa riots in

---

16 Daniel Tödt, *Elitenbildung und Dekolonisierung: Die Évolués in Belgisch-Kongo 1944–1960* (Göttingen: Vandenhoeck & Ruprecht, Kritische Studien zur Geschichtswissenschaft, Band 228, 2018); Michael Oliver West, *The Rise of an African Middle Class. Colonial Zimbabwe, 1898–1965*. (Bloomington: Indiana University Press, 2002).
17 Cooper, *Africa since 1940*. Schicho, "Das Scheitern von Demokratie und Staat."
18 For an excellent treatment of that transition, with particular reference to the French Empire, see Frederick Cooper, *Citizenship between Empire and Nation: Remaking France and French Africa, 1945–1960* (Princeton: Princeton University Press, 2014).
19 A wave of strikes and unrest hit the Northern Rhodesian Copperbelt, railway and mines in the 1930s, Mombasa and Dar es Salaam in 1939, Katanga in 1941, Cameroon in 1945, and Gold Coast in 1948.

1939 was lack of proper housing, and similar causes have been found to be responsible for the more recent strikes and disturbances."[20] Herewith, the very existence of two vital determinants of colonial rule, namely order and productivity, was threatened. Colonial Zambia went through a similar period of unrest and dissatisfaction on the part of the workers. Yet the Northern Rhodesia Government was in a position to contain the situation and channel the quest for housing into a differing direction as compared to Kenya.

Colonial governments were particularly reluctant to accommodate Africans within emerging cities and towns for longer than just temporary sojourns of formal employment. Once the short-term contract terminated, the workers had to return to their areas of origin. The authorities attempted to regulate mobility of Africans by passing and amending laws and regulations. In times of labor shortage, Africans were forced to move to urban areas, for instance, through the imposition of various taxes. Adversely, if their numbers became excessive, pass and eviction laws were issued to ban them from the urban sites.[21] The stay of Africans there, especially if they were poor, was deemed illegal and illegitimate, unwanted and provisional, and authorities on many occasions demolished their (interim) dwellings. As the authorities were not able to cope with the situation and the budgets were overstrained, the provision of accommodation for the masses of urban wage earners was generally neglected. In many places, deplorable conditions of living and dwelling prevailed for the majority, and in urban centers Africans were often restricted to "native locations", which is where government and employees' housing was built. If one was not housed by one's employer or under a municipal scheme, it was extremely difficult to find private accommodation within the boundaries of the town. Most accommodation was "overcrowded, filthy and unweather proof."[22] In 1941 in Pumwani, one of Nairobi's locations, houses "of mud and wattle construction with scrap-iron roofs, with small windows and inadequate ventilation," with a permitted number of occupants of 171, were illicitly sheltering 481 persons.[23] Africans occupied but did not own the urban space.

---

20 G. C. W. Ogilvie, *The Housing of Africans in the Urban Areas of Kenya* (Nairobi: Kenya Information Office, 1946), 15.
21 Eviction procedures differed in respective colonies and in the long run. Colonial governments often proved reluctant to enforce evictions in Kenya or Northern Rhodesia, whereas in Southern Rhodesia the policies were carried out more immediately. This aspect of labor control and its connection to the availability of housing is ongoing work in progress in our project.
22 Nairobi Housing Scheme, 1941, CO 533/528/17, The Kenya National Archives (hereafter KNA).
23 Ogilvie, *The Housing of Africans*, 15.

The colonial authorities recognized that to a significant degree the housing situation was caused by the prevailing socioeconomic conditions, in particular by the low wages the majority of unskilled African workers received: "A low wage economy does not permit an African to pay more than Sh. 6.50 per month in Nairobi for a bed space, if and when he can get it. Very often he cannot and sleeps wherever he can, wet or fine."[24] A survey of wage conditions conducted in November 1952 in Nairobi revealed that 27 percent of unskilled workers were being paid the minimum wage of 56.5 shillings per month and 47 percent were being paid not more than 60 shillings. As for the more skilled type of industrial worker, monthly wages varied between 100 to 250 shillings per month.[25] The economic rent per bed space, the unit of measurement in Nairobi, was 17 shillings per month, but the housing allowance in the wage structure did not exceed 7 shillings.[26] Furthermore, as the minimum wage was calculated on the minimum requirements of a single man, it did not take into account the worker's family. The "single man" wage policy and "bed space" housing made it virtually impossible for any but the highly paid African to bring up a family decently in Nairobi. As George Atkinson, the Colonial Office Liaison Housing Officer, noted in internal correspondence, "[t]he discrepancy between the low wages of the Africans and the high rents is one of the biggest obstacles of housing provision."[27] At the same time, the high rents were to be blamed on the "greedy, unscrupulous" private African and Asian landlords charging excessive rents or tenants who sub-let their dwellings.[28]

Followed by an unprecedented boom in urbanization, the postwar housing shortage was massive, especially in hubs of industrialization and commercial centers. Still, the housing shortage, though most acute in Nairobi and Mombasa in the Kenyan context, was not confined to these two cities. Some government officials in smaller townships, for instance in Kisumu, noted lack of housing in particular for the "superior grades" of African employees: "The educated man

---

[24] George Tyson, "The African Housing Problem: A Memorandum submitted to the Nairobi Chamber of Commerce," Nairobi City Council, 1953, in: CO 822/588 African Urban Housing in Kenya, 1953, The National Archives, Kew (hereafter TNA).

[25] Summary of Information for Royal Commission: Number of Africans in Employment, in: CO 892/7/1 East African Royal Commission: Miscellaneous Papers, 1953, TNA.

[26] Tyson, "The African Housing Problem," CO 822/588. Improved Housing in Kenya, *East Africa and Rhodesia*, 10 September 1953, in: CO 822/588 African Urban Housing in Kenya, 1953, TNA.

[27] Letter from Atkinson to Rogers, 4 January 1953, in: CO 822/588 African Urban Housing in Kenya, TNA.

[28] Harris, "From Trusteeship to Development," 317. East African Royal Commission, 1953, CO 892/7/1, TNA.

with a wife finds it impossible to obtain adequate accommodation in Kisumu at the present time unless he is a Government employee."²⁹ In 1953, the chairman of the Central Housing Board, the statutory body responsible for housing policies, referred to the fact that the higher-paid Africans throughout the colony were complaining that they were being ignored in the matter of housing. "Schemes were being prepared and carried out for laborers, but nothing was being done to accommodate clerks and artisans."³⁰ Public opinion was critical of the government's lack of initiative. There was a rising awareness that, with the development of industrial areas and the emergence of the industrial worker, "it is essential that housing policies should give the maximum aid to the town African in establishing not only himself but his family in decent living conditions, and doing so within his income."³¹

Challenged by this pressure and the increased number of labor-related unrest due to, among other factors, inadequate housing and living conditions, the colonial state made a determined effort to find alternatives. The 1940s thus marked a shift in official colonial housing discourse and policy. The political context within which decisions were made changed; in a number of colonies, permanent living and housing for male, working Africans in major urban centers became inevitable. The metropolitan centers were frightened. The loyalty of Africans was needed.³² In Kenya, once again, to reflect the social and political changes and the inclusion of Africans into urban life, specific attention was given to the construction of municipal housing schemes, replacement of bachelor with family housing, launching of aided self-help schemes, in particular in the form of home-ownership and tenant-purchase.³³ In addition, employers were to become more active in the provision of housing. The employers were a very heterogeneous category and there was a great variety both in type and quality of accommodation they offered to their employees.

---

29 Municipal Board of Kisumu, Housing Committee, 9 August 1951, in: DC/KSM/1/16/53 Vasey Kisumu Housing Committee, 1948–1956, KNA.
30 Kisumu Municipal Board, 3 December 1953, in: DC/KSM/1/16/53 Vasey Kisumu Housing Committee, 1948–1956, KNA.
31 "Housing." *East African Standard*, 28 June 1951, in: ABK/17/6 Vasey African Housing General File, 1951–1953, KNA.
32 Richard Harris and Susan Parnell, "The Turning Point in Urban Policy for British Colonial Africa, 1939–1945," in *Colonial Architecture and Urbanism in Africa: Intertwined and Contested Histories*, ed. Fassil Demissie (Aldershot: Ashgate, 2012), 150.
33 Such a policy was in line with globally connected efforts towards the promotion of home-ownership and finance on the basis of private capital. See Nancy Kwak, *A World of Homeowners: American Power and the Politics of Housing Aid* (Chicago: University of Chicago Press, 2015).

Although the contribution of employers in Kenya towards addressing the housing shortage never truly satisfied the demand,[34] it was substantial. According to a 1959 survey, 67 percent of employed Africans in Nairobi were housed by their employers.[35] As Anderson noted, the need for more housing was recognized by the Town Council as early as 1911. However, nobody was willing to dedicate resources to build housing for African workers and a constant battle between central government, municipal authorities, and employers characterized the housing scene.[36] These categories were often one and the same as government departments were, for a long time, the largest employers in the town. Although it was a legal obligation in Kenya upon an employer to provide either suitable housing for his African employees or an allowance for rent,[37] the housing facilities provided by individual employers varied greatly:

> [O]nly the larger firms such as the railway, bus companies, etc. have provided housing. Employees not so housed find accommodation in municipal housing schemes and African-owned lodging houses. Domestic servants, who comprise about one-sixth of the urban population, are usually housed on the employers' premises, and the type of housing provided varies greatly, the usual accommodation consisting of one small hut without cooking or bathing facilities.[38]

The state, by far the largest employer,[39] provided housing for its African employees, with several state agencies, such as the Public Works Department, Posts and Telegraphs Department, or the Health Office, building houses at the same time. For decades, the Kenya and Uganda Railways, the largest employer in the country, was considered exemplary both in terms of quantity and quality

---

[34] A 1951 report noted 10,000 bed spaces shortage despite all the efforts. N.M. Deverell, *Social Conditions Arising out of the Growth of Large Urban Populations in East Africa* (City Council of Nairobi: Annual Report of the African Affairs Department, 1951).

[35] Richard Harris and Allison Hay, "New Plans for Housing in Urban Kenya, 1939–1963," *Planning Perspectives* 22 (2007): 199. This was counted on the then conventional bed space. The survey included only those within city limits and informal employment.

[36] David Anderson, "Corruption at City Hall: African Housing and Urban Development in Colonial Nairobi," *Azania: Archaeological Research in Africa* 36–37 (2001).

[37] Section 41 of the Employment Ordinance made it obligatory to provide housing for those employees whose earnings did not exceed 100 shillings per month or else to provide in addition to the wage a sufficient allowance *in lieu* to enable an employee to rent appropriate accommodation.

[38] Ogilvie, *The Housing of Africans*.

[39] According to available statistical information, in 1951, approximately one quarter (93,361) of the total employed population of 412,416 Africans were employed either by the Kenyan Government or the East Africa High Commission. East African Royal Commission, 1953, CO 892/7/1, TNA.

of housing.⁴⁰ As for the private employers, only larger industries and companies could afford to create separate housing estates for their workers; small businesses housed their staff in quarters that were attached to, or part of, their business premises.⁴¹

The employees were at least as diverse and multiple as their employers. There were professional and commercial middle classes, clerical and skilled manual workers, workers in commerce and industry, petty traders and hawkers, white-collar workers in government service, laborers, domestic servants, semi-skilled and unskilled – the largest group of all, and the formally unemployed.⁴² Notwithstanding their differences, ethnic and professional backgrounds, all had one thing in common: they were in need of housing. The housing survey conducted by the Labour Department in Nairobi in 1950 found alarming conditions regarding housing provision:

> A very great proportion of these employees, in fact, had no form of roof at all: 15% were found to be sleeping in places where they should never be in at all, such as railway landhies, Nairobi Club area, Indian and European residential areas etc. A further 20% lives at the expense of others, paying no rents but moving about from place to place every few days. 30% shared rooms with friends and paid rent in proportion to the number of people in the room, while 25% are tenants in African locations. The remaining 10% have their own houses.⁴³

Women present in urban areas were categorized along different lines. Rather than being thought of in terms of wage employment and economic contribution,

---

40 Cooper, for instance, noted that the railway housed 80 percent of Mombasa's railway workers. Frederick Cooper, *On the African Waterfront: Urban Disorder and the Transformation of Work in Colonial Mombasa* (New Haven & London: Yale University Press, 1987), 48. Railways were also one of the very few employers, which provided family quarters instead of the ubiquitous bed space typical for municipal and council housing schemes (Deverell, *Social Conditions*). In contrast, the Rhodesia Railway's compounds in colonial Zambia were a permanent focus of critique. Politicians, medical officers and town councilors argued that Government should set a better example in their own housing to push Rhodesia Railways towards providing accommodation of required standards: "At the moment when the Municipal Council is building much better houses in the Maramba and we are endeavouring to persuade the Rhodesia Railways to improve their African quarters it is disheartening to find Government still setting the lowest standard of all." Senior Medical Officer, J.A. McGregor, Livingstone, to Provincial Commissioner in Livingstone, 24 March 1941, in: LGH 3/5/1 Livingstone: African Housing, 1937–1946, National Archives of Zambia.
41 Harris and Hay, "New Plans for Housing in Urban Kenya," 199.
42 Memorandum on Housing in Africa, 1953, in: CO 859/490 Housing and Town Planning in Africa, 1953, TNA.
43 Letter from Carpenter to Editor of *East African Standard*, 22 August 1950, in: ABK 17/13 Vasey Inquiry into African Housing, 1949–1965, KNA.

a 1951 report listed Nairobi's women as (a) genuine wives, resident with their husbands, mainly of the higher paid groups; (b) concubines; (c) prostitutes, and (d) migratory Kikuyu wives and children.[44]

As stated above, the low-wage economy meant that ordinary African workers were not in a position to pay the rent. They needed supplementary income, which they ordinarily obtained from the land owned by them in the rural areas. The constant commuting between rural and urban areas lowered the efficiency of the workforce, and made it more difficult to impose order:

> We can no longer take it as the normal state of affairs that a man works in Nairobi and his wife and family scratch a livelihood out of an allotment in the Reserve. [...] The losses in the turnover of labour due to these divided households and the periodical visits of the African to his plot in the Reserve must cost the country and industry generally, considerable sums.[45]

Converting migrant casual labor into a stabilized urban workforce was directly linked to the consequent need for social services and, in particular, improved housing conditions. Permanent building materials replaced temporary ones. The minimum allotted space per occupant was increased. To be able to cater for a family, a wage increase, regular employment, a house and security for retirement all became part of the social and political engineering programs. It was believed that a stabilized, disciplined, and urbanized working class would lead to increased efficiency and suppress the unrest that threatened the social order. Such a "powerful pacification device"[46] was hoped to maintain control by deliberately creating "responsible" dwellers, loyal and committed to the colonial government.

Inadequate housing was understood as "a known menace to health, to social stability and to the maintenance of law and order."[47] Poor housing conditions were seen as "ideal for subversive activities" and directly contributing to unrest. While describing the living conditions of Africans in Nairobi's shanty towns, the Sunday Post reporter noted "distinct signs of unrest and dissatisfaction, [...] this is the stuff of which rebellion is made, [...] toilet is the bush, they draw their water from puddles, swamps. [...] It stinks of filth and hate."[48]

---

44 Deverell, *Social Conditions*.
45 Tyson, "The African Housing Problem," CO 822/588.
46 Viviana d'Auria, "In the Laboratory and in the Field: Hybrid Housing Design for the African City in Late-colonial and Decolonising Ghana (1945–57)," *The Journal of Architecture* 19 (2014): 330.
47 "Housing," *East African Standard*, 28 June 1951, ABK/17/6.
48 "Rebellion's Nursery: Quarry Shanty Towns," *The Sunday Post*, 27 May 1956, in: NHC/1/381 Nairobi County Council African Housing, 1952–1958, KNA.

The local media readily amplified the link between housing and revolutionary thinking: "there is no better breeding ground for crime, no better forum on which real and imaginary grievances can be ventilated and enlarged, than an overcrowded hovel of 'bedspaces' dimly lit by a flickering oil tin light, with nothing to do in the early hours of the evening after work but grumble."[49]

Economic thinking was as important as the imposition of law and order. In the 1940s and 1950s, the situation in Nairobi was considered so bad that an embargo on recruitment of any more workers was being contemplated.[50] Industrial firms and commercial employers were also told they would be refused land for the erection of new factories and offices unless they built housing estates for the workers they intended to employ.[51] That such a drastic measure would bear catastrophic consequences was obvious; the financial loss, in particular during the scarcity caused by war conditions, would have had an overly dramatic impact, not only on the colonies but on the metropolis itself, at times highly dependent on exports from the colonies.

As a consequence, urban housing became a priority. Special funds were created for housing projects. Interestingly enough, in many British colonies, including Kenya, although the low-paid workers and poor dwellers were the most numerous group and thus in the direst need of housing, the provision of dwellings for the poor was not at the center of attention. Colonial housing policy in Kenya was meant for the more stable: the white collar, civil servants, government workers, municipality employees and better-off workers such as railway men. As Cooper argued, "these policies attempted to fix a working class into a direct, long-term relation with capital and the state."[52] Even site-and-service or tenant-purchase schemes were reserved for those with a certain level of income.[53]

The wish of colonizers to establish "decent" living conditions surely indicates how their technocratic perspective was imbued with concepts of morality, ideas of discipline, and the notions of imposing order and hierarchy: people

---

49 "The Root of the Trouble," *Sunday Post Reporter*, 15 February 1953, in: CO 822/588, African Urban Housing in Kenya, 1953, TNA.
50 Letter from Vasey to Norton, 13 November 1952, in: CO 822/136/3 African Housing Plans, 1947, TNA.
51 East African Royal Commission, 1953, CO 892/7/1.
52 Frederick Cooper, "Urban Space, Industrial Time, and Wage Labor in Africa," in *Struggle for the City: Migrant Labor, Capital, and the State in Urban Africa*, ed. Frederick Cooper (Beverly Hills: Sage Publications, 1983), 3.
53 Ernest A. Vasey, *Report on the Housing of Africans in Townships and Trading Centres* (Nairobi, 1950). Karen Tranberg Hansen, "Lusaka's Squatters: Past and Present," *African Studies Review* 25 (1982). Richard Stren, "Underdevelopment, Urban Squatting and the State Bureaucracy: A Case Study of Tanzania," *Canadian Journal of African Studies* 6 (1982).

with supposedly superior knowledge provided the means to help others emerge from "non-civilization", poverty and chaos – in brief: from circumstances which rendered society "illegible" and thus a challenge to the emerging modern state.[54] At the same time, the focus on housing as a technical matter depoliticized the debate and avoided discussion of controversial political issues, such as emerging civil rights, entitlement to private property or to political representation. The coming into being of a political voice and the emergence of a particular modern African urban identity through access to urban housing is thus one dimension of housing the volume explores. As Rüther states in this volume: "The debate had shifted from issues of labor stabilization to more openly expressed complaints of residents with self-asserted urban identities." By the very act of laying claim to their urban homes, the new dwellers assumed new notions of self-understanding, worth, personhood, and family.

Despite imperial attempts to impose control, there were no uniform, linear master-housing plans implemented in practice. The gatekeeper colonial states had only "weak instruments for entering into the social and cultural realm over which they presided."[55] The social, economic, political, and cultural networks created by Africans thus often remained beyond the state's reach. As a result, a multiplicity of inter/re/actions, such as resistance and accommodation, or appropriation and independent communication, occurred when designed policies were actually implemented. In consequence, as demonstrated in this volume's contributions, a rather heterogeneous and "unplanned" set of housing forms and designs emerged. Where the authorities or employers failed to provide housing, dwellers took matters into their own hands. What emerged, often described as "slums", "squatter settlements" or "unauthorized housing", were spontaneous reactions to formal urban planning deemed illegal, irregular, and informal by those in power:

> An urban sub-proletariat was coming into being all over Africa, swollen by the influx of jobless people driven out of the rural areas by the war effort, with its forced labour, compulsory crops and heavy taxation: they consisted of ill-paid workers, rootless individuals from here, there and everywhere, and the unemployed. Temporary accommodation became permanent, with hardly any roads, public services or sanitation.[56]

---

[54] James Scott, *Seeing Like A State: How Certain Schemes to Improve the Human Condition Have Failed* (New Haven: Yale University Press, 1998).
[55] Cooper, *Africa since 1940*, 5.
[56] Catherine Coquery-Vidrovitch, "Economic Changes in Africa in the World Context," in *General History of Africa: Africa since 1935*, ed. Ali A. Mazrui (California, UNESCO: James Currey, 1999), 295.

Africans came into cities without waiting for the blessing of the colonial state.[57] They brought their families along with them and had no intention of returning. The state was forced to find a solution. Instead of using force to push them out, the state opted for co-optation: stable employment, stable families, stable housing, stable communities, and – in due time, even though perhaps never fully achieved – a stable political system.

A multiplicity of actors has characterized the housing field. As the central government lacked the required resources and capacity to meet the demand for new urban housing,[58] other players such as local government actors, municipalities or private companies and estates were encouraged to provide housing facilities for the ever-increasing numbers of new urban residents.[59] None of the actors, though, seemed keen on taking the lead in housing questions. As Cooper noted, "everyone was in favor of a stabilized African work force but no one wanted to pay for it."[60] The administrative burden of housing and the responsibility for it was transferred between different echelons of colonial government or to other players, mostly employers. Except for the mining sector, employers, in turn, were often interested in the devolution of this task back to the municipalities. Notwithstanding the increased investments and new strategies, the resources made available for the provision of housing were always too short, the demand never satisfied. If finances were made available, housing policies, as Boonen and Lagae demonstrate in their chapter, often failed in many aspects in large part due to "the unwillingness of the metropole-based officials, architects and planners who promoted general solutions to the problem of housing shortage, based on abstract ideas of rationality and cost-efficiency, [...] to adapt to local specificities."

The communication between these various actors and echelons of the colonial government, as archival sources reveal, was oftentimes highly bureaucratic and centralized with an insufficient exchange of information between the metropolis and the colonies. The procedures were lengthy and time-consuming; the decision-making was marked by internal conflicts. The institutions were ill-prepared and, though working simultaneously, they were poorly coordinated. The multiplicity of actors stood in contrast with the constant lack of qualified personnel.[61]

---

57 For a detailed analysis of this train of thought consult Cooper, "Urban Space", and Cooper, *On the African Waterfront*.
58 See, for instance, Tipple, "The Need for New Urban Housing in Sub-Saharan Africa."
59 See also Robert Home, "From Barrack Compounds to the Single-Family House. Planning Worker Housing in Colonial Natal and Northern Rhodesia," *Planning Perspectives* 15 (2000).
60 Cooper, *On the African Waterfront*, 123.
61 See also Luce Beeckmans, "Editing the African City: Reading Colonial Planning in Africa from a Comparative Perspective," *Planning Perspectives* 28 (2013): 619.

To sum up, institutional fragmentation, malfunctioning departments, and administrative glitches were not uncommon encounters in the housing field. The ideas of the empire and the reality of the colonies often clashed.

This ambiguous and indeed conflicting situation between different actors was rendered visible not only in the provision of urban housing, but also with regard to infrastructures and services. Ultimately, it also touched upon the conceptualization of urban forms and their transformation. The morphogenesis of urban areas between the late nineteenth century and the 1930s was based on the garden-city model of urban planning in combination with an economic planning rationale that was intended to meet the needs for industrial developments of different sectors such as mining, agriculture, and transportation.[62] Throughout colonial sub-Saharan Africa planning and development of urban structures were initially pursued by military planners and engineering staff mostly based in the colonial metropolises. They were only gradually adopted by civil engineers and urban planners working from inside the colonial territories in the last two to three decades of colonial rule.[63] Physical and socio-spatial segregation along racial lines were legitimized based on the logics of hygiene and public health as well as on notions of establishing and fostering spatial dominance and control.[64] Differences in the degrees of segregation between colonies and colonial rulers were balanced out by increasing exchanges of knowledge and cooperation in matters of tropical medicine and later architecture and urban planning.[65] Sanitary corridors and physical boundaries or barriers in the form of railway lines and industrial zones, or green belts and rivers, structured urban spatial forms.

Later, colonial planning rationales were replaced by ideas of developmentalism, modernism, and the discourse of urban planning unfolding in the context of the network emerging from a succession of international conferences on

---

[62] Robert Home, "Town Planning and the Garden Cities in the British Colonial Empire 1910–1940," *Planning Perspectives* 5 (1990): 25.
[63] Carlos Nunes Silva, "Urban Planning in Sub-Saharan Africa: An Overview", in *Urban Planning in Sub-Saharan Africa: Colonial and Postcolonial Planning Cultures*, ed. Carlos Nunes Silva (London: Routledge, 2015), 9–10.
[64] Garth Andrew Myers, "Designing Power: Forms and Purpose of Colonial Model Neighborhoods in British Africa," *Habitat International* 27 (2003), 193–204; Ambe Njoh, "Ideology and Public Health Elements of Human Settlement Policies in Sub-Saharan Africa," *Cities* 26 (2009): 9–18; Ambe Njoh, "Urban Planning as a Tool of Power and Social Control in Colonial Africa," *Planning Perspectives* 24 (2009): 301–317.
[65] Catherine Coquery-Vidrovitch, "From Residential Segregation to African Urban Centres: City Planning and the Modalities of Change in Africa South of the Sahara," *Journal of Contemporary African Studies* 32 (2014): 1–12.

modern architecture.⁶⁶ The rationale of segregation and exclusion, however, was basically kept untouched, less so on principles of hygiene, but rather on economic and technical grounds. While the political and social transformations between the 1930s and 1960s did not radically scrape off the urban tissue of earlier decades, they continued to influence the theory and practice of late colonial and postcolonial urban planning. As a result, planning often proved ineffective and inefficient in the light of rising urbanization rates and its increased demand for housing and infrastructures. Many urban planning initiatives and ideas were only partly operationalized or not at all. In fact, different branches and departments (technical, economic, legal, social welfare, etc.) of urban development were acting parallel to each other or in little, sometimes no, knowledge of each other. Moreover, the political struggles of the pre-independence era complicated urban planning even further as technocratic policies and legislations were readily questioned by African political classes who could hold against them not only their inefficiencies, but more so the unevenness and inequalities of infrastructural service distributions and urban densities.

The "inefficiencies and inequities created by the colonial city"⁶⁷ outlived the transition to postcolonial African urbanities. The divide between low- and high-density areas and between the availability and lack of urban infrastructures and services shifted from being based on racial to social segregation and exclusion.

As the complexity of the tasks was growing, so was the vastness of the network of actors dealing with housing. Kooiman argues that "interdependencies between these actors [...] must be recognized, as no single actor has the knowledge and information required to solve complex, dynamic, and diversified societal challenges; no single actor has sufficient potential to dominate unilaterally."⁶⁸ New bodies, ministries, departments, and institutes specializing in housing, both in the metropolitan centers and the colonies, such as the Building Research Station, Tropical Building Section, the Colonial Housing Research Study Group, or the Housing Advisory Committee for British Colonies (oftentimes duplicating their efforts) were established. Knowledge and experiences were exchanged and shared across the regional boundaries; study tours were organized. Our archival research at the National Archives in Kew, the State Archives in Brussels, and the Archives of the *Union Minière du Haut-Katanga* in Brussels revealed rich information on

---

66 Nancy Odendaal et al., "Planning Education in Sub-Saharan Africa," in *Urban Planning in Sub-Saharan Africa. Colonial and Postcolonial Planning Cultures*, ed. Carlos Nunes Silva (London: Routledge, 2015), 285–300.
67 Home, *Of Planting and Planning*, 227.
68 Jan Kooiman, *Governing as Governance* (Los Angeles: SAGE Publications, 2003), 11.

social mobility, the circulation and exchange of ideas, concepts, and experts, in particular through housing conferences, implementation of city master plans, or appointments of town planning advisers. One of the aims of this volume is to encompass this large network and the multiple interactions within.

When speaking about actors, what do we know about dwellers and their preferences? What building materials and how many rooms did they desire for their houses? Was indoor or outdoor cooking the preferred choice? What do dwellers expect from housing and what does housing mean to them? Martina Kopf, in this volume, states that housing has been

> a source of constant stress and strain [for the dwellers]. On the one hand, this concerns the quality of living space – represented by smells, the lack and malfunctioning of sanitary services and narrowness – and on the other hand, this concerns the precariousness and instability of housing, as a consequence of insecure tenancies, the illegalization of housing and the resulting threat of eviction.

A 1951 report on social conditions in Nairobi is a testimony to how housing in urban centers was a dream imagined by each and every dweller in a very specific way:

> [w]here each individual seeks primarily his own interest and where apparently passive acceptance of bleak living conditions is coloured by the fact that the young men dream dreams of self-government with ministerial posts for all, the old men see visions of a return to pastoral or agricultural life surrounded by rich crops and large herds and the women secretly hanker after economic independence. Few, as yet, conceive that they might be 'builders of cities.'[69]

Notwithstanding the precarious conditions, residents did their best to improve their houses, or beautify their homes, so as to make the most of an adverse or even oppressive system. At all times, to some extent, many Africans put a lot of effort into managing space and diversity to their own benefit. Some managed to endow places with their own insignia of power, faith, and custom and found sufficient ways around imposed rules and orders.[70] The chapters in this book establish what happened along the often meandering paths from conceptualizing housing down to implementing it in late colonial and early postcolonial settings in terms of social or political change.

---

[69] Deverell, *Social Conditions*.
[70] Laurent Fourchard, "Between World History and State Formation: New Perspectives on Africa's Cities," *Journal of African History* 52 (2011). Achille Mbembe and Sarah Nuttall, "Writing the World from an African Metropolis," *Public Culture* 16 (2004). Myers, *Verandahs of Power*.

We are fully aware that this period, 1930s–1960s, cannot be described equally well from all points of view. Whereas the official sources representing the metropolitan centers and colonial state are rich, others remain silent or, if available, are buried deep in archival records. By carefully browsing through files of numerous archives and by conducting elaborate field research, the contributors of this volume were able to reconstruct, at least partially, the intentions, initiatives, criticisms, and (hi)stories from below of the residents, dwellers, and inhabitants. Such an endeavor is of crucial importance because how people were housed is a reflection of how they were integrated into society.

Structure

The cover photo, taken by Carl-Philipp Bodenstein during his field research in Livingstone, Zambia, in 2018, has been selected for its depiction of the multiple yet interwoven ways housing can present itself. The picture symbolically reflects the dimensions and aspects of housing that the contributions in this volume revolve around. It highlights, among others, the continuities in housing and urban processes from the colonial to the post-independence era.[71] The colonial buildings in the back, evidently still occupied today, are a manifestation of spatial appropriation by dwellers. The construction site in the foreground provides ample maneuvering space for transformations. To a careful observer, the photograph reveals part of a high-density area with too little open space left between individual houses, non-availability of financial, material, and possibly personal resources to complete the foundations, and even lack of privacy. Did the owner dream too big and is now awaiting additional cash flow from remittances? Did administrative hurdles come up along the way with the municipal council questioning the soundness of the construction? We can only speculate as the shot was made in passing. What we can claim with certainty though is that the complex processes of provision and building this particular house have undergone multiple alternations since the conception of its original plan. The picture gives testimony to the fact that housing as a built environment in the making never turns out in reality as what it was originally intended.

The dimensions of housing are approached at different levels of analysis in this volume. The first three chapters, contributions by Kirsten Rüther, Sofie Boonen and Johan Lagae, and Martina Kopf on Zambia, the Democratic Republic

---

[71] See Carole Rakodi, *Harare: Inheriting a Settler-Colonial City: Change or Continuity?* (New York: John Wiley, 1995), 8.

of Congo, and Kenya place the becoming urban dwellers and their interactions with other actors of the housing network at the focus of analyses. The authors examine conflicting interests, interactions, and processes of negotiation as players were claiming their spaces to maneuver, attempting to make the best of their living and housing conditions. The selected foci – compliance or denial to pay rent, appropriation and transformation of space, and household formations according to dwellers' ideas – are all expressions of agential power on the side of the residents. Residents tried to engage with the openings and opportunities that housing offered.[72]

The main entry point of the three next chapters is worker housing – according to Home,[73] the commonest built element of the colonial landscape. The two case studies set in Lubumbashi, former Elisabethville by Donatien Dibwe dia Mwembu and Daniela Waldburger respectively, and Cameroon by Ambe Njoh and Liora Bigon explore how employment-tied housing served as an instrument for the projection and articulation of state power during the colonial era and has remained an important tool for the exercise of societal domination and control by the postcolonial state up to the present day. All three contributions testify to how vital employers are to our narrative. For decades, they were accorded a central role by colonial and independent governments in the provision of housing for permanently employed Africans in urban centers and workplaces.[74] Nevertheless, the reach of their control was by far not omnipotent. As Cooper[75] claimed, the initiatives of workers to gain control of their own lives and those of the state and capital to remake the workplace, living place, and colonial society all shaped each other. The final part of the introduction depicts each contribution in more detail.

Innovatively, *in lieu* of an epilogue, we included, in a form of an interview, the views of an architect and a civil engineer who, while on construction sites, transform interdisciplinary (theoretical) approaches into daily negotiations with on-site people and communities. While studying housing from an interdisciplinary perspective – a central endeavor in our research – we saw it as an enriching opportunity to involve housing practitioners into the debate. At the same time, this exchange of ideas and input from colleagues enabled us to further reflect on our preliminary research findings and served as a potential outlook for the future. Opening up the field to housing practitioners is an invitation to participate in an ongoing conversation. After all, research is a continuing process and we

---

[72] See Robinson, "Global and World Cities."
[73] Home, "From Barrack Compounds."
[74] See, for instance, Harris and Hay, "New Plans for Housing in Urban Kenya."
[75] Cooper, *On the African Waterfront*.

think it is worth stressing the procedural character of research unfolding with regard to (post)colonial housing politics.

Kirsten Rüther explores in her chapter the interwoven complex relations between the colonial state, various employers, and the becoming urban dweller in Northern Rhodesia. At the center of her analysis is the concept of rent: rent paid, rent complied with, rent delayed, rent omitted, rent resisted, rent collected. Rent serves here as a lens through which multiple conflicts playing out between a variety of actors at different levels, be they landlords, tenants, or state agencies, got articulated in practice. Her selected timeframe, from 1948 to 1962, is chosen with precision, as it is in this period that the meaning of rent changed dramatically as it reflected the shifting political, economic, and social circumstances.

By tying the multiplicity of actors together in a so-called "societal field of force" through the concept of rent, Rüther is able not only to capture their interactions and mutual relations but, even more importantly, to explore how power was enforced and rule established and how these carefully balanced constellations of power changed over time. Rent was a manifestation of power as it regulated access to housing. Unaffordable rent often led to subject-citizen mobilization in the form of resistance, boycott or unrest. As the meaning of rent shifted in the context of rising African nationalism, the paying of rent served as a manifestation of individual, political responsibility and made a precondition to the enjoyment of citizenship rights and African representation in elected bodies. Ultimately, the main contribution of the chapter is that, by tracing back the changes of meaning of rent shifts in conceptions of power, rule and obedience can be better understood.

In the second contribution, Sofie Boonen and Johan Lagae illustrate how the urban landscape of one particular *Office des Cités Africaines* (OCA) neighborhood of Ruashi in Lubumbashi in the 1950s speaks of the manifold ways in which its inhabitants have responded to a physical environment shaped according to western dwelling patterns and introduced in the context of colonialism. Deeply rooted in the paternalistic rationale underlying postwar colonial policies in the Belgian Congo, in particular the first Ten-Year Plan for the Economic and Social Development of the Belgian Congo (1949–1959), the OCA houses were not merely intended to provide shelter for the booming African population in Congo's major urban centers. They were also a major element in a broader project of social engineering, aimed at the "emancipation" of the African household defined in terms of a nuclear family. As such, the houses underwent major alterations over time, for instance, through the addition of informal structures or privatization of public spaces.

Boonen and Lagae skillfully depict the complexity of the designing and building process and highlight the tensions between the central and local administration which were characteristic of the process. The authors' interpretation of the convoluted process of appropriation, adaptation, and transformation that took place in Ruashi by its inhabitants is pleasingly refreshing. They read this transformed urban landscape neither in terms of a failed modernist project nor as merely an act of resistance against an imposed colonial order. Instead, in line with Philippe Boudon's 1969 study of Le Corbusier's *Cité Frugès* in Pessac, they approach Ruashi – but also other OCA-neighborhoods in other Congolese cities – as an example of an *architecture habitée activement*, an "actively lived-in architecture" providing maneuvering space for transformations. Instead of condemning or regretting the change of the original concept, this alternative view understands the modifications as a positive contribution. As the authors argue, addressing the complexities of the "actively lived-in architecture" helps to gain a better appreciation of everyday struggles OCA inhabitants undergo up to the present day.

Martina Kopf "reads" the city and the urban households of post-independence Kenya in the 1970s from a different perspective, through literature – such a crucial narrative and source for understanding post-independent perceptions of politics and the everyday. Analyzing two literary works by Meja Mwangi, *Going Down River Road* and *The Cockroach Dance*, portraying the lives of the urban poor living in unstable and informal working and housing conditions, she demonstrates the potential of fiction and literary analysis as means to question and disrupt objectifying approaches towards people in low-income livelihoods prevalent in Western (academic) literature. Kopf approaches fiction and narrative as tools giving meaning to the realities people live in and argues that Mwangi's novels contribute to a better understanding of the housing conditions of Nairobi's working poor by, among others, "offering a window into the history of urban settlement and of social and ethnic stratification at the shore of the Nairobi river."

Through Mwangi's novels, Kopf shows the emergence of a particular modern African urban identity. The household, a key concept in her analysis, is understood as a fluid, dynamic, and short-lived concept which manifests itself in multiple constellations, be it a household managed and financed by an African woman in her early twenties, a shack occupied by male buddies or a polygamous household. Housing, Kopf argues, emerges in Mwangi's novels as a subject of narration which on a literary level connects to larger stories of urbanization and urban development. It can be read and interpreted as a microcosm which reflects hierarchies not only of class and "race" but also of gender in post-independence Nairobi. In her analysis, she touches upon colonial patterns of labor migration continuing into postcolonial capitalist development and the continued restriction of urban space for Africans in the Nairobi of independence. Even though published four decades ago, Mwangi's texts are still relevant for the way they tell stories of urban life from below.

Donatien Dibwe dia Mwembu takes us to Katanga Province, Lubumbashi (Elisabethville) in Congo. In his own words, a child of *Union Minière du Haut-Katanga* (UMHK) himself, in Mwembu's contribution we feel the real *connoisseur* of living, working, and housing conditions talking. He knows every street, every building, and every corner of Lubumbashi; the city becomes alive through his descriptions. His contribution traces the evolution of Lubumbashi since its foundation in 1910 up to the independence of Congo in 1960. He explores the attempts of the Belgian colonial state to implement full political segregation of the city along racial lines into three separate zones: white, black, and the so-called *zone neutre*, separating the two by at least 700 meters which, according to official medical reports at that time, would prevent the transmission of malaria from the African to the European part of town.

Dibwe dia Mwembu interlinks the city's development, in particular *la ville noire*, with that of the region's biggest employer, the mining company UMHK. Through his detailed description, we get enriching insight into UMHK's workers' camps which served mostly as reservoirs of African labor force for the booming industry. Established to stabilize and discipline the workforce and to protect them from the "backward" influence of the rural areas, the founders' intention was to create a feeling of social community and belonging or, as Mwembu says, to craft a *grande famille discipline et saine*. This socialization led to a creation of a new collective identity which had far-reaching implications, among others, on the language usage: people employed in the UMHK were referred to as *ba Union Minière* or children as *batoto ba Union Minière*, and people referred to each other as "brother" and "sister".

Daniela Waldburger takes the discourse of Donatien Dibwe dia Mwembu further and scrutinizes the concepts of hygiene and health the UMHK used from the 1940s onwards as a stabilization tool to discipline its workers. She displays how the UMHK's decisions and strategies in the project of social engineering mirrored the Belgian Colonial state's ideas of development for the colony. Waldburger draws parallels between the *zone neutre*, on the scale of the city, and the house, on a smaller scale – both of which became core objects of the Belgians' concern for cleanliness and hygiene. Her research focuses on the worker and his house. She argues that the house "was one if not the central element of the experience of the good life."

Waldburger pays special attention to the "civilizing" measures of the UMHK associated with the topics of home, house, hygiene, and health. Hygiene was directly linked to the health condition of workers; they needed to be both physically fit and emotionally balanced to sustain productivity levels. As a linguist, she explores the prevalent discourse, language usage, and communication strategies that key actors, such as the colonial state, the UMHK or workers, selected to make themselves understood and to (re)negotiate their respective individual interests. By analyzing a variety of primary archival materials, including official propaganda materials of the UMHK and the Belgian colonial state, she illustrates the strategies these players used to exercise control over the workers. Waldburger's contribution is multifaceted and gives voice to a whole range of actors; a valuable element of her research is the detailed description of demands the workers posed on the company. These varied from requests for electric light in the house to running water for toilets, or the installation of doors that can be locked from the inside to secure more privacy.

In one more contribution of the volume, Ambe Njoh and Liora Bigon trace the development and use of company towns – settlements built, owned and operated by corporations or individual investors – as an instrument of social engineering employed by the European colonial powers. Their detailed analysis of one such establishment, the workers' camps of the Cameroon Development Corporation (CDC) in Cameroon created by the British colonial government in 1946, illustrates how workers' camps were constructed to articulate power and maintain social order in built space, and at the same time how they served as transmitters of Eurocentric ideals of work and general conduct to the workers. Through close supervision, it was hoped to instill in the workers the Western work ethic, minimize absenteeism and, above all, facilitate employee retention.

One of the main challenges for the CDC was the provision of housing for these workers, amounting up to some 20,000 men. The facilities maintained racial (and later socioeconomic) residential segregation and, as Njoh and Bigon illustrate, different types of housing were provided for different categories of workers. The spacious parcels of land complete with lawns and gardens reserved for European employees of the corporation were typically far-removed from African employees' quarters (usually military barrack structure like) and perched atop higher elevations overlooking these quarters. This constituted just one example of how workers were disciplined and their movement controlled. Njoh's and Bigon's contribution is of particular contemporary relevance as, with the demise of colonialism, the indigenous leadership of the corporation has continued the colonial practice of articulating power and maintaining social order through built space.

This collection concerns itself with the specific role of housing in colonial and postcolonial Africa. In particular, it seeks to uncover and reconstruct the multiple ways in which housing served as a means to achieve other "higher" ends, be it increased efficiency and productivity, or stability and tranquility. Ultimately, permanent housing, rooting Africans both politically and geographically, was meant to create a stabilized, obedient urban middle class – a class of citizens to which the political and economic power was to be handed over in due time. By restructuring African class and gender relations and by creating a stabilized (male) working class, racial ideologies gave place to categorizing Africans along socioeconomic lines. Housing served as a disciplining instrument, an attempt by the colonial state to exercise some authority over all dimensions of dwellers' lives, private, residential, and social aspects included. Studying housing as a reflection of colonial and development discourses and practices provides an excellent opportunity to understand fundamental urban transformations and the shaping of physical spaces under colonialism and post-independence.

References

Archival sources

The National Archives, Kew, UK (TNA)
CO 533/528/17 Nairobi Housing Scheme, 1941.
CO 822/136/3 African Housing Plans, 1947.
CO 822/588 African Urban Housing in Kenya, 1953.
CO 859/490 Housing and Town Planning in Africa, 1953.
CO 892/7/1 East African Royal Commission: Miscellaneous Papers, 1953.

The Kenya National Archives, Nairobi, Kenya (KNA)
ABK/17/6 Vasey African Housing General File, 1951–1953.
ABK 17/13 Vasey Inquiry into African Housing, 1949–1965.
DC/KSM/1/16/53 Vasey Kisumu Housing Committee, 1948–1956.
NHC/1/381 Nairobi County Council African Housing, 1952–1958.

Government reports

Deverell, N. M. *Social Conditions Arising out of the Growth of Large Urban Populations in East Africa*. Nairobi, 1951.
Ogilvie, G. C. W. *The Housing of Africans in the Urban Areas of Kenya*. Nairobi: Kenya Information Office, 1946.
Vasey, Ernest A. *Report on the Housing of Africans in Townships and Trading Centres*. Nairobi, 1950.

Secondary literature

Anderson, David M. "Corruption at City Hall: African Housing and Urban Development in Colonial Nairobi." *Azania: Archaeological Research in Africa* 36–37 (2001): 138–154.
Ansprenger, Franz. *Geschichte Afrikas*, 2nd edition. Muenchen: C.H. Beck, 2004.

Beeckmans, Luce. "Editing the African City: Reading Colonial Planning in Africa from a Comparative Perspective." *Planning Perspectives* 28 (2013): 615–627.
Boudreaux, Karol. "Urbanization and Informality in Africa's Housing Markets." *Institute of Economic Affairs* 28 (2008): 17–24.
Cooper, Frederick. *Citizenship between Empire and Nation: Remaking France and French Africa, 1945–1960*. Princeton: Princeton University Press, 2014.
Cooper, Frederick. *Africa since 1940: The Past of the Present*. Cambridge: Cambridge University Press, 2002.
Cooper, Frederick. *On the African Waterfront: Urban Disorder and the Transformation of Work in Colonial Mombasa*. New Haven & London: Yale University Press, 1987.
Cooper, Frederick. "Urban Space, Industrial Time, and Wage Labor in Africa." In *Struggle for the City: Migrant Labor, Capital, and the State in Urban Africa*, edited by Frederick Cooper, 7–51. Bevery Hills: Sage Publications, 1983.
Coquery-Vidrovitch, Catherine. "From Residential Segregation to African Urban Centres: City Planning and the Modalities of Change in Africa South of the Sahara." *Journal of Contemporary African Studies* 32 (2014): 1–12.
Coquery-Vidrovitch, Catherine. "Economic Changes in Africa in the World Context." In *General History of Africa: Africa since 1935*, edited by Ali A. Mazrui, 285–317. California, UNESCO: James Currey, 1999.
D'Auria, Viviana. "In the Laboratory and in the Field: Hybrid Housing Design for the African City in Late-colonial and Decolonising Ghana (1945–57)." *The Journal of Architecture* 19 (2014): 329–356.
Fourchard, Laurent. "Between World History and State Formation: New Perspectives on Africa's Cities." *Journal of African History* 52 (2011): 223–248.
Gilbert, Alan G. "Home Enterprises in Poor Urban Settlements: Constraints, Potentials, and Policy Options." *Regional Development Dialogue* 9 (1988): 21–37.
Hansen, Karen T. "Lusaka's Squatters: Past and Present." *African Studies Review* 25 (1982): 117–136.
Harris, Richard. "From Trusteeship to Development: How Class and Gender Complicated Kenya's Housing Policy, 1939–1963." *Journal of Historical Geography* 34 (2008): 311–337.
Harris, Richard, and Allison Hay. "New Plans for Housing in Urban Kenya, 1939–1963." *Planning Perspectives* 22 (2007): 195–223.
Harris, Richard, and Susan Parnell. "The Turning Point in Urban Policy for British Colonial Africa, 1939–1945." In *Colonial Architecture and Urbanism in Africa: Intertwined and Contested Histories*, edited by Fassil Demissie, 127–153. Aldershot: Ashgate, 2012.
Headrick, Daniel R. *The Tools of Empire: Technology and European Imperialism in the Nineteenth Century*. Oxford: Oxford University Press, 1981.
Home, Robert. *Of Planting and Planning: The Making of British Colonial Cities*. 2nd edition. New York: Routledge, 2013.
Home, Robert. "From Barrack Compounds to the Single-Family House Planning Worker Housing in Colonial Natal and Northern Rhodesia." *Planning Perspectives* 15 (2000): 327–347.
Home, Robert. "Town Planning and the Garden Cities in the British Colonial Empire 1910–1940." *Planning Perspectives* 5 (1990): 23–37.
Huchzermeyer, Marie. *Cities with 'Slums.' From Informal Settlement Eradication to a Right to the City in Africa*. Cape Town: University of Cape Town Press, 2011.

Kooiman, Jan. *Governing as Governance*. Los Angeles: SAGE Publications, 2003.
Kusow, Abdi. "The Role of Shelter in Generating Income Opportunities for Poor Women in the Third World." In *Shelter, Women and Development*, edited by Hemalata C. Dandekar, 218–224. Michigan: George Wahr, 1993.
Kwak, Nancy. *A World of Homeowners: American Power and the Politics of Housing Aid*. Chicago: University of Chicago Press, 2015.
Mbembe, Achille, and Sarah Nuttall. 2004. "Writing the World from an African Metropolis." *Public Culture* 16 (2004): 347–372.
Myers, Garth Andrew. *African Cities: Alternative Visions of Urban Theory and Practice*. London & New York: Zed-Books, 2011.
Myers, Garth Andrew. *Verandahs of Power: Colonialism and Space in Urban Africa*. New York: Syracuse University Press, 2003.
Myers, Garth Andrew. "Designing Power: Forms and Purpose of Colonial Model Neighborhoods in British Africa." *Habitat International* 27 (2003): 193–204.
Njoh, Ambe. "Ideology and Public Health Elements of Human Settlement Policies in Sub-Saharan Africa." *Cities* 26 (2009): 9–18.
Njoh, Ambe. "Urban Planning as a Tool of Power and Social Control in Colonial Africa." *Planning Perspectives* 24 (2009): 301–317.
Odendaal, Nancy et al. "Planning Education in Sub-Saharan Africa." In *Urban Planning in Sub-Saharan Africa: Colonial and Postcolonial Planning Cultures*, edited by Carlos Nunes Silva, 285–300. London: Routledge, 2015.
Oliver, Roland, and Anthony Atmore. *Africa since 1800*. 5th edition. Cambridge: Cambridge University Press, 2004.
Otiso, Kefa, and George Owusu. "Comparative Urbanization in Ghana and Kenya in Time and Space." *GeoJournal* 71 (2008): 143–157.
Parker, John, and Richard Rathbone. *African History: A Very Short Introduction*. Oxford: Oxford University Press, 2007.
Pieterse, Edgar, and AbdouMaliq Simone, editors. *Rogue Urbanism: Emergent African Cities*. Johannesburg: Jacana Media, 2013.
Rakodi, Carole. "Addressing Gendered Inequalities in Housing." In *Gender, Asset Accumulation and Just Cities: Pathways to Transformation?*, edited by Caroline O. N. Moser, 81–99. London: Routledge, 2015.
Rakodi, Carole. *Harare: Inheriting a Settler-Colonial City: Change or Continuity?* New York: John Wiley, 1995.
Robinson, Jennifer. "Global and World Cities: A View from off the Map." *International Journal of Urban and Regional Research* 26 (2002): 531–554.
Schicho, Walter. "Das Scheitern von Demokratie und Staat." In *Afrika: Geschichte und Gesellschaft im 19. und 20. Jahrhundert*, edited by Ingeborg Grau, Christian Mährdel, and Walter Schicho, 211–241. Wien: Promedia, 2003.
Scott, James. *Seeing Like A State: How Certain Schemes to Improve the Human Condition Have Failed*. New Haven: Yale University Press, 1998.
Silva, Carlos Nunes. "Urban Planning in Sub-Saharan Africa: An Overview." In *Urban Planning in Sub-Saharan Africa: Colonial and Postcolonial Planning Cultures*, edited by Carlos Nunes Silva, 8–40. London: Routledge, 2015.
Stren, Richard. "Underdevelopment, Urban Squatting and the State Bureaucracy: A Case Study of Tanzania." *Canadian Journal of African Studies* 6 (1982): 93–123.

Tipple, Graham A. "The Need for New Urban Housing in Sub-Saharan Africa: Problem or Opportunity." *African Affairs* 93 (1994): 587–608.

Tödt, Daniel. *Elitenbildung und Dekolonisierung: Die Évolués in Belgisch-Kongo 1944–1960*. Göttingen: Vandenhoeck & Ruprecht, Kritische Studien zur Geschichtswissenschaft, Band 228, 2018.

West, Michael Oliver. *The Rise of an African Middle Class: Colonial Zimbabwe, 1898–1965*. Bloomington: Indiana University Press, 2002.

Kirsten Rüther
2 The Rule of Rent: The State, Employers and the Becoming Urban Dweller in Northern Rhodesia Acting Across a Societal Field of Force, c. 1948–1962

Introduction

Urbanization means that people come to town.[1] Their houses, all too often representing a promise rather than a materially available choice, have long become a staple of urban politics. After Northern Rhodesia had become implicated in the metropolitan war effort in the 1940s,[2] it experienced one of the highest urbanization rates throughout the African continent. Moreover, ever since the first step of public investment in the colonies, the 1940 Colonial Development and Welfare Act, made available metropolitan loans, standards, accessibility, and politics of African housing incurred recurring debate and regulation, not only with regard to the Copperbelt region but with regard to other rapidly growing towns as well. At this time, the colonial state was fully established in Northern Rhodesia – albeit the number of expat administrators at no stage exceeded 300 persons.[3]

Even though the majority of white residents, be they from Britain, Germany, Greece, South Africa, Southern Rhodesia or other countries, did not have sustained experience in living in cities, the urbanization of Africans was frowned upon with particular suspicion by planning authorities, town clerks, district commissioners, representatives of municipal ratepayers, and town councilors officially in charge of turning the towns into livable space. While the so-called stabilization of labor became a declared aim of the time, a fundamental reservation pertained against African people's permanent residence in towns, let alone their entitlement to active social and political participation right there. The provision of social and infrastructural amenities was imaginable and, over time, consent emerged that it

---

[1] This paper was written as part of the FWF-granted project "Employment-tied Housing in (Post) colonial Africa" (Project no. P29566–G28). For further information see: housing.univie.ac.at.
[2] Kusum Datta, "Farm Labour, Agrarian Capital and the State in Colonial Zambia: The African Labour Corps, 1942–52," *Journal of Southern African Studies* 14, no. 3 (1988).
[3] Jan-Bart Gewald, "Researching and Writing in the Twilight of an Imagined Conquest: Anthropology in Northern Rhodesia 1930–1960," *History and Anthropology* 18, no. 4 (2007): 483.

∂ Open Access. © 2020 Kirsten Rüther, published by De Gruyter. [CC BY-NC] This work is licensed under a Creative Commons Attribution-NonCommercial 4.0 International License.
https://doi.org/10.1515/9783110601183-002

could be wise to have appointed Africans – less so elected ones – on advisory boards and committees.⁴ This was a paternal gesture along the lines that to advise was to learn while to rule was to teach. Hence, it was not intended to incorporate Africans politically or as fully rights-bearing citizens into the country's emerging conviction "that modern life and improved living standards could be open to all, regardless of race or history of subjugation."⁵ As a result, housing policies consciously withheld resources towards self-assertion or security of tenure. They made available accommodation in the form of social benefits and welfare tokens. Although today housing experiences are dominated by private renting, a free market philosophy, and the use of housing property to achieve financial gain, for the purpose of this paper, we have to engage with a completely different logic. State and employers who had no particular purview of investment or financially gainful speculation provided housing jointly and with a view of "stabilizing" labor.

In this scenario, the payment of rent became a relation that tied up in a web of power the metropolitan colonial state, its Northern Rhodesia government, urban bureaucracies, small as well as internationally operating employers, and the becoming urban dwellers – be they European, African or otherwise, be they immigrants from the South or elsewhere, colonial staff, industrial workers, or anyone else. This paper aims to show how a considerable number of acting bodies and individuals became tied up in the politics of rent. It sets out to detail how and to which effect these actors perceived each other through the experiences of rent payment and collection, and how they tried to make the best out of a system that was complicated and fraught with power biases as well as loopholes. The paper will furthermore assess the changes of some of these constellations as they occurred between 1948, when the African Housing Ordinance was passed, and 1962, when (after a complicated general election) European dominance ended and, with the installation of the first "black government", the path for Zambia's independence was set.⁶

---

4 Draft memorandum of an unnamed member of Livingstone Municipality's Native Affairs Committee, June 1948, in: SP 4/1/33 Municipality of Livingstone, Minutes of Native Affairs Sub-Committee 1948, National Archives of Zambia (hereafter NAZ).
5 Frederick Cooper and Randall Packard, "Introduction," in *International Development and the Social Sciences: Essays on the History and Politics of Knowledge*, ed. Frederick Cooper and Randall Packard (Berkeley, CA: University of California Press, 1997), 9.
6 David Mulford, *Zambia: The Politics of Independence 1957–1964* (Oxford: Oxford University Press, 1967), 56–106, 143–197; Bizeck Jube Phiri, *A Political History of Zambia: From Colonial Rule to the Third Republic, 1890–2001* (Trenton, NJ: Africa World Press, 2006), 31–130, quoted term p. 113.

Approaching the Field of Study

How did the variously implicated acting bodies and individuals relate to each other? Throughout the period under review, rent tied together a multitude of participants in what may be described as a "societal field of force."[7] This concept captures how, between more than just two participants and their mutual relations, power biases and rule became enacted and shifted as a result of interactions.

> Rule, authority and mastery (Herrschaft) [conceived of] as a social practice – this phrase indicates a 'field of force' in which players establish relations between each other. They handle and deal with each other, even if at times they evade or try to ignore each other. It should be noted that this 'field' is not a static entity; its space and its contours change as players act out relations or refrain from them. Moreover, players are not autonomous subjects entering this 'field' from the outside. They evolve in exchange and negotiation to make other maneuvering forces feel their power, the stimuli they set and the demands they wish to impose or thwart. [...] This concept of a 'field of force' in which power is enforced and rule established or queried cannot be grasped in dual poles. Rulers and power holders face the ruled and the overpowered – rulers and power holders define themselves by means of holding sway over the ruled. And yet, rulers and power holders may depend on others while the ruled are more than passive recipients of rule(s) from the powerful. Most importantly, there are inequalities, contradictions, and differences between and among the rulers as well as between and among the ruled.[8]

This concept helps to capture the Northern Rhodesian situation where the state, various urban dwellers, administrations, engineers, the country's Municipal Association, and many more actors forced relations among each other – none of whom acted in either isolation, or an unchallenged power-holding position, or in hopeless subservience. Once an actor moved, the forces between the others in this matrix were recalibrated as well and, as a consequence, so were the exercise, experience, and expectations of legitimate power and rule. Rent and, more particularly, the acts of paying, withholding, or collecting rent worked as a medium that, as a material relationship as well as a more abstract idea, tied together actors in the variously emerging urban settings where people turned into urban dwellers. Thus, rent provides a useful lens through which to grasp the changing

---

7 E. P. Thompson, "Eighteenth-Century English Society: Class Struggle without Class?" *Social History* 3, no. 2 (1978): 151; Alf Lüdtke, "Einleitung: Herrschaft als soziale Praxis," in *Herrschaft als soziale Praxis: Historische und sozial-anthropologische Studien*, ed. Alf Lüdtke (Göttingen: Vandenhoek & Ruprecht, 1991). For reasons of readability and because I take over this term into my own vocabulary, I hereafter refrain from using inverted commas.
8 Lüdtke, "Einleitung", 12–13.

constellations of power and scopes for negotiation. The second section of this chapter will focus on these constellations.

Northern Rhodesia became a protectorate that was taken over from the British South Africa Company by the Colonial Office with an administration headed by a Governor in 1924. It was ever more successfully claimed as "their own" by settlers from various backgrounds, many of whom were British or Afrikaans-speaking farmers from Southern Rhodesia or South Africa. Increased European immigration – again from various parts of Europe, Southern Rhodesia, and South Africa – had prompted the consideration of improved housing for "Europeans" as early as 1942.[9] Almost simultaneously, the Colonial Office in London circulated a position paper on the "General Aspects of the Housing Problem in the Colonial Empire" to its colonial governments. It pressed for reviewing existing housing legislation and recommended the introduction of town planning procedures and housing committees in each territory.[10] In the colonial metropole, the Colonial Housing Research Group was initiated and chaired by the newly appointed director of the recently established Building Research Station to advise the Colonial Office on the organization of housing research in the colonies. Knowledge about building "in the tropics" became efficiently centralized, especially once each British colony assigned a technical officer henceforth to correspond with the metropolitan chief liaison officer. In southern-central Africa, the Central African Council appointed a Standing Committee on African Housing in 1945. It met consecutively in the respective capitals of Salisbury, Lusaka, and Limbe.[11] Finally, in 1948, the African Housing Ordinance compelled employers to either build houses for their employees, including their legal wife and family, or pay rent for their accommodation to be erected under the aegis of local and municipal authorities. Funds were transferred from London to Lusaka and from there into the apparatus of colonial bureaucracy.

A significant number of areas became filled with houses by 1952.[12] Concomitantly, a "Report of Committee to Inquire into the African and Eurafrican

---

9 Telegram from Sir J. Waddington, Northern Rhodesia, to Secretary of State for the Colonies, 2 June 1942 and further correspondence, in: CO 795/123/4 Copperbelt Labour Supplies. Housing Question, 1942–1943, The National Archives, Kew (hereafter TNA).
10 Colonial Office, *Housing in British African Territories* (London: Her Majesty's Stationary Office, 1954), 10–11, in: LGH 1/16/53 African Housing. Atkinson Report, 1953, NAZ.
11 Minutes of the first meeting of the Standing African Housing Committee, Salisbury, 3–5 September 1945, in: CO 927/35/3 Housing Research, Central Africa, 1945–1947, TNA.
12 "Col. Wilson gives housing figures for Africans," *Northern News* 4 December 1952, and further records, in: LGH 1/16/52 Local Government: African Housing. General Policy, 1952–1953, NAZ.

Housing Position in Lusaka" confirmed that much more housing was needed.[13] Perhaps predictably, the number of houses built would always lag behind demand. In addition, despite increased government spending on African welfare, especially on housing, it was always much less than it could have been and, visibly for all, it was unimpressive compared with spending on services for Europeans.[14] The standard of African housing[15] projected buildings to last some 20 or 25 years, whereas loans were repayable over a period of 40 years. In the long run, this would develop into "an extremely serious position,"[16] especially when the metropolitan and central governments divested themselves of the financial and administrative burdens of housing by transferring it to the responsibility of Local Authorities and individual municipalities. It was in fact in the mid-1950s, against the backdrop of housing provision becoming more burdensome and mounting political pressure from African nationalist politicians, that Africans became increasingly welcome into the Township Management Boards through which rent from so-called self-payers and fees or charges and services were to be collected. Such boards, staffed by Europeans and some Africans of honorary appointment, first existed for larger townships which were promised that, in case of successful development, they could develop into a municipality and establish their own municipal council. Up to that point, they would be subject to another municipal council.[17]

Even though rent represented a crucial form of tenure and mutual entanglement in towns, in academic literature it has largely been neglected.[18] Where it was paid, rent was imbued with conflicts between private (and, to speak more

---

13 "Report of the Committee to Inquire into the African and Eurafrican Housing Position in Lusaka" [Nightingale Committee], discussed 5 May 1953, in: LGH 1/16/49 Housing for Eurafricans, 1949–1953, NAZ.
14 Andrew Roberts, *A History of Zambia* (London: Heinemann, 1976), 215–216.
15 Due to the idea that Africans would live in geographically determined zones, the so-called "African areas", the administration used "African housing" as a predominantly spatially related category. Africans who lived on educational establishments, in hospital wards, in police camps within European zones, or along the boundaries between officially designated zones (also called "open areas" according to Phiri, *Political History of Zambia*, 41) lived in buildings which were not necessarily submitted to the regulations of African housing.
16 Acting Commissioner for Local Government, S. W. Coleman, to Member for Lands and Local Government, 7 October 1958, in: LGH 1/8/1 Local Government: Municipal Association General, 1952–1963, NAZ.
17 Emmanuel Mutale, *The Management of Urban Development in Zambia* (Farnham: Ashgate, 2004), chapter 4 (book not paginated).
18 Carole Rakodi, "Rental Tenure in the Cities of Developing Countries," *Urban Studies* 32, no. 4–5 (1995).

bluntly, often greedy) landlords, (usually impoverished) tenants, and state agencies incapable of or unwilling to provide housing. Not only in Tanzania or in Kenya, such landlords were often of Indian descent which contributed to rent becoming an important ingredient for racialized post-independent policies regulating housing property.[19] Even though the state introduced rent limits or expropriated Indian landlords, this usually did not help the tenants if no additional housing became available. In Nairobi, for instance, unprecedentedly exploitative relations emerged after independence. They were an immediate result of a neglect of building houses for African workers in the colonial period. The persistent focus on ownership issues, however, has resulted in a distorted thinking in terms of tenement housing. Instead, the current debate focuses on unwanted "slums" rather than on achieving secure tenure through tenant-protecting rental agreements.[20]

Where rent was experienced as exploitative, boycotts became an issue. In South Africa, for instance, they turned into nationwide civil unrest throughout the 1980s and represented dwellers' responses to unaffordable rents and imminent eviction. Such boycotts also helped create a group awareness and a readiness to confront the state and municipality more generally.[21] In Kenya, as well, where living conditions in the major cities were harsh, rent boycotts represented a moment of citizen mobilization.[22] With regard to Northern Rhodesia, however, it is striking that colonial powers initially took rent-paying by tenants out of the power equation – to reduce conflict and to "deprive" urban dwellers of the reason for turning to organized protest against rent. Instead, Africans becoming urban dwellers in colonial Zambia boycotted in concerted action Asian and European shops, butchers selling bad meat wrapped in greasy paper, and elections, but there was no mobilization against rent issues.[23] This aspect will be taken up in the subsequent section on the payment of rent as a relational force.

---

19 James R. Brennan, *Taifa: Making Nation and Race in Urban Tanzania* (Athens, OH: Ohio University Press, 2012), 1–20; see also William Cunningham Bissell, *Urban Design, Chaos, and Colonial Power in Zanzibar* (Bloomington, IN: Indiana University Press, 2011), 174, 238.
20 Marie Huchzermeyer, "Tenement City: The Emergence of Multi-Storey Districts Through Large-Scale Private Landlordism in Nairobi," *International Journal of Urban and Regional Research* 31, no. 4 (2007).
21 Matthew Chaskalson, Karen Jochelson, and Jeremy Seekings, "Rent Boycotts, the State and the Transformation of the Urban Political Economy in South Africa," *Review of African Political Economy* 40 (1987).
22 For a literary engagement with this important issue see, for instance, Meja Mwangi, *The Cockroach Dance*. 2nd edition (Columbus, Ohio: HM Books Intl., 2017).
23 Stephen A. Mpashi, *Betty Kaunda* (Lusaka: Longmans, 1969), 38–39.

Only where residents looked back on long histories of settlement and tenancy, tenant associations emerged. This was the case in Bulawayo where, after 1951, a Rent Payers Association not only started to engage critically with the activities of the Location Advisory Board but also offered a platform for women to enter urban politics when board members were all male.[24] For the majority of becoming urban dwellers, however, actual access to housing remained the more acute problem.[25] People had to become rent payers first before they could organize as such and claim rights. As employers paid the rent for the majority of their generally low-paid African workforce, it remained difficult for tenants to position themselves independently and away from a stifling "master-servant" relation. It took a long time before they developed a self-conception as payers of rent and rates, despite the efforts of proponents of African nationalism who, immediately after the formation of the Central African Federation in 1953, forcefully drove social and political dynamics towards this direction.

A distinct situation emerged for African civil servants, many of whom aspired to occupy the same, or at least a similar, class position as their often Oxbridge-educated colonial peers and superiors. Their rent was less subjugated to a master-servant relationship and at times not even to the specific regulations of an officially denominated "African area". Quite frequently, and more tangibly however, a so-called "color bar" hampered their aspirations as will be described later. Many of these civil servants had a clear understanding of how Africans lived in most cases and how, at the same time, privileged white members of the Colonial Service lived, dwelled and resided. This is also the reason why the latter group's housing will come under scrutiny in the third section of this contribution on people moving places and residences. Of course, rent changed its significance over time and against the backdrop of heightened political tensions which occurred towards the imminent expectation of Zambian independence. This will be addressed in the fourth section of this contribution with a view to looking at political change through the vantage point of what happened with regard to housing and rent.

The contribution is based on documentary evidence gained from the National Archives in London and Lusaka respectively. Various departments of the colonial administration dealt with issues of housing. They collected evidence, papers, and memoranda from other interest groups, filed minutes from advisory councils,

---

24 Terence Ranger, *Bulawayo Burning: The Social History of a Southern African City, 1893–1960* (Suffolk: Boydell & Brewer, 2010), 171–174.
25 Amin Y. Kamete II, "Civil Society, Housing and Urban Governance: The Case of Urban Housing Co-operatives in Zimbabwe," in *Associational Life in African Cities: Popular Responses to the Urban Crisis*, ed. Arne Tostensen, Inge Tvedten, and Mariken Vaa (Stockholm: Nordiska Afrikainstitutet, 2001).

legislation drafts and paid careful attention to newspaper coverage. This makes up for a rich and friction-bearing variety of perspectives and the documentation of controversies on issues related to the provision of housing and the ways tenants used and appropriated it. A serious impediment arises from the fact that the perspectives of the people for whom the houses were provided are rendered indirectly only. Moreover, the individuals and bodies that documented and archived material about housing were not necessarily inclined to use the same terms with reference to the same meaning. Planners, for instance, spoke of "African housing" as a spatially or typologically determined category, whereas settler politicians used the term "Africans" as a racial category intended to apply to people of color whom they did not want to differentiate either ethnically or with regard to social standing. Engineers referred to "housing types" rather than areas, people, or building projects, especially when houses were built and where the need for repair occurred. The colonial administration was interested in controlling areas and less so in how particular housing projects developed, at least not once they had been finished and started to expand or collapse. The Urban Advisory Boards, in turn, took individual houses and individuals' complaints as the starting point for dealing with housing issues and particular buildings. Today these individual houses cannot easily be identified, as there are often no street names or other indicators which would facilitate such a tracing.

This has major implications for the historian who wishes to trace the path of either a group of tenants or a set of houses allocated to one particular employer in a larger municipal area. Usually, we cannot follow a stringent trace but have to "hop around" between incidents, fragments, moments, and perspectives. Comprehending the categories pre-determined in the archival documentation, to read, in combined efforts, along and against the grain, we have to engage with the existing order as well as to try and overcome it.[26] It is basically impossible to follow one set of actors, houses, or problems through multifaceted documentation which, each in itself, produces its own paper trails, categories, and units of observation. It is also not always clear how the key categories, terms, and phrases are to be wound down into clear racial, ethnic, social, or gender equivalents. Many denotations remain murky. As a result, as researchers and readers, we sometimes have to put up with a certain unease and remaining vagueness when we write and read about the rule of rent.

---

[26] Ann Laura Stoler, *Along the Archival Grain: Epistemic Anxieties and Colonial Common Sense* (Princeton: Princeton University Press, 2009).

The Payment of Rent as a Relational Force

In Northern Rhodesian towns, actors such as employers, the colonial and local governments, municipalities, engineers and, last but certainly not least, the workers and their families, as well as the aspiring African civil servants, enforced their powers, interests, and skepticisms upon each other. After the 1948 African Housing Ordinance ruled that employers would have to house their labor force or pay for its accommodation, this became accepted policy. It was seconded by the Employment of Natives Ordinance which dated back to 1929 and was amended in 1953. The ordinances bound large employers, such as the mines, the Zambesi Saw Mills or the Rhodesia Railway Company, in the same way as it bound the colonial government itself in whose service clerks, policemen, teachers, public work laborers, health officers, men in the postal and communication services, and many more stood. They also bound small employers such as market gardening companies, charcoal burning enterprises, fish or tobacco farming as well as small entrepreneurs in the transport business. With the Ministry of Mines and Labour (later renamed into Mines, Labour and Social Services) an agreement existed that, for workers earning less than £10 per month, employers paid the rent directly to local authorities or to the municipality, and only in 1963, as part of an incessant debate about paying an all-in wage, discussions started that this should perhaps be shifted to the amount of £15.[27] The very few men whose earnings exceeded this amount were expected to pay themselves – again, only after exemption had been granted through the Commissioner of Labour and Mines. Rent thus tightened relations between state and employers and turned workers into recipients of the fruits of that power web – as long as they were formally employed. In cases of unemployment, prolonged sickness, and after retirement they were removed from that tripartite relation and had to fend for themselves.[28]

The system did not run smoothly. The legislation was modeled on an understanding of paternalist rule, as in idealized circumstances it assumed legitimacy between a well-meaning, perhaps even feudal, master and obedient and, in the best of cases, cared-for servants. Colonial paternalism may have proved attractive from the viewpoint of the British colonizers for whom it produced a re-encounter with their own pre-modern past and a largely outmoded form of rural social organization.[29] It was inappropriate, in many ways, to meet African

---

[27] Report of the Secretary to the Executive Committee, 1 October 1963, in: LGH 1/2/72 Township Regulations, 1963–66, NAZ.
[28] For a general overview see Roberts, *History of Zambia*, 187–194.
[29] On paternalism as a backward-looking myth or ideology see Thompson, "Eighteenth-Century English Society," 134–137.

people's expectations and aspirations to move towards modern life and improved living standards. It was also inappropriate for employers' capitalist-driven ambitions. Reading across a multitude of files it appears that in most cases employers other than the internationally operating mines were reluctant to bind capital in company housing and organize resources for the upkeep of that asset. They generally preferred to pay rent and keep the wages accordingly low. Sometimes they offered housing allowances if municipal housing was unavailable. For employers, generally, it virtually paid much more and would have sufficed that, in dealing with the moderate trade union leader Lawrence Katilungu, in the decade between 1949 and 1959 the Northern Rhodesia Government successfully kept trade union affairs and politics in separate compartments. The government's effective curbing of trade unionism secured the persistence of a low-wage economy, and workers had no possibility of falling back onto an organization which would have pushed the expression of their frustrations.[30] In fact, better schooling would have assisted employers far more than housing offers to get hold of the labor and skills they required.

Once the Central African Federation had come into existence and the African nationalist parties asserted their position between 1953 and 1957, it would turn out that large employers, such as the mining companies, devised their own policies to maintain power in the region. Rather than using housing for their political agendas they started to talk to leaders and to support the Federation government and offered to African nationalist politicians loans or financial incentives.[31] They allowed skilled African miners into jobs previously held by Europeans – albeit for a third or even less of what white miners had earned.[32] Even though rent was an issue of daily concern, it did not become a topic "appropriated" by the workers. Smaller enterprises went on as before. In the end, none of all these employers' art of domination really depended on the provision of houses. They went by it as long as the colonial legislation required them to do so. They refrained from undermining the authority of the colonial state, which supported the interests of various employers and tried to get them on board, as best as they could. However, the more mobile employers, such as

---

30 Mulford, *Zambia*, 170–177.
31 Andrew Cohen, "Business and Decolonisation in Central Africa Reconsidered," *Journal of Imperial and Commonwealth History* 36, no. 4 (2008).
32 Ian Phimister, "Proletarians in Paradise: The Historiography and Historical Sociology of White Miners on the Copperbelt," in *Living the End of Empire: Politics and Society in Late Colonial Zambia*, ed. Giacomo Macola, Jan-Bart Gewald, and Marja Hinfelaar (Leiden: Brill, 2011), 151–152; and Jane Parpart, *Labor and Capital on the African Copperbelt* (Philadelphia: Temple University Press, 1983), 136–137.

the Rhodesia Railways, the Zambesi Saw Mills or the various construction companies always lagged behind with the provision of housing according to standards due to their changing sites of business activity.

The postwar colonial state, despite its paternal gestures, extended control over subjects and becoming citizens to demonstrate its rationality and efficiency. Disciplining the populace, bettering their living conditions and making male labor subservient and content in the comforts of family homes became important initiatives in order to intensify the state's outreach. Colonialism represented an authoritarian form of rule. More acutely than before, the state was felt in personal surroundings. As a result, workers became eager to participate in the promises which existed nevertheless and claimed opportunities for themselves.[33] However, even though liberally minded sections of the colonizers promoted the idea of a new African middle class to emerge, colonial authorities more generally lacked the inclination to let an independent and rights-demanding African citizenry emerge. Ideally, the majority of Africans would arrange themselves and cooperate with colonial rule, so that despite discontent and friction they would not have to face open challenges or resistance. To achieve this, it had to leave enough scope for subservient people to carve out and make use of economic, cultural, and social niches in which they could pursue family life and indulgence in social welfare activities (even though these social welfare clubs became the very foundations of organized political activities). For this reason, it definitely made sense to make rent a concern to be agreed upon between employers and local authorities and to turn housing into a social benefit rather than an asset that families would consider their own. Naturally, this was resource-intensive. Over the years, the official housing policy improved housing and enhanced certain standards for some rather than for all.[34] The majority of the urban working-class people continued to make their own housing arrangements.[35] And yet, as long as rent was not paid by a

---

33 James Ferguson, *Expectations of Modernity: Myths and Meanings of Urban Life on the Zambian Copperbelt* (Berkeley: University of California Press, 2001).
34 It has been argued that in rural development policies, the minority of "modernizing" farmers, the so-called "emergent farmer," rather than the majority of poor and small-scale producers were intended as recipients of support. See Kate Crehan and Achim von Oppen, "Understandings of 'Development': An Arena for Struggle. The Making of a Development Project in North-Western Province," in *Planners and History: Negotiating 'Development' in Rural Zambia*, ed. Kate Crehan and Achim von Oppen (Lusaka: Multimedia Publications, 1994). This pertains to the urban situation as well, where a small number of formally employed African workers became the recipients of housing.
35 Karen Tranberg Hansen, *Distant Companions: Servants and Employers in Zambia, 1900–1985* (Ithaca, NY: Cornell University Press, 1989), 120.

large number of employees themselves, it remained difficult for them to claim permanence in their new surroundings.

Of course, there was the wish of those who came to the towns as workers to achieve entitlement to their new place, to be able to pay the required rates and taxes, to live in decency, and to be able to support a family as well as other aspirations pursued either in town, back home, or in both places. These people were prepared to submit to the supervision and tutelage of employers and towns. As evidently public spending went into urban and industrializing areas rather than into rural areas and agriculture, cash and the promises of wage employment were to be tapped right there – often to the detriment of rural areas. Rent, paid by others, inhibited permanence in the towns. It tied Africans, especially formally employed African workers, to political authorities as clients rather than independent town dwellers. And in fact, once direct political representation became a concerted claim in the colony, the paying of rent was used to denigrate African tenants as unpropertied and thus unqualified for the franchise.

In a perfectly controlled setting, rent thus enacted would have kept tenants in check. Laborers, however, who lost their families' accommodation in the case of unemployment, when they changed employers or when official housing was unavailable, arranged to live in what the colonial administration labeled as "private locations," "unauthorised settlements" or, in the case of Livingstone, even "loafers' compounds."[36] As many stayed in such places even after taking up work with another employer, these sub-scenarios of power and dependency substantially inhibited the purview of the state-employer dominance in the Northern Rhodesian field of force. Building standards and living conditions of "unauthorised housing" did not receive official approval. The places were often, though not always, overpriced. Colonial state departments were prone to losing grip of the situation.

> There are always difficulties about having little islands in a Government area leased to private individuals. Arguments start over the length of term of the lease before it is granted, continue about the type of building to be erected, and only cease when the lease is surrendered or falls in – and even then only after a final haggle about payment of compensation.[37]

---

36 MLSS 1/24/7 Labour Department. African Housing (Unauthorised Locations), 1955–1961, NAZ; LGH 1/1/30 Unauthorised Locations, 1960–1968, NAZ; MLSS 1/24/2 Housing. Native Locations. Private Locations, 1944, NAZ; SP 4/1/30 Municipality of Livingstone. Minutes Native Affairs Sub-Committee Meetings, 1947, NAZ.
37 Director of Lands and Surveys, Livingstone, to Secretariat, Lusaka, 13 March 1950, in: LGH 3/2/9 Livingstone: Areas and Boundaries, 1951–59, NAZ.

Employers protested against having to pay rent to the Local Authorities for workers who lived in such surroundings.[38] They actually found it difficult to keep track of where their laborers lived just as rent-collecting Local Authorities did not always know which laborers were paid for by their employers, who had to pay rent themselves, and how many workers might live in one house (and would have had to pay rent for it, too). Thus, the collection and payment of rent evolved into a highly arbitrary activity:

> Half the men in Kalingalinga are unemployed, I was told by Africans there. So when the rent collector comes round for the 10s. a month rent, the jobless Africans have to borrow from their employed 'brothers'. The rent collector, incidentally, lives in 'Capital House', as Africans described his abode to me. The rent collector is the agent of the landowners – chiefly Indians – and besides collecting rent he visits each house giving any orders or instructions the landlords of the five sections of the compound wish to make.[39]

As problematic as living in such places proved to be, it opened up scope for self-employment, for living near one's relatives and, perhaps, some other advantages not documented in the archival fold. The documents, rich as they are, absorb and swallow much of what we would like to establish with more clarity. We cannot actually retrieve from the archival documentation how many workers preferred to pay higher rent for standardized homes. Many Africans, though, workers, civil servants, and incipient entrepreneurs, so it appears from reading the debates across the files, would have preferred to pay their own rent. They wanted to pay less rent for old houses with leaking roofs and in need of repair – houses they could probably have afforded more easily in comparison to the newer two- or three-roomed houses of different standards.[40] Others argued that they preferred to receive a cash allowance they could have spent on items more desirable than rent. Such responses indicate a wish on the part of workers and town dwellers to assume control over resources. They also indicate changing expectations with regard to necessary expenses and desirable commodities. From the record, it is unfathomable when and how exactly such attitudes may have changed. But attitudes in 1957 differed from what they used to be in 1948. People then consistently complained about a lack of infrastructure, wished to retain their houses in times of unemployment, had more encompassing consumer wishes and desired to take

---

38 Labour Officer's Office to Labour Commissioner, Lusaka, 9 February 1956, in: MLSS 1/24/7, NAZ.
39 "Rough – But Alive", *Central African Post*, 26 October 1960, in: MLSS 1/24/7, NAZ.
40 SP 4/6/10 Urban Advisory Councils and Welfare Associations. General, 1952–1956, NAZ.

decisions about the areas in which they lived.[41] As becoming urban citizens, they claimed entitlement and expressed their aspiration towards participation in the towns. A sense of entitlement, participation, and access to consumer commodities crystallized around rent, which was paid in money, but again, at least in the archival record, rent did not arise as a topic of contention pushed from either town dwellers, workers, civil servants or the advisory councils. Rent was a tie, and it was tied itself to many other, more immediate claims to living rightful in an urban context.

Between the metropolitan government committing itself to a rhetoric of multiracialism, the operations of the settler immigrants, many of whom openly favored either racist policies or liberal positions, the Federation government which insisted on independent action from the metropole, and the locally situated municipalities, an inherent web of tensions is worth of note. The colonial bureaucracy was staffed with Oxon graduates who seldom feared job competition and who were often more well-disposed to African people's aspirations. They frequently resorted to open paternalism and to patronizing attitudes.[42] This was different with European and South African whites who envisaged their lives and prosperity permanently in Northern Rhodesia and who were particularly suspicious of any political interference from the Colonial Office back in London. London, in turn, even though critical of growing settler antagonism, also felt the ambiguous task to protect this group. Lacking desired liberality, they were nevertheless deemed superior to Africans who, notwithstanding, had a right to progress and advance.

With the introduction of the Central African Federation's racially discriminatory legislation, a fear of a legally inscribed racism into Northern Rhodesia's society prompted the rise of African nationalism. This African nationalism was borne by the African National Congress (ANC) in the initial years. After the breakaway of the more radical Zambia African National Congress (ZANC) in 1958 (which a year later became the United Independence Party (UNIP)), competition between two versions of African nationalism intensified. With regard to urban policy and planning, white and European settlers from the South were much more effectively represented in the Municipal Association of Northern Rhodesia. This body campaigned ruthlessly for privileges along the lines of South African apartheid rules. They advocated spatial separation and segregated administration setups and did not encounter serious resistance in the Urban Advisory Councils and

---

41 "Take-note motion" of the Brown Report, Mr. Cousins, Nominated Official, *Hansard* 7 August 1957, in: MLSS 1/24/14 Employment of Natives and "Housing Conditions", 1957–1959, NAZ.
42 Gewald, "Researching and Writing," 35.

African Affairs Committees, which were often toothless tigers on the basis of contested legitimacy among the constituency they were due to represent.

After 1940, in an act of welfare and development, the Colonial Office in London had started to channel funds to the colonies, more particularly, to the newly founded Department of Local Government and Social Welfare (at times also named the Department of Local Government and Housing), for the erection of housing. For a brief period, the philosophy of cost-recovery was substituted: to overcome the problems attached to a low-wage economy, and to persuade employers into the scheme, they suggested the provisional introduction of sub-economic rents.[43] When the metropolitan government became more reluctant to colonize, because it had to keep settlers at bay and to finance increasing welfare commitments, housing was transferred into the responsibility of the colonies themselves. This included the handling of finances. Debates changed almost immediately once it became clear, shortly after 1957, that central funds would soon be withdrawn. All of a sudden, by 1959, arguments about economic rents and the payment of rent surfaced as a precondition for turning tenants into rights-bearing citizens – as will be commented upon further below. Rent then became a strand tied to which the more important issue of citizenship moved to the fore.

There is at least one more force to be taken into consideration on the Northern Rhodesian field of force. For the implementation of housing programs, the colonial administration relied on techno-scientific expertise. Already in its initial stages of the late nineteenth century, the planning professions had reflected a strengthened role for the state which went hand in glove with techno-scientific management approaches to growing populations in rapidly industrializing nations.[44] After the ending of the Second World War, engineering and planning professionals tapped the new knowledge emerging from building research and coordinated it through the metropole. When engineers entered the Northern Rhodesian societal field of force, they advocated "modern" means, such as zoning, to achieve the control of the urban population. This was a tool of control which was detached and worked through de-emphasizing the logic of personalized rule. The South African writer Ivan Vladislavic crisply captures this attitude

---

43 Northern Rhodesia Colonial Governor, J. Waddington, to A. B. Cohen, Colonial Office, 13 February 1946, in: CO 927/35/3 Housing Research, Central Africa, 1945–1947, TNA. For the debate in Livingstone see, for instance, Municipality of Livingstone's Report of meeting with Commissioner for Local Government and African Housing, L. W. G. Eccles, and Executive Engineer, A. M. Dibble, 17 October 1946, in: SP 4/3/6 Municipality of Livingstone, Native Affairs Sub-Committee, 1946, NAZ.
44 Robert K. Home, *Of Planting and Planning: The Making of British Colonial Cities*. 2nd edition (Oxford: Routledge, 2013), 36–61.

in two of his fictional characters, a sanitary engineer who "always found it strange to set foot for the first time in a place he knew from the plans," and a public planner who pondered that "we don't have relations with the public. We have relations with local governments."[45] This was another strategy to conceptualize the power biases of urban planning without the tenant or urban dweller being represented in government institutions or in the colony-wide Municipal Association.

Couched in a lexicon of rationality and neutrality – thus overriding conflict, interest and bias – the language of planning and engineering left a significant imprint on the way in which actors in the Northern Rhodesian field of force were able to engage with regard to housing and spatial planning. Even well-meaning politicians learned with surprise from some of their African colleagues that, for instance, rather than speaking of different zones and areas, Africans referred to "going down Colour Bar Road" when commenting upon racialized urban planning legislation.

> You talk to an African, a fairly leading citizen, perhaps an African Civil Servant or something like that, and he suddenly says, 'I was going down Colour Bar Road the other day'. Well now, you learn something that you did not know before. You have seen the road, you never realised that the tarmac stopped at one place and it went on as an earth road; you never even noticed it. [...] [Y]ou realise that something should be done about it; and in fact it . . . was taken up by the hon. Member for Lands and Local Government.[46]

Mr. Franklin, the Member for Education and Social Services in the Northern Rhodesia Legislative Council, who made this remark, still thought in terms of material infrastructure and built environment, while his interlocutor probably meant to describe racial discrimination more generally. In fact, the language of engineering earned itself a reputation for de-emphasizing the human element which, up to today, remains a major effort to reintroduce.[47] Instead, their lexicon and discourse revolved around standards, building material, and measurements, not even rent, ownership, and subsidization which preoccupied colonial politicians in the first instance. Hardly ever did anyone mention African people's right to permanence in the towns as urban dwellers. But Africans, civil servants, workers, and councils pressed hard to shift the more technically phrased debates to

---

45 Ivan Vladislavic, *The Exploded View* (Cape Town: Umuzi, 2017), 52, 56.
46 Mr. Franklin, Member for Education and Social Services, in LegCo debate, *Hansard* 92x, 7 August 1957, in: MLSS 1/24/14, NAZ.
47 Nicholas Sungura, "Der Faktor Mensch bei der Risikosteuerung öffentlicher Bauvorhaben in Kenia" (Dr. Eng. diss., University of Hannover, 2016). See also the interview with Nicholas Sungura and Marlene Wagner in this volume.

agendas in which they demanded their employers and fellow politicians to account for policies of inequality in appropriate language.⁴⁸

A group whose interactions with European holders of power intensified towards the late 1950s, and who represented yet another player on the Northern Rhodesian field of force, was African civil servants. The ways they voiced their aspirations is therefore particularly indicative with regard to the evolvement of power relations as crystallized through understandings of housing and rent. With the exception of hospital staff, police, and teachers at higher educational institutions, civil servants were not housed in their own compounds but lived interspersed with other Africans to whom they were intended to serve as role models. Safeli Chileshe, member of the First African Representative Council and elected to the Legislative Council in 1954, did not receive accommodation in a township when starting his career as a teacher but was put up in a hurriedly constructed house on the western side of the township, on Burma Road, which served as a dividing line between African compounds on the West and artisans of European extraction on the East. Chileshe remembers this abode as "no-man's land house."⁴⁹ In the medium and higher ranks, African civil servants were entitled to better-type housing. This was built in distinct places, sometimes in the in-between spaces bordering either European residential areas or large roads leading up to European housing areas. The accommodation of individual Africans of senior rank would become even more complicated once African civil servants became integrated into civil service in larger numbers and at higher ranks. It was through them that the privileged housing circumstances for Europeans come into view, as they served as a reference for those to whom this kind of housing was not (yet) available but who attained prospective entitlement to it through the years. It was in this group that the racism of housing policies mattered tangibly, as many Africans aspired to higher ranks but were outdone in terms of material wealth by whites of lower social or educational rank. As John Mwanakatwe, who achieved a distinguished record in government service, first as an education officer and later as the first African secondary-school principal in Northern Rhodesia, noted in his autobiography:

> I had serious reservations about the attitude of the less educated white clerical officers and businessmen. Such white men and women enjoyed privileges – salaries, housing and

---

48 Various minutes and reports in: SP 4/1/26 Municipality of Livingstone. Minutes. Public Works – Sub-Committee, 1946–1955, NAZ.
49 Jonathan H. Chileshe, *Alderman Safeli Hannock Chileshe: A Tribute to (the Man), His Life, and History* (Ndola: Mission Press, 1998), 65.

social amenities not because of their superior abilities or qualifications, but simply because of the colour of their skin.[50]

In Northern Rhodesia, society was interdependent, even though by far not integrated. It therefore helps to look at housing involvements not just of Africans but of others as well. Housing for Africans was indeed embedded in a polarized society in which a plurality of extremes and nodes, an unevenly structured fabric soaked with inequality, channeled access to housing. The issue at stake was not primarily rent, but housing itself, its physical provision as well as the way it signified privilege.

People Moving Places and Residence

What was this privilege demonstrated in the colony? Fresh from the British metropole, the young colonial servants' discourse was all about largeness, unavailability, and being prepared to move when they talked about housing. They were a "wandering flock," part of "Northern Rhodesia's migrating herds."[51] For young men, Lusaka nevertheless was a place of promise as compared, for instance, to any of the dull Lancastrian towns back home. If unmarried, colonial servants were not entitled to housing of their own immediately upon their arrival in the colony. While being based in the Government Rest House, some took it as a virtual sport to find opportunities for house-sitting the most splendid and well-staffed mansions of senior colleagues for the time they went on leave. For the occupiers of such large state-provided homes, in turn, it was advantageous to hand over their house to a known or trusted person. This ensured that they would not have to fully move out of the allotted house. As leaves were long – colonial servants acquired five days of holiday per month so that after three years these accumulated up to 180 days plus 42 days of travel – housing committees were keen on putting new arrivals or people from the waiting list into the empty houses.[52] Sparing the host the burden of having to pack personal items away and offering them the opportunity to repossess the same house after their

---

50 John M. Mwanakatwe, *Teacher, Politician, Lawyer: My Autobiography* (Lusaka: Bookworld Publications, 2003), 67. In this memoir, it becomes clear that at least in later years members of the African new elite also read the memoirs of the older British civil servant group, see especially pp. 44–45.
51 Frank Bennett, *Under an African Sun: Memoirs of a Colonial Officer in Northern Rhodesia* (London: Radcliffe, 2005), 97, 98.
52 Bennett, *African Sun*, 31–33, 72.

return, the young Frank Bennett managed to dive into the promises of colonial abundance so that, already in youthful years, he enjoyed a status unaffordable to him back home. While his life was (still) impermanent, he moved into the appropriate networks. This set him on the track of upward social mobility. Other people also moved in and out in a world that held more than permanent possessions. And even though in the living room of expatriates' houses the furniture was hard, once having received some curtains for adorning at least the windows, the houses received a personal touch and became the basis for the pursuit of an unknown lifestyle, with cooks, gardeners, and other servants.[53] Rent was calculated on the basis of these civil servants' salaries rather than in relation to the luxuriousness of the respective house they had grabbed from colleagues. If they wished, they moved across a masculine imperial world in which they were able to "fl[ee] from domesticity."[54] They added adventure to their lives or, if they preferred otherwise, created promises to their evolving families.

Housing experiences of British colonial officers in Northern Rhodesia thus resembled what "empire families" felt elsewhere and conveyed an important experience via letters back home. They moved from one place to another, packed repeatedly and each time filled new accommodations with another set of cheaply purchased furnishings. They always rented houses, or had the government rent the houses for them. Accumulating relatively few pieces of furniture and keeping a small quantity of portable decorative objects only, many of them, however, looked forward to being rewarded with a small English house upon retirement.[55] The house "at home" represented an expectation. More than once, this turned into plain disappointment, as returnees from Northern Rhodesia soon realized.

---

[53] Mick Bond, *From Northern Rhodesia to Zambia: Recollections of a DO/DC 1962–73* (Oxford: Gadsden Publishers, 2014), 13–28.
[54] John Tosh, "Imperial Masculinity and the Flight from Domesticity in Britain, 1880–1914," in *Gender and Colonialism*, ed. Timothy P. Foley et al. (Galway: Galway University Press, 1995). Tosh's observation has been made for an earlier period, but it holds for this context as well.
[55] Elizabeth Buettner, *Empire Families: Britons and Late Imperial India* (Oxford: Oxford University Press, 2005), 189–194. As regards the situation of workers in Northern Rhodesia classified as "European", it is a commonplace that white immigrants from South Africa were less secure in their social position and used racism and racial politics in different ways to better and back up their position. For most of the 1950s, the real earnings of white artisans were approximately 20 times greater than those of the black workers they supervised; see Phimister, "Proletarians in Paradise", 154. On the mines, earnings were good, housing was provided, European workers could buy cars and go to bars or sports facilities. Sixteen percent of them envisaged in the late 1950s to stay beyond retirement; see p. 157. So, settlement remained largely temporary – albeit lengthening – sojourns. In our project work, up to now, we have not been able to locate documentation in which they would have voiced their particular grievances or aspirations.

Returning civil servants, even after brief spells only in colonial territories, stumbled into "the smallest living room I had ever seen in my life" back home or despaired when, on leave, they had to share places with their nagging parents.[56]

For others, housing functioned as a way of beginning to feel settled. This was especially the case if officers wished to start a family and adamantly preferred any short-term placement to boundless rootlessness. Mick Bond, a district commissioner who joined the Colonial Service when it was already clear that the empire would soon dissolve, rejoiced that "Mporokoso quickly became *ku mwesu* (at ours, at home). This was where we were to spend our first two years in Africa, the first two years of our married life, and for me my first paid employment."[57] Once transferred to another place, however, he and his wife would lose sight of those with whom, for a couple of years, they had dined and maintained the ties of neighborly communion. The world of the colonial service was mobile. In the archival files, though different from individually published memoirs, letters are replete with requests submitted by men who were tired of being shifted around and of living in desolate buildings nobody regarded as their own.

> The difficulty of residing in temporary premises, will, I am sure, be appreciated by all members of the Housing Committee, the comfort of one's home and the satisfaction of good permanent housing reflects not only in the creature comforts, but also in the efficiency, enthusiasm, and concentration that one can apply to the daily task.[58]

Despite urgently needed housing on all sides, the government spent visibly more resources on white privilege than on the needs and demands arising from Africans. Moreover, while housing requests by Europeans became part of the archival documentation, the requests by Africans directed to the African Urban Advisory Councils are available in mediated form only. On the advisory councils, members spoke to the district officers about complaints they had received but these spokespersons often did not enjoy much trust or high regard in the eyes of the dwellers whose concerns they represented.[59]

---

56 Bennett, *African Sun*, 240; Bond, *From Northern Rhodesia*, 147.
57 Bond, *From Northern Rhodesia*, 13.
58 H. Bradford to Mazabuka Housing Committee, 20 December 1957, in: SP 4/3/14 Housing Committee, Mazabuka, 1955–1958, NAZ.
59 For Southern Province, for instance, see LGH 3/25/17 Urban Advisory Councils, Welfare Associations General, and Other Associations, 1956–1960, NAZ; SP 4/6/10 Urban Advisory Councils and Welfare Associations – General, 1952–1956, NAZ; SP 1/4/14 Livingstone African Urban Advisory Council 1958–1959, NAZ.

There is additional evidence in a handful of memoirs, popular biographies, and autobiographical accounts written by Zambians – often with a view to building and strengthening the independent nation. More than one of them emphasized that their fathers actively built the colony in brick and stone. Safeli Chileshe's father, for instance, used to be a bricklayer. His family recalled that he had helped erect the Livingstone statue which faced the Victoria Falls Hotel and that he had built the very steps which, years back in 1947, the British royal family used to disembark from the Flying Boat onto the banks of the Zambezi River. The Chileshes understood this as their founding father's contribution to the forming of the country's landscape.[60] John M. Mwanakatwe's father worked with the Public Works Department and thus contributed to the building of the first secondary educational establishment, Munali School, an institution from which the aspiring post-independence elite, and also Mwanakatwe himself, emerged as some of the men responsible for building the independent nation.[61] And Robinson Nabulyato, member of the Northern Rhodesian Legislative Council and later speaker of the National Assembly of Zambia, self-confidently stated that

> [i]n colonial Zambia, the missionaries who brought education and medical care to the rural people never had to put up schools or clinics or the houses for their teachers and medical workers. These were built by the villagers, who appreciated the services rendered on to them. The colonial government, too, drew upon self-help, especially when 'Native Courts' were built in many chiefly capitals from the late 1920s. Even when permanent materials were required, the local people provided the bricks, while the government gave them the corrugated iron sheets, doors, windows and so on.[62]

Nabulyato's narrative comprises a pinch of rhetoric about so-called self-help, an important phrase in the 1970s and 1980s when everybody would speak about development in a language that differed from previous discursive patterns.

Read against the playful grabbing of houses by greenhorn colonial officers, these statements mark a counter position which points out that even though Africans did not share the same availability of resources as their colonial rulers, it was them who actually commanded building expertise and that it was them who actually built the houses materially – with their labor, accommodating openness, and dignity. To a certain degree, it shows the reluctance, even though not outspoken resistance, to accept being drawn into the colonial relations of power and rule via rent, not just by avoiding and evading it, but by formulating

---

60 Chileshe, *Alderman Safeli Hannock Chileshe*, 29.
61 Mwanakatwe, *Teacher, Politician*, 1–5, 9.
62 Robinson M. Nabulyato, *African Realities: A Memoir*, ed. Giacomo Macola (Lusaka: The Lembani Trust, 2008), 63. More autobiographies wait to be investigated.

an alternative discursive trope. Certainly, rule was not omniscient. There were options and avenues of circling around. There was, in fact, an "addressivity that neither vilified nor vindicated colonialism."[63] Even if individuals did not own a house and even if they were not able to claim participation through the payment of rent, some at least were in a position to lay claim to the nation, the town and its surroundings through their fathers' occupations one generation back. In the political debate, however, one major argument to prevent people from participation in urban issues and direct representation was that they were no proper ratepayers. It is to this scenario that the next section will turn.

The Changing Significance of Rent Against the Backdrop of Heightening Political Tensions

The significance of rent changed over time, and its meaning needed to be worked out against shifting political, economic, and social circumstances which were tightening after the establishment of the Central African Federation in 1953 and especially towards the achievement of independence after 1957. One perspective that has, as of yet, been neglected in this contribution is how relations, mutual perceptions, and obligations as well as efforts to set new agendas evolved over time, thus reshaping the temporal dimensions of the Northern Rhodesian societal field of force. A field of force is not just spatial. It has temporal dimensions as well. In this regard it is especially rewarding to trace the meaning of rent in the intensifying debate about political responsibility and (direct) African representation in municipal, federal or colonial governing bodies and, more particularly, the way it was entangled with handling rent issues.

Prior to 1953, neither the educated African minority nor politically mobilized workers and unions were keen on overthrowing the colonial state. To some extent, they yielded into the dictum that sitting on advisory boards would train and instruct them in administrative procedures even though it barred them from proper decision-taking and did not necessarily make them popular with the mass of people they represented. The majority being largely subservient African members of governing and consultative bodies, many accepted their roles as informants, brokers, and go-betweens rather than

---

[63] Harri Englund, "Anti Anti-Colonialism: Vernacular Press and Emergent Possibilities in Colonial Zambia," *Comparative Studies in Society and History* 57, no. 1 (2015): 231.

being rebels when it came to issues such as education, sanitation, and township organization. The African Representative Council, established as the highest African consulting body in 1946, was presided over by the Secretary of Native Affairs and, after 1948, elected two of its members to sit on the Legislative Council but had no executive powers. The members of that council articulated African opinion and criticized the so-called "color bar" but did not grab the chance to act as immediate achievers of African interests and aspirations. In the end, however, it was here that official delegates of the African people fiercely protested against the establishment of Federation, as they were even weaker represented on lower boards and municipal councils.[64]

Impending voicelessness was worse with other bodies, such as the Housing Area Boards, established after 1954 in an advisory capacity to Local Authorities. Assigned to European or white chairmanship, the boards were responsible to the African Affairs Committees, adjunct to each Municipal Council and becoming largely impotent under the Federal Government in Salisbury which, in the end, decided about the ordering and well-being of the town, its infrastructure, and its African areas. African township residents could take their problems, sorrows, and complaints to these official forums. Most Housing Area Boards, however, suffered from a lack of legitimacy with the constituencies they were supposed to represent.[65] Township dwellers were especially suspicious of the nominated members, particularly when they turned out to be puppets of the powers that appointed them rather than advocates acting on behalf of the evolving needy urban African constituency. Becoming politically aware and increasingly articulating their voice through better-organized parties (ANC and ZANC/UNIP), many Africans of Northern Rhodesia became less compromising about direct representation. Consequently, the ratio between nominated and elected members became an issue of dispute – white officeholders arguing they were the ones who financed the towns as ratepayers while Africans, devoid of property, did not qualify for the franchise.[66] It is interesting to note that in South Africa, for instance,

---

64 Jotham C. Momba and Fay Gadsden, "Zambia: Nonviolent Strategies Against Colonialism, 1900s–1960s," in *Recovering Nonviolent History: Civil Resistance in Liberation Struggles*, ed. Maciej J. Bartkowski (Boulder, CO: Rienner, 2013).
65 Draft press communiqué after 1958 elections, in: LGH 1/2/1 Urban African Housing Area Boards Regs., 1948–1961, NAZ.
66 See, for instance, debate about African representation at Ndola, 30 October 1956, in: LGH 1/18/19 African Affairs. African Representation. Written Evidence, 1956, NAZ; Mr. Roberts, Member for Lands and Local Government, in LegCo debate, *Hansard* 92x, 7 August 1957, in: MLSS 1/24/14, NAZ; "Widening Municipal Franchise", *Central African Post*, 14 November 1961, in: LGH 1/5/17 Participation of Africans in Local Government. Report and Minutes of Evidence, 1961–1962, NAZ.

the provision of housing was kept under control because authorities feared people could form strong communities, no longer migrating, which could instigate a feeling of community. As members of such a community they could feel entitled to vote.[67] In Northern Rhodesia the discourse focused on urban Africans paying neither rent nor property rates and thus not being entitled to the franchise.

Yet things were in transition. There was a tendency towards the later 1950s already for councils and urban advisory bodies dominated by both colonial and settler interests to nominate members of the newly educated elite at the expense of representatives of the so-called traditional elite who had originally dominated these bodies. The hope was that this way nationalist leaders and their politics would be barred from advancing into political office. This, in turn, weakened the institutions in the eyes of those constituencies which, in accordance with the idea of "indirect rule," expected African representatives to be connected to royal families.[68]

In February 1957, four years into the existence of the Central African Federation, the Brown Report was presented. It had been commissioned by the Legislative Council in December 1955 and responded to pressure emerging from the demands of people taking to African nationalist parties. For the first time in the Northern Rhodesian history of government commissions, all members of the working group were resident in Northern Rhodesia, many of them throughout their lives, and in this composition, so the eager expectation, they captured a multiracial and deep local experience. The Brown Report suggested that African workers receive an all-in wage, including a cash element from which they would pay their own rent. To the disappointment of the more liberally minded, the Brown Report refrained from recommending direct African representation – even though it did consider more active parts for Africans to play in the administration of their housing areas.[69] In the subsequent debate of the Legislative Council, the argument arose that the recommendations provided strong incentives for Africans who wanted to live in town permanently, who were among the aspiring and interested in social and political participation in the urban setting and its institutions. The conservative counter-argument held that still too many unwanted Africans would people the towns:

---

[67] Adam Ashforth, *The Politics of Official Discourse in Twentieth-Century South Africa* (Oxford: Clarendon Press, 1990), 114–148.
[68] Walima Kalusa, "Traditional Rulers, Nationalists and the Quest for Freedom in Northern Rhodesia in the 1950s," in *Living the End of Empire: Politics and Society in Late Colonial Zambia*, ed. Giacomo Macola, Jan-Bart Gewald, and Marja Hinfelaar (Leiden: Brill, 2011), 81.
[69] Mr. Botha, Nkana representative, and Mr. Sokota, African Member, in LegCo debate, *Hansard* 92x 7 August 1957, in: MLSS 1/24/14, NAZ.

We have the other type of African who comes into the townships in order to have a look at the lights, to fit himself out with a new outfit, and to go back to the village with his pocket duly lined; he does not require a house of any particularly good standard. If, therefore, the employee himself is responsible for paying his rent he himself will choose which type of house he wants to live in and not merely accept that his employer is paying for it and so not have any regards whatsoever as to what it costs or as to what type is to be supplied.[70]

The debate had shifted from earlier issues of labor stabilization to more openly expressed complaints of residents with self-asserted urban identities. Over the years, it had become evident that African workers did not need an incentive to come and stay in the towns. Instead, they needed means and an infrastructure to stay there and in their houses once they got unemployed or changed employers. All of a sudden, discussions around rent implied the reconceptualization of African representation – and vice versa. Should Africans become part of the administration by making them collect the rents, or should they take on complete financial responsibility? Would this endow them with the right of political representation? These considerations merged with a debate whether the strengthening of urban administrative structures should be achieved through Area Boards, on which nominated members would sit, or through actual Area Committees into which a certain proportion of Africans would be elected.[71] As was the case with many debates at this time, arguments were intense for the time being but it took much longer to redesign the actual ways politics and board compositions unfolded in practice. Irrespective of their outcome, however, they indicate that political change was a slow, tough, and tenacious process and that issues of housing and rent had become deeply implicated in future rights to permanence in the towns and political representation in the country.

Perhaps not coincidentally, the debate gathered pace once the Colonial Office announced to withdraw funds which, for the municipalities, made the arrangement of sub-economic rents a policy not worthwhile pursuing. The situation was exacerbated because African residents pressed for electricity, water points, roads, and other services. In fact, another commission had to take up the question of African representation a few years onwards again. This time, direct representation was inevitable. That Africans should be allowed to vote for Africans on the African Area Housing Boards was conceded without much

---

70 *Hansard*, Legislative Council transcript, 7 August 1957, in: MLSS 1/24/14, NAZ.
71 *Hansard*, Legislative Council transcript, 7 August 1957, in: MLSS 1/24/14, NAZ. Area Boards or Area Committees would engage with the African Affairs Committee of the Municipal Council. The African Affairs Committee would bring African and township issues into the main body where decisions were taken.

opposition. Immediately, however, the ratio of representation on committees, boards, and other bodies came under dispute. More liberal proponents of direct representation considered a 50-50 representation possible. Others advocated for one-third of Africans and two-thirds of European members in each committee.

Debates about rent and representation were also tied up with ideas about responsible citizenship and consumption in a society in which an increasing number of commodities became available through cash payment. In fact, one of the argumentative strands in the ongoing controversy about whether to pay wages on a weekly or monthly basis was that by adding a housing allowance to the wage, and by perhaps even paying monthly rates, authorities and Northern Rhodesian settler society more generally would lose grip on how people would spend their wealth. Would they rent decent houses? Would they not get indebted? Africans were eager to get higher cash lump sums into their hands and employers were favorably disposed towards disciplining workers through wages rather than providing them with accommodation.[72]

Meanwhile, the payment of rent itself had become more complex. Even though employers had paid for housing, they were not necessarily responsible for paying charges and service fees for water, electricity, and other amenities. However, as long as water was received through public pipes and no metering took place, people could only understand it as part of charges covered by others for them.[73] To them, it did not matter whether employers, local authorities or the municipality paid for these expenses. They themselves contributed to the wealth of the colony by making their labor cheaply available – and expected a return in the form of services.[74] Technically, if meters were installed in houses, a certain amount of water was free of charge for tenants, and only if these limits were exceeded, households had to pay.[75] To measure this was not a straightforward affair, either. As it turned out, electricity was sometimes part of the rent,

---

[72] *Hansard*, Legislative Council transcript, 7 August 1957, in: MLSS 1/24/14, NAZ.
[73] Report of the Working Party Appointed to Examine the Implications of Providing Electrical Reticulation in Certain African Housing Areas (1960), 17 March 1960, in: LGH 1/1/26 African Housing Areas – Working Party on Electricity. Reticulation, 1960–1962, NAZ; or Report of the Proceedings of the Thirteenth Annual Conference of the Municipal Association of Northern Rhodesia and Nyasaland, held at Kitwe, 4–6 May 1960, and several other minutes in: LGH 1/8/5 Local Government. Municipal Association. Annual Conference, 1961, NAZ.
[74] Memorandum "African Representation on Municipal and Township Councils", dated 1956 and submitted by R. M. Nabulyato, in: LGH 1/18/19, NAZ.
[75] Municipal Association of Northern Rhodesia and Nyasaland, Report of the Secretary to the Executive Committee, 5 July 1962, in: LGH 1/8/9 Municipal Association of Northern Rhodesia, Executive Committee: Minutes, 1961–1962, NAZ.

sometimes it was not. This inscrutable situation turned into an issue of debate when the collection of rent, fees, and charges became the first responsibility handed over to the so-called Township Management Boards – and one understands why settler-dominated bodies wanted to get rid of such affairs.

In a next step, after June 1958, the Colonial Office and, consequently, the colonial government in Lusaka finally ceased to subsidize rents. Like in some earlier fruitless efforts, for a moment, house ownership for Africans was more prominently discussed, promoting the idea that, freed from rent and elevated into being propertied persons, house owners would gain security in their class position and evolve as a group "who can play a useful part in local government."[76] Yet, reality played out in a different way. Local governments and municipalities had to increase rents which were – as in Livingstone, for instance – mainly met by smaller and middle-sized employers anyway.[77] There was no way of knowing who of the residents were self-payers so that the collection of rent remained, if not impossible, at least very difficult. Some four percent of it, so the estimate, had to be written off monthly.[78] The fact that after 1958, workers were expected to pay their own rent (or were entitled to pay it) did not mean that employers automatically added a housing allowance to their workers' wages. Sometimes, increased rent was deducted from laborers' tickets or their weekly pay. In other instances, laborers paid rent to the Local Authority and were compensated by their employers with a limited proportion only. Workers who, in view of these inconsistencies, complained to the Labor Officer were instantly sacked.[79] This prevented rent from becoming a responsibility of citizens claiming, through the act of rent-paying, rights, and security of dwelling in town.

Again, the debate around African civil service differed from how African workers' situation was affected. African civil servants and clerks were a large and diversified group whose earnings could be as small as a few shillings paid per day or as substantial as some £50 per month. This grand variety of scale proved complicated to translate into general housing allowances or entitlements to housing classified to each respective rank.[80] The situation created

---

[76] Municipal Association of Northern Rhodesia, Minutes of the Eleventh Annual Conference, Livingstone 21–23 May 1958, in: LGH 1/8/2 Municipal Association of Northern Rhodesia. Annual Conferences, 1957–1960, NAZ.
[77] Minutes of a Meeting, 6 May 1958, in: SP 1/4/14, NAZ.
[78] Report of the Secretary to the Executive Committee, 1 October 1963, in: LGH 1/2/72, NAZ.
[79] *Hansard* 94, 5 May 1958, and broadcast speech of C.E, Cousins, Labour Commissioner, 28 April 1958, as well as Mr. Sokoto's remark in MLSS 1/24/14, NAZ.
[80] Minute to Brown Report, 1 March 1957, in: MLSS 1/24/14, NAZ.

debate when the civil service became more thoroughly Africanized. While the opinion of African civil servants as of now seems irretrievable from the archival record, for the state it was clearly untenable to continue the provision of overpaid rental housing for all Africans entering the ranks of the service previously held by Europeans. There were ideas to subdivide existing houses of European standards into units fitting three or four African families.[81] This is to assume, however, that expectations were more difficult to curb than standards. It was evident that the government would have to further provide rental rather than owner-occupied accommodation for its staff due to the numerous transfers while in office.[82] For years to come, civil servants remained reluctant to "sink ... large sums in long-term investment."[83]

It was in 1959 that a three-year period started when

> the future of Northern Rhodesia was ultimately decided [...] as Britain, the increasingly reluctant colonial power, was squeezed by rising white settler calls for a racially-based Dominion, on the one hand, and nationalist demands for a rapid transition to independence on the other.[84]

As finances became more difficult to consolidate on the spot, the Minister of Local Government and Social Welfare admonished the African Township Management Boards sharply about failing to make township residents pay the rates and rents they were supposed to contribute. In all explicitness, he stressed that this would preclude them from claiming rights-bearing citizenship.[85] While most African nationalists and liberal British observers imagined the future of Northern Rhodesia as a unified territory governed by majority self-rule, white rulers of the Federation and some conservative British officials contemplated the redrawing of borders and separating the Copperbelt and urban commercial areas along the railway line from the rest of the colony. A lengthy period of delicate negotiations ensued with intensive lobbying on all sides. Danger loomed that settler hostility against a constitution, which granted Africans substantial political power, would thwart the whole

---

81 Some Notes on Housing for the Local Civil Service, c. 1962, in: LGH 1/24/20 Housing Local Civil Service, 1961–62, NAZ.
82 Various correspondence and minutes, in: MLSS 1/24/20, NAZ.
83 Notes on Housing for the Local Civil Service, c. 1962, in: MLSS 1/24/20, NAZ.
84 Miles Larmer, *Rethinking African Politics: A History of Opposition in Zambia* (Farnham: Ashgate, 2011), 32.
85 "Township 'Confab'," *Central African Post*, 20 November 1959 and "Africans must realise the basis of citizenship is to pay its way," *Northern News*, 20 November 1959, as well as opening speech printed in Minutes of the Tenth Annual Conference of the African Township Management Boards, Mukubeko, 20 October 1960, in: LGH 1/9/2 Local Government: Conference – African Townships, 1959–1963, NAZ.

process. In the end, a complex electoral system was agreed upon. It ensured that for part of their candidates, African national parties had to attract support from European settlers as well and vice versa – that certain seats could only be required for Europeans if they secured a minimum number of African votes. Accelerated progress towards self-rule in the colony rested on the defense of the privileged political representation of white settlers and hence, an African nationalist majority in the new Legislative Council was virtually impossible.[86] Yet, despite these stumbling blocks, the mid-1962 elections set the colony on its path towards independence.

The provision of rented accommodation or houses available on alternative terms never ceased to run as a debate in the background. To ease transitions, the Government introduced a scheme which provided for the long-term lease of land in African townships. The newly organized leases were intended to add security to tenure and to make the collection of rent a possible venture. In October 1962, preparations started that by July the following year, tenants should have, at a minimum, a one-year Crown Annual tenancy issued by the Ministry of Land and Natural Resources. Generally, however, the idea was to issue ten-year leases.[87] It was also planned that with the new leases local authorities would become responsible for the handling of rent – well knowing that "the income collection systems of African Township Management Boards have, unfortunately, proved to be one of the weakest parts of their administration."[88] The wording of the notices intended to end the current system of renting, while introducing the new one was strict and bore a tone of authoritarianism. Officials from the local bureaucracy, whose attitudes on the spot were guided by pragmatism and knowledge of what was possible to achieve, objected and suggested to "tone [the wording] down a little to avoid much ill-will in the Townships at a time when we are surely hoping to foster good-will."[89] This intervention reveals that at this stage the

---

86 Mulford, *Zambia*, 178–197, 229–300.
87 Circular of Ministry of Land and Natural Resources, Lusaka, 27 October 1962, to Senior Provincial Commissioners, District Officers, Township Officers, Ministry of Local Government and Social Welfare, in: LGH 1/2/60 African Townships. Building Schemes under Section 14B Township Ordinance, 1963, NAZ.
88 Correspondence of Permanent Secretary, Ministry of Lands and Natural Resources, to Permanent Secretary, Ministry of Local Government and Social Welfare, 9 October 1962, in: LGH 1/2/60, NAZ; Finance Circular No. MF/3640/2 Vol. II, 16 January 1961, in: MLSS 1/24/18 Housing Government Employees. General, 1960–1968, NAZ.
89 Circular of Ministry of Land and Natural Resources, 27 October 1962, in: LGH 1/2/60, NAZ; for quote refer to S. L. G. F .O., Ndola, to Permanent Secretary, Lusaka, 13 November 1962, in: LGH 1/14/33 Leases African Townships, 1961–1962, NAZ.

scope to maneuver in a field of forces was evidently biased towards township residents rather than in the hands of colonial agents. In fact, it soon turned out that the tenants' responses to this incentive were disappointing.[90] This was partly due to the cost involved. People had to pay rent plus a fee for the agreement plus additional board fees. Many did not want long-term leases but preferred the option of changing places and staying mobile. They had learned through experience that any new scheme would last only sporadically.[91] So why invest resources this time? There were good reasons to first wait and see.

This notwithstanding, the ruling powers insisted on redefining the meaning of housing:

> In nearly all countries individuals are responsible for providing their own housing. The standard of the house in which they live and the area in which it is situated is a matter of personal choice and is dictated almost entirely by the proportion of his income which the individual is prepared to devote to housing himself and his family. The present system of Government-provided housing inevitably produces pressures, both from individual and the Civil Service organisations, for Government to provide ever increasing standards.[92]

As usual, the blame went on African tenants irrespective of the new conviction that "[t]he best hope of achieving new and realistic levels in housing is for the Companies to divest themselves of the responsibility of providing houses so that normal economic factors come into play and employees occupy houses of their choice in accord with their earnings."[93]

In this transition period, the building of medium grade African houses to be leased in the same manner as European houses proved especially problematic. It was impossible to bill tenants for rent, electricity, and water charges if before they had not sought exemption from the regulations of the Employment of Natives Ordinance. There was no rule as to what tariffs had to be applied. The Commissioner for Local Government and, in a somewhat different vein, the Ministry of Labour and Mines decided that even if water was to be metered and paid for, electricity would perhaps be payable through the employer – provided he consented to this. If, however, some of the houses would be occupied by

---

90 Circular of Ministry of Land and Natural Resources, 27 October 1962, in: LGH 1/2/60, NAZ.
91 District Commissioner, N. A. Baguley, to Secretary, Ministry of Local Government and Social Welfare, Ndola, 26 November 1962 and S. L. G. F .O., Ndola, to Permanent Secretary, Lusaka, 13 November 1962, in: LGH 1/14/33, NAZ.
92 Notes on Housing for the Local Civil Service, c. 1962, in: MLSS 1/24/20, NAZ.
93 Notes on Housing for the Local Civil Service, c. 1962, in: MLSS 1/24/20, NAZ.

African civil servants, other rules would apply as yet another set of rules would have to be considered if self-employed African entrepreneurs moved in.[94]

Almost concomitantly, a debate emerged with regard to voting rights. In the process of incorporating more Africans, especially urban ones, into the system of a qualified franchise, H.J.E. Stanley, Member of Legislative Council, suggested to reduce the limit of property or earned income to £300 (instead of previously £750). This would have allowed owners of a normal two-bedroomed house to qualify for the franchise.[95] Moreover, self-payers of rent came within the reach of the vote. No longer should it matter whether people actually owned property or whether they paid rent for such a property. As long as they had been resident in town for at least six months, paid rent regularly, and were not in arrears they should receive the vote.[96] Stanley's radical re-evaluation showed that the towns both lacked funds and needed to integrate a new clientele eager to participate in urban politics. About this time, rent ceased to be a medium through which to assess how colonial rule unfolded between most actors in the Northern Rhodesian societal field of force. It had changed its meaning, and colonial rule would henceforth be graspable through other relations of power.

Conclusions

As people came to town and had to look for accommodation, once they did not stay with kin rent was woven into their daily affairs. It was a tie kept by the various authorities and by employers as a bond of dependence and remained under the grip of formal employers and the municipalities. Rent also kept the municipalities tied to the subsidies paid and forwarded by the central government as financially and economically the management of rent was not a gainful endeavor. Throughout the late colonial period rent did not become a publicly politicized concern in the immediate sense. Tied to it, however, was a range of political debates such as permanence in towns, voting rights, and achievement of status through ownership, or alternative forms of tenure security.

Between 1948 and 1962, rent dramatically changed its meaning. It had evolved from being an intended tool of keeping workers acquiescent into a

---

94 Report of the Secretary to the Executive Committee, 5 July 1962 – Bancroft, in: LGH 1/8/9, NAZ.
95 For changing qualifications to achieve the vote see Mulford, *Zambia*, 49, 56–61; for debate see Minute of oral evidence and written memoranda submitted to the Committee appointed to inquire into "The Participation of Africans in Local Government in Municipal and Township Areas," October 1960, in: LGH 1/5/17, NAZ.
96 Stanley's evidence and memorandum in a written report, undated, in: LGH 1/5/17, NAZ.

payment considered empowering to participate in responsible urban politics and the national franchise. From being an element of social welfare, which enforced a union between state and employers, it became a burden the late colonial state was unable to handle and employers reluctant to shoulder. The focus on rent provides a telling lens on understanding shifts in conceptions of power, rule, good-will, and obedience. To talk about rent opens up possibilities to think about power and rule more independently from the established master narrative of ownership housing schemes mattering elsewhere.

To use the notion of power, rule, and obedience unfolding in a Northern Rhodesian societal field of force allows looking, through rent, at relations unfolding and shifting power biases between multiple actors. Rent in Northern Rhodesia itself was an indication of a paternalist form of rule. This paternalism did not completely cease throughout the period under review. But after the establishment of the Central African Federation – and while the African nationalist movement was gathering momentum by protesting against the unification of the three territories – paternalism lost ground, and against this backdrop the payment of rent became ever more complex and complicated until it even served as a means of thinking about it as equivalent to property values. Employers, yet again, needed to rely on other means than housing to safeguard their companies' position in the colonial economy.

Rent thus provides a lens through which to assess the changing dynamics of power and rule. It is a lens heavily entangled with a number of debates which all feed into the amalgamated, and at time convoluted, experience of colonialism in Northern Rhodesia. In the end, this convoluted nature of the debates protruding into the lens alerts us to the fact that the history of rent cannot be told as a history of its own. It is deeply ingrained in the political as well as in the everyday spheres of what housing under colonialism meant to a society moving towards independence.

References

Archival sources

National Archives of Zambia, Lusaka (NAZ)

Ministry of Mines and Labour and Social Services (MLSS)
1/24/2 Housing: Native Locations. Private Locations, 1944–1955.
1/24/7 Labour Department: African Housing (Unauthorised Locations), 1955–1961.
1/24/14 Employment of Natives and "Housing Conditions", 1957–1959.

1/24/18 Housing Government Employees. General, 1960–1968.
1/24/20 Housing Local Civil Service, 1961–1962.

Ministry of Local Government and Housing (LGH)
1/1/26 African Housing Areas – Working Party on Electricity. Reticulation, 1960–1962.
1/1/30 Unauthorised Locations, 1960–1968.
1/2/1 Urban African Housing Area Boards Regs., 1948–1961.
1/2/60 African Townships. Building Schemes under Section 14B Township Ordinance, 1963.
1/2/72 Township Regulations, 1963–1966.
1/5/17 Participation of Africans in Local Government. Report and Minutes of Evidence, 1961–1962.
1/8/1 Local Government: Municipal Association General, 1952–1963.
1/8/2 Municipal Association of Northern Rhodesia. Annual Conference, 1957–1960.
1/8/5 Local Government. Municipal Association. Annual Conference, 1961.
1/8/9 Municipal Association of Northern Rhodesia, Executive Committee: Minutes, 1961–1962.
1/9/2 Local Government: Conference – African Townships, 1959–1963.
1/14/33 Leases African Townships, 1961–1962.
1/16/49 Housing for Eurafricans, 1949–1953.
1/16/52 Local Government: African Housing, General Policy, 1952–1953.
1/16/53 African Housing, Atkinson Report, 1953.
1/18/19 African Affairs. African Representation. Written Evidence, 1956.
3/2/9 Livingstone: Areas and Boundaries, 1951–1959.
3/25/17 Urban Advisory Councils, Welfare Associations General, and Other Associations, 1956–1960.

Southern Province (SP)
1/4/14 Alienation of Land and Township Plots, 1948–1952.
4/1/30 Municipality of Livingstone. Minutes of Native Affairs Sub-Committee Meetings, 1947.
4/1/26 Municipality of Livingstone. Minutes. Public Works – Sub-Committee, 1946–1955
4/1/33 Municipality of Livingstone. Minutes of Native Affairs Sub-Committee Meetings, 1948.
4/3/6 Municipality of Livingstone, Native Affairs Sub-Committee, 1946.
4/3/14 Housing Committee, Mazabuka, 1955–1958.
4/6/10 Urban Advisory Councils and Welfare Associations – General, 1952–1956.

The National Archives, Kew (TNA)

Colonial Office (CO)
CO 795/123/4 Copperbelt Labour Supplies. Housing Question, 1942–1943.
CO 927/35/3 Housing Research, Central Africa, 1945–1947.

Secondary literature

Ashforth, Adam. *The Politics of Official Discourse in Twentieth-Century South Africa*. Oxford: Clarendon Press, 1990.

Bennett, Frank. *Under an African Sun: Memoirs of a Colonial Officer in Northern Rhodesia*. London: Radcliffe, 2005.
Bissell, William Cunningham. *Urban Design, Chaos, and Colonial Power in Zanzibar*. Bloomington, IN: Indiana University Press, 2011.
Bond, Mick. *From Northern Rhodesia to Zambia: Recollections of a DO/DC 1962–73*. Oxford: Gadsden Publishers, 2014.
Brennan, James R. *Taifa: Making Nation and Race in Urban Tanzania*. Athens, OH: Ohio University Press, 2012.
Buettner, Elizabeth. *Empire Families: Britons and Late Imperial India*. Oxford: Oxford University Press, 2005.
Chaskalson, Matthew, Karen Jochelson, and Jeremy Seekings. "Rent Boycotts, the State and the Transformation of the Urban Political Economy in South Africa." *Review of African Political Economy* 40 (1987): 47–64.
Chileshe, Jonathan H. *Alderman Safeli Hannock Chileshe: A Tribute to (the Man), His Life, and History*. Ndola: Mission Press, 1998.
Cohen, Andrew. "Business and Decolonisation in Central Africa Reconsidered." *Journal of Imperial and Commonwealth History* 36, no. 4 (2008): 641–658.
Cooper, Frederick, and Randall Packard. "Introduction." In *International Development and the Social Sciences: Essays on the History and Politics of Knowledge*, edited by Frederick Cooper and Randall Packard, 1–41. Berkeley, CA: University of California Press, 1997.
Crehan, Kate, and Achim von Oppen. "Understandings of 'Development': An Arena for Struggle. The Making of a Development Project in North-Western Province." In *Planners and History: Negotiating 'Development' in Rural Zambia*, edited by Kate Crehan and Achim von Oppen, 257–305. Lusaka: Multimedia Publications, 1994.
Datta, Kusum. "Farm Labour, Agrarian Capital and the State in Colonial Zambia: The African Labour Corps, 1942–52." *Journal of Southern African Studies* 14, no. 3 (1988): 371–792.
Englund, Harri. "Anti Anti-Colonialism: Vernacular Press and Emergent Possibilities in Colonial Zambia." *Comparative Studies in Society and History* 57, no. 1 (2015): 221–247.
Ferguson, James. *Expectations of Modernity: Myths and Meanings of Urban Life on the Zambian Copperbelt*. Berkeley: University of California Press, 2001.
Gewald, Jan-Bart. "Researching and Writing in the Twilight of an Imagined Conquest: Anthropology in Northern Rhodesia 1930–1960." *History and Anthropology* 18, no. 4 (2007): 459–487.
Hansen, Karen Tranberg. *Distant Companions: Servants and Employers in Zambia, 1900–1985*. Ithaca, NY: Cornell University Press, 1989.
Home, Robert K. *Of Planting and Planning: The Making of British Colonial Cities*. 2nd edition. Oxford: Routledge, 2013.
Huchzermeyer, Marie. "Tenement City: The Emergence of Multi-Storey Districts Through Large-Scale Private Landlordism in Nairobi." *International Journal of Urban and Regional Research* 31, no. 4 (2007): 714–732.
Kalusa, Walima. "Traditional Rulers, Nationalists and the Quest for Freedom in Northern Rhodesia in the 1950s." In *Living the End of Empire: Politics and Society in Late Colonial Zambia*, edited by Giacomo Macola, Jan-Bart Gewald, and Marja Hinfelaar, 67–90. Leiden: Brill, 2011.
Kamete II, Amin Y. "Civil Society, Housing and Urban Governance: The Case of Urban Housing Co-operatives in Zimbabwe." In *Associational Life in African Cities: Popular Responses to*

the Urban Crisis, edited by Arne Tostensen, Inge Tvedten, and Mariken Vaa, 162–179. Stockholm: Nordiska Afrikainstitutet, 2001.

Larmer, Miles. *Rethinking African Politics: A History of Opposition in Zambia*. Farnham: Ashgate, 2011.

Lüdtke, Alf. "Einleitung: Herrschaft als soziale Praxis." In *Herrschaft als soziale Praxis: Historische und sozial-anthropologische Studien*, edited by Alf Lüdtke, 9–63. Göttingen: Vandenhoek & Ruprecht, 1991.

Momba, Jotham C., and Fay Gadsden. "Zambia: Nonviolent Strategies Against Colonialism, 1900s–1960s." In *Recovering Nonviolent History: Civil Resistance in Liberation Struggles*, edited by Maciej J. Bartkowski, 71–88. Boulder, CO: Rienner, 2013.

Mpashi, Stephen A. *Betty Kaunda*. Lusaka: Longmans, 1969.

Mulford, David C. *Zambia: The Politics of Independence 1957–1964*. Oxford: Oxford University Press, 1967.

Mutale, Emmanuel. *The Management of Urban Development in Zambia*. Farnham: Ashgate, 2004.

Mwanakatwe, John M. *Teacher, Politician, Lawyer: My Autobiography*. Lusaka: Bookworld Publications, 2003.

Mwangi, Meja. *The Cockroach Dance*. 2nd edition. Columbus, Ohio: HM Books Intl., 2017.

Nabulyato, Robinson M. *African Realities: A Memoir*. Edited by Giacomo Macola. Lusaka: The Lembani Trust, 2008.

Parpart, Jane. *Labor and Capital on the African Copperbelt*. Philadelphia: Temple University Press, 1983.

Phimister, Ian. "Proletarians in Paradise: The Historiography and Historical Sociology of White Miners on the Copperbelt." In *Living the End of Empire: Politics and Society in Late Colonial Zambia*, edited by Giacomo Macola, Jan-Bart Gewald, and Marja Hinfelaar, 141–160. Leiden: Brill, 2011.

Phiri, Bizeck Jube. *A Political History of Zambia: From Colonial Rule to the Third Republic, 1890–2001*. Trenton, NJ: Africa World Press, 2006.

Rakodi, Carole. "Rental Tenure in the Cities of Developing Countries." *Urban Studies* 32, no. 4–5 (1995): 791–811.

Ranger, Terence. *Bulawayo Burning: The Social History of a Southern African City, 1893–1960*. Suffolk: Boydell & Brewer, 2010.

Roberts, Andrew. *A History of Zambia*. London: Heinemann, 1976.

Stoler, Ann Laura. *Along the Archival Grain: Epistemic Anxieties and Colonial Common Sense*. Princeton: Princeton University Press, 2009.

Sungura, Nicholas. "Der Faktor Mensch bei der Risikosteuerung öffentlicher Bauvorhaben in Kenia." Dr. Eng. diss., University of Hannover, 2016.

Thompson, E. P. "Eighteenth-Century English Society: Class Struggle without Class?" *Social History* 3, no. 2 (1978): 133–165.

Tosh, John. "Imperial Masculinity and the Flight from Domesticity in Britain, 1880–1914." In *Gender and Colonialism*, edited by Timothy P. Foley et al., 72–85. Galway: Galway University Press, 1995.

Vladislavic, Ivan. *The Exploded View*. Cape Town: Umuzi, 2017.

Sofie Boonen and Johan Lagae
3 Ruashi, a Pessac in Congo? On the Design, Inhabitation, and Transformation of a 1950s Neighborhood in Lubumbashi, Democratic Republic of the Congo

Introduction

In the 1950s, the *Office des Cités Africaines* (OCA) built a number of neighborhoods for Africans around the major cities of Congo, Rwanda, and Burundi, at the time all territories under Belgian rule.[1] Built within the broader context of the first *Ten-Year Plan for the Economic and Social Development of the Belgian Congo* (1949–1959), these "satellite cities" were conceived as a direct response to the emergence of *bidonvilles* or slums in urban centers like Kinshasa, Lubumbashi, Kisangani, or Bujumbura during the immediate postwar years. Evoking the motto *Vers l'Avenir* that underscored the then policy of the colonial government, these neighborhoods were celebrated in the national and international architectural press of the time as a successful example of the application of modern architectural and urban design principles to the urgent housing needs in Central Africa. The OCA *cités* featured prominently in a survey

---

[1] A preliminary version of this paper was first presented at the 4th European Conference on African Studies (ECAS), Uppsala, 15–18 June 2011. The paper draws on research conducted in the context of the FWO-funded project "City, architecture and colonial space in Matadi and Lubumbashi, Congo. A historical analysis from a translocal perspective" (FWO n° G.0786.09N, 2009–2012; main researcher: Sofie Boonen; main supervisor: Johan Lagae; co-supervisors: Baz Lecocq, Ghent University; Jacob Sabakinu, University of Kinshasa; Donatien Dibwe, University of Lubumbashi). Moreover, this paper benefitted in a substantial way from the unpublished master's dissertation of Céline Fenaux, "L'Office des Cités Africaines in Lubumbashi. Ruashi. Architecturale analyse en studie van de toe-eigening van een Congolese wijk uit de jaren 1950" (Ghent University, 2010; supervisors: Johan Lagae & Sofie Boonen, Ghent University). We sincerely want to thank professor Donatien Dibwe dia Mwembu and assistant Serge Songa Songa Mitwa of the University of Lubumbashi, whose help has been crucial during all our fieldwork trips in Lubumbashi over the many years of research since 2000, and especially those missions in 2006, 2008, and 2010 during which Johan Lagae, Sofie Boonen, and Céline Fenaux investigated the Ruashi neighborhood

Ə Open Access. © 2020 Sofie Boonen and Johan Lagae, published by De Gruyter. [CC BY-NC] This work is licensed under a Creative Commons Attribution-NonCommercial 4.0 International License.
https://doi.org/10.1515/9783110601183-003

documenting the achievements of the Ten-Year Plan that was published in 1950 under the title *Investir c'est prospérer*.[2]

In quantitative terms, however, the OCA *cités* did not provide a real solution, as the albeit impressive number of houses that were actually built remained far too limited to cover actual needs. Moreover, the OCA houses proved to be too expensive to be affordable for the targeted African inhabitants. Finally, as they were modeled on the modest single-family home in Belgium, their design did not meet the dwelling needs and practices of the common African household. No surprise then that the OCA neighborhoods have undergone major transformations over time. Parts of the original public spaces of the OCA *cités* have been re-appropriated or even privatized, and original OCA-type houses have in many cases been radically altered through the addition of informal structures.

In this chapter, we will focus on one particular example, the Ruashi neighborhood, built by the *Office des Cités Africaines* in the mining city of Lubumbashi. We will map its design phase with its underlying ideological agenda of colonial social engineering as well as modes of inhabitation and transformation, illustrating how the urban landscape of this particular OCA *cité* speaks of the manifold ways in which its inhabitants have responded to a physical environment shaped according to western dwelling patterns that were introduced in the context of colonialism. Instead of reading this transformed urban landscape in terms of a failed modernist project, let alone as an act of resistance against an imposed colonial order, we will approach it as an example of an "actively lived-in architecture," in line with Philippe Boudon's famous 1969 study of Le Corbusier's *Cité Frugès* in Pessac.[3] Doing so, we argue, opens up alternative ways of thinking the future of the OCA *cités* as an African, rather than as a mere colonial built, legacy.

Countering the *bidonville*

As in many other colonies, the Second World War gave rise to a massive migration wave of Africans from the hinterlands to the main urban centers of the Belgian Congo. Large enterprises based in the cities significantly increased the number of recruited African workers to respond to a booming economy in

---

[2] Georges J. Plumier, ed., *Investir c'est prospérer: Les réalisations du plan décennal pour le développement économique et sociale du Congo belge 1949–1959* (Brussels: Imifi, 1959).
[3] Philippe Boudon, *Pessac de Le Corbusier 1927–1967: Étude socio-architecturale* (Paris: Dunod, 1977).

the immediate postwar years while an intensified agricultural production and the resulting distortion of the social structure of rural communities, which had occurred during the war years, also incited thousands of Africans to move to Kinshasa, Lubumbashi, Kisangani, and other urban centers.[4] The sharply increasing growth rate of the African urban population quickly resulted in the emergence of *bidonvilles* popping up in the peripheries of the main urban centers. This forced colonial authorities to radically rethink their policies and strategies of urban governance. The provision of decent housing for Africans thus constituted one of the main objectives of the postwar *Ten-Year Plan for the Social and Economic Development of the Belgian Congo* which was launched in 1949.[5] The colonial government undertook several initiatives in order to create sufficient housing facilities for the growing urban African population in a relatively short time frame. At the start of the Ten-Year Plan, it established the semi-governmental *Office des Cités Indigènes* (OCI) whose task was to build new so-called "Cités Indigènes" or "native towns" in the proximity of the main cities of the Belgian Congo and Ruanda-Urundi.[6] In order to solve the managerial problems related to its decentralized structure, the OCI was already replaced in 1952 by the new semi-governmental *Office des Cités Africaines* (OCA) which was directed by a Brussels-based head office.[7]

As the Ten-Year Plan aimed at improving the well-being and welfare of both Europeans and Africans, it required an active socioeconomic state policy. It hence marked an important shift in housing policy in the Belgian colony. For the first time, the colonial government presented itself as the main provider of housing facilities for Africans, while previously colonial enterprises had taken

---

[4] Between 1940 and 1945, Lubumbashi's African population knew its highest growth rate in the city's history (18%) with a rise of approximately 26,000 to 65,000 African inhabitants. Bruce Fetter, *The Creation of Elisabethville, 1910–1940* (Stanford: Hoover Institution Press, 1976), 173.

[5] Ministère des Colonies, ed., *Plan décennal pour le développement économique et social du Congo belge* (Brussels: Les Editions de Visscher, 1949). For a brief discussion of the plan and its objectives, see Guy Vantemsche, "Le Plan Décennal et la modernisation du Congo belge (1949–1959)," in *La mémoire du Congo: Le temps colonial*, ed. Jean-Luc Vellut (Gent/Tervuren: Snoeck/MRAC, 2005).

[6] For a genealogy of the OCI and the OCA, see Xavier Lejeune de Schiervel, *Les nouvelles cités congolaises: L'architecture et le logement* (Brussels: Académie Royale des Sciences coloniales, 1956), 38.

[7] For a historical discussion of the OCA, see Bruno de Meulder, *Kuvuanda Mbote: Een eeuw architectuur en stedenbouw in Kongo* (Antwerpen: Hautekiet/deSingel, 2000), 185–251. Bruno De Meulder, "OCA (Office des Cités Africaines, 1952–1960) and the Urban Question in Central Africa," accessed October 17, 2017, https://archnet.org/system/publications/contents/4922/original/DPC1635.pdf?1384787195.

up the largest responsibility in this domain of construction, building many workers' camps.[8] The housing policy also shifted gradually towards the accommodation of African families rather than of single male laborers. Particular attention was given to the living standards in the African quarters, and initiatives were deployed to offer house ownership to the African dweller. This shift in policy is clearly reflected in the domain of action entrusted to the OCA which was assigned to organize the complete urbanization of new African quarters, from the design and implementation of the urban plans and dwellings to the attribution of the built houses to the African inhabitants.[9] Moreover, the new "native towns" were not only to provide housing but also had to include all necessary public infrastructure, from roads and sewage systems to various facilities (administration, police, education, cult etc.). As Xavier Lejeune de Schiervel, the then director-general of the OCA, stated, this was a task that went far beyond a technocratic operation, for it was about providing "decent and hygienic accommodation in sufficient numbers"[10] which required an apt response in both quantitative and qualitative terms.

In its eight years' existence, the OCA built a significant number of African neighborhoods in cities such as Kinshasa, Lubumbashi, Kisangani, and Bujumbura, constructing a total of 40,000 new houses. Based on the model of the "neighborhood unit," the quarters were realized as fully-equipped satellite cities for approximately 30,000 inhabitants in the cities' peripheries. This large-scale enterprise testifies of the particular position of the OCA within the official sphere. Indeed, as it worked as a *parastatale*, the OCA profited from substantial financial means and was able to operate with a relative autonomy vis-à-vis the colonial government. Moreover, Xavier Lejeune de Schiervel had attracted some prominent figures from the more progressive circles of Belgian architects and urban planners, giving them opportunities to create work on a scale that most of their colleagues, who worked in the colony at the time, could only dream of.[11] As Bruno de Meulder has argued, the OCA actually succeeded in building *cités* that not only stood out as remarkable achievements in the field of housing in the Belgian colonial context, but that also surpassed – in scale, quality, and

---

8 See Bruno De Meulder, *De Kampen van Kongo: Arbeid, kapitaal en rasveredeling in de koloniale planning* (Amsterdam/Antwerpen: Meulenhoff/Kritak, 1996).
9 For the decree of 30 March 1952 on the creation of the OCA, see Lejeune De Schiervel, *Les nouvelles cités congolaises*, 49.
10 Lejeune de Schiervel, *Les nouvelles cités congolaises*, 10. All translations from French are by the authors.
11 Most of the designers working for the OCA were linked to or had been trained at La Cambre, an architectural school in Brussels that was considered as the "Bauhaus belge" at the time.

coherence – most of the then current architectural production in the mother country itself.¹² In the national and international architectural press of the time, the realizations of the OCA were highly praised (Fig. 3.1). Despite the social context and ambitions of the OCA projects, these neighborhoods remained very much "colonial projects": conceived as "satellite cities", at a significant distance from the existing urban centers, they were in tune with the segregationist logic that had characterized the urban planning policies in the Belgian Congo as well as elsewhere in sub-Saharan Africa since the 1910s and 1920s.¹³

The *Office des Cités Africaines* in Lubumbashi

From 1954 onwards, the OCA started to design the Ruashi neighborhood in Lubumbashi for a population of approximately 32,000 inhabitants. It was also involved in designing and constructing several public facilities, such as schools, churches, communal offices etc. in the other African neighborhoods of the city. While following the overall guidelines of the OCA's urban operations in other parts of Congo, the design and building process of the Ruashi neighborhood nevertheless was also influenced by the local particularities of Lubumbashi, the mining city situated in the southern province of Katanga and economic heart of the Belgian colony.¹⁴

Compared to other cities in Congo, Lubumbashi constitutes one of the clearest and most explicit illustrations of the binary colonial city, with clearly segregated areas for Europeans and Africans.¹⁵ Already in the city's first urban

---

12 De Meulder, *Kuvuande Mbote*, 189.
13 For a discussion of spatial segregation along racial lines in Belgian colonial urban planning, see Luce Beeckmans and Johan Lagae, "Kinshasa's Syndrome-planning in Historical Perspective: From Belgian Colonial Capital to Self-constructed Megalopolis," in *Urban Planning in Sub-Saharan Africa: Colonial and Post-Colonial Planning Cultures*, ed. Carlos Nunes Silva (Abingdon: Routledge, 2015), 201–224. For a concise but fundamental discussion of the segregationist logic of colonial urban planning in a comparative perspective, see Carl Nightingale, *Segregation: A Global History of Divided Cities* (Chicago: University of Chicago Press, 2012).
14 In this paper, we will refer to contemporary place names instead of colonial ones, thus using Lubumbashi instead of Elisabethville to refer to the city, and Commune Kamalondo instead of *Cité* Albert Ier for the first *cité indigène* or "native town" of the city. The place names of the other three "native towns" (Kenya, Katuba, and Ruashi) have not changed over time.
15 On segregation in Lubumbashi, see Johan Lagae, Sofie Boonen and Maarten Liefooghe, "Fissures dans le 'cordon sanitaire': Architecture hospitalière et ségrégation urbaine à Lubumbashi, 1920–1960," in *Lubumbashi: Cent ans d'histoire*, ed. Maurice Amuri Mpala-Lutebele (Paris: L'Harmattan, 2013).

3 Ruashi, a Pessac in Congo? — 71

Figure 3.1: Cover of a theme issue of the Belgian architectural journal *Rythme*, devoted to the work of the *Office des Cités Africaines*, issue #30, 1960.
Source: collection of Johan Lagae.

plan, drawn up in 1911, such neat distinction was visible, with the settlement for Africans separated from the *ville européenne* by a 170-meter-wide buffer zone. This spatial division was to become much more explicit during the 1920s when the then governor-general Maurice Lippens requested that the first African settlement was to be razed because of what he described as a *saleté repoussante* ("disgusting filthiness").[16] A new *cité indigéne Albert Ier*, today Commune Kamalondo, was constructed at a larger distance of 700 meters which, according to contemporary sources, would prevent the transmission of malaria from the African to the European part of town.[17]

Already during the 1930s, the colonial government was confronted with a strong demographic pressure on the *commune Kamalondo* requiring an expansion of the neighborhoods for Africans. But it was only during the immediate postwar years that a project for a new "native town", the so-called *commune Kenya*, was realized.[18] This, however, immediately proved to be insufficient as well, inciting the local policymakers to undertake new actions. The debates occurring within the colonial administration at the time help explain the peripheral situation of the Ruashi neighborhood: within the *Comité Urbain*, whose members represented the various power groups and communities within Lubumbashi's urban society,[19] various locations for building new neighborhoods for Africans were discussed, taking into consideration two principles. First, it was considered necessary to break up the African community into small, manageable groups in an attempt to implement a "divide and rule" policy; and second, an encircling of the European city by African neighborhoods was to be avoided at all cost. While the creation of the commune Katuba, adjacent to the already existing *cités* of *Kamalondo and Kenya*, was in accordance with the second principle, the creation of the satellite city of

---

16 Lippens quoted in Ferdinand Grévisse, *Le Centre Extra-Coutumier d'Elisabethville: Quelques aspects de la politique indigène du Haut-Katanga industriel* (Brussels: Institut Royal Colonial Belge, 1950), 5.

17 For the hygienic argument underlying this urban operation, see R. Hins, "L'Urbanisme au Katanga," *Essor du Congo* (1931), special edition on the occasion of the international exposition of Elisabethville, [s.p.].

18 A historical analysis of the development of this neigbourhood is provided by Simon de Nys-Ketels, "Koloniaal beleid en stedelijke ruimte in een Congolese stad: De wijk Kenya in Lubumbashi, Congo" (Master diss., Ghent University, 2011).

19 From the interwar period onwards, the urban planning of main urban centers as Kinshasa, Lubumbashi or Kisangani was mainly in hands of an "Urban Committee" (*Comité Urbain*), containing different services (e.g. the Public Health Service, Public Works Service, Services of the General Governor etc.) For more information on the "Urban Committee", see Crispin Mulumba, "Origines et Evolution des institutions communales et urbaines au Congo," *Congo-Afrique* 29 (1968).

Ruashi, situated to the northeast of the existing city center, can be explained by the first (Fig. 3.2).[20]

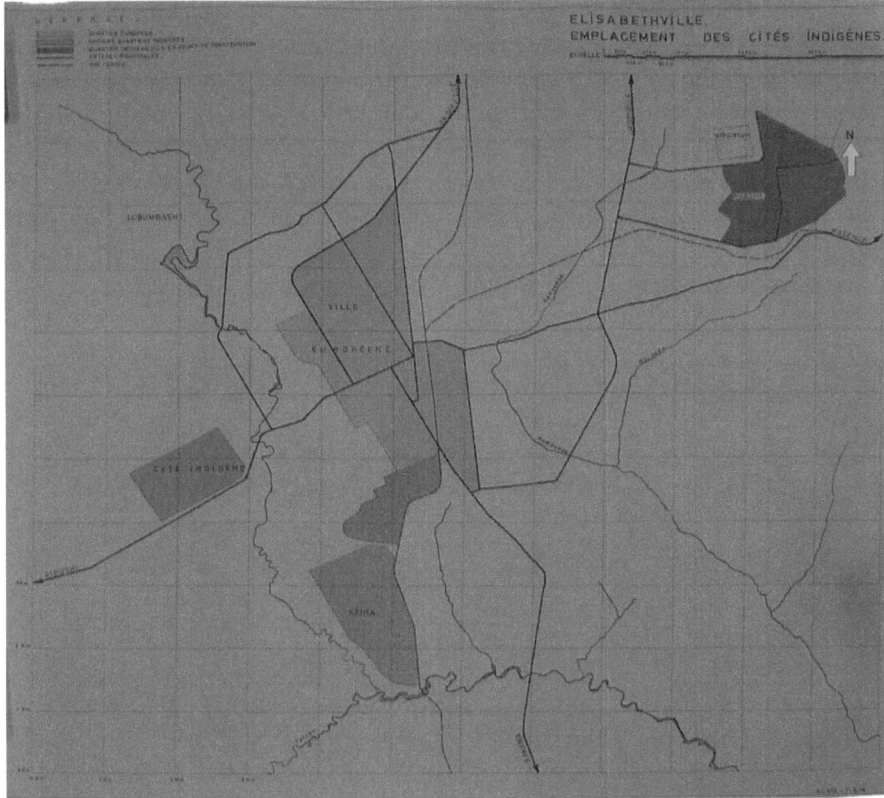

Figure 3.2: "Elisabethville. Emplacement des cites indigènes." Map showing the spatial organization of Lubumbashi with: in the middle the "European city," to the south, the two "native town" of Kamalondo and Kenya (the third one, Katuba, not existing then), to the west, along the road to Kipushi, the mining camp of the Union Minière (here indicated as a "cité indigène") and, to the north-east, the OCA neighborhood of Ruashi.
Source: Africa Archives, Ministry of Foreign Affairs, Brussels; Fund OCA, Courtesy Africa Archives.

Ruashi not only differed from Lubumbashi's other *cités* because of its oppositional geographical location, but it also had, as we shall discuss below, a spatial layout which contrasted with the grid-pattern structuring the other *cités* of

---

20 GG.20.400. Congo Belge. Nouveaux emplacements – Urbanisme, 1945–1949, Africa Archives Brussels (hereafter AA).

Kamalondo, *Kenya* and *Katuba*. In terms of housing, the *Katuba* neighborhood was based on the so-called *Système Grévisse*, which encouraged the African population to participate in the construction of their own residences, albeit under strict supervision and following a predefined list of restrictions and obligations on technical issues.[21] In the *Système Grévisse*, the foundations of the houses were constructed by the colonial administration itself in order to keep control of the precise dimensions and the exact positioning of the house on the parcel. The main body of the house was then to be erected by the future inhabitants themselves, with materials provided by the government at favorable prices (Fig. 3.3). This construction method allowed the bypassing of qualified construction firms and promoted the use of prefabricated mass-produced elements, such as windows, doors, and roof elements, reducing the building costs significantly.

Figure 3.3: Building with the *Système Grévisse* in Lubumbashi.
Source: Archives of the Soeurs de la Charité, Gent, file A 76-CON Lubumbashi.

For Ferdinand Grévisse, the then district commissioner and fervent promoter of this method, its real importance did not reside in the technical aspects or in the architectural quality of the houses alone. He rather accentuated its social

---

21 The *Système Grévisse* was called after Ferdinand Grévisse, the then district commissioner, who published a study on the "native towns" of Lubumbashi: Grévisse, *Le Centre Extra-Coutumier d'Elisabethville*.

dimensions. By encouraging the future inhabitants to participate in the construction and, in addition, giving them the possibility to become owners of their residence, the *Système Grévisse*, he argued, would introduce order and stability in the life of the African urbanite, and, moreover, anchor him more firmly to the colonial project as "he would no longer be the simple proletarian who is condemned to an absolute dependency on his employer."[22] In that sense, this housing policy was (very) similar to the promotion of individual home ownership that the Catholic party and related associations were developing at the time in Belgium to turn the laborer into a docile member of Belgian society by stimulating him to buy and build his own house.[23]

Already in 1950, Grévisse argued that, given the immediate success of his approach (at the time over a thousand houses had been built according to the *Système Grévisse*), it provided the ultimate solution to Lubumbashi's housing crisis. Yet, the construction method was also harshly criticized because of the poor technical quality of houses built by laymen, the underestimation of real costs as well as the minimal surface that left little flexibility for spatially organizing the house. Some of the more acerbic critiques were, not surprisingly, formulated by those who were in favor of the OCA approach to the housing problem, such as G. Mosmans.[24] Lubumbashi quickly became the stage of conflicts and tensions between the promoters of both housing schemes which presented fundamentally divergent positions regarding the role of the state in responding to the housing crisis. While the *Système Grévisse* granted a large initiative to the future African inhabitants themselves, the OCA schemes favored a top-down approach allowing close monitoring of each step in the planning and building process.

Implementing the Model

The OCA *cités* were based on the urban concept of the "neighborhood unit", a particular kind of spatial organization of settlements which gained a strong currency in circles of modernist architects and planners in the immediate postwar

---

[22] Grévisse, *Le Centre Extra-Coutumier d'Elisabethville*, 204.
[23] This approach was institutionalized by the notorious law De Taeye, that formed a major cornerstone of postwar housing policies in Belgium, see Tom Avermaete et al., eds., *Wonen in Welvaart: woningbouw en wooncultuur in Vlaanderen 1948–1973* (Antwerpen: deSingel, 2006).
[24] For a contemporary comparison between the two approaches, see Georges Mosmans, "Elisabethville – Méthodes Grévisse et OCA, September 18, 1955," in file 566, portfolio 96, Inventory OCA dossiers, AA.

years.²⁵ It was premised on the creation of a qualitative urban environment which required a spatial organization that took into account the human scale as well as the provision of community enhancing facilities and public spaces. Ruashi was originally conceived to house approximately 32,000 inhabitants, with the whole neighborhood being divided into five autonomous sub-quarters of each around 6,000 inhabitants, spatially separated from each other by large roads (Fig. 3.4a, b). While this sub-structuring had its roots in some of the modernist planning principles of the time, it also echoed the preference of Lubumbashi's *Comité Urbain* for splitting the growing African urban population into separated communities in order to better control and discipline it.

In line with the original concept, however, the "neighborhood unit" was used by the OCA on the basis of social grounds which are clearly described in a late 1963 article written by the architect and urban planner Ernest Scaillon, a prominent former member of OCA's main architectural section. In contrast to the earlier modernist urban planning principle of the functionalist city, which aimed at a clear separation of the different functions of life (dwelling, work, transportation, recreation), Scaillon presented the advantage of the "neighborhood unit" concept as its capacity to enable an interlocking of various urban functions, thus creating a coherent and harmonious living environment which would stimulate a sense of community and belonging.²⁶ To that end, not only housing but also a variety of public facilities needed to be provided, both on the scale of the whole neighborhood and on that of its constituent sub-quarters (Fig. 3.5). The Ruashi neighborhood was thus organized around a communal center, comprising the communal administrative center, a tribunal, a police station, a main market, and a church, while the sub-quarters had their own centers with, among others, a local school, medical facility, market and/or shops, a sports field, a church and a *foyer social*, where Congolese women could be trained to become "respectable and devoted" housewives (Fig. 3.6).²⁷ In their

---

25 The concept of the "neighborhood unit", which has its origin in US urban planning practices of the 1920s, became a key concept in discussions on modern urban planning in Europe in the late 1940s and was explicitly discussed in the 6th *Congrès International d'Architecture Moderne* (CIAM), held in Bridgewater in 1947. For an elaborate discussion, see Auke Van der Woud, *CIAM: Housing Town Planning* (Delft: Delft University Press, 1983). Eric Mumford, *The CIAM Discourse on Urbanism, 1928–1960* (Cambridge, Mass.: MIT Press, 2000).
26 Ernest Scaillon, "La rénovation urbaine et l'unité de voisinage," *Rythme* 37 (1963).
27 On the role of the *foyers sociaux* as instruments to create "respectable, devoted housewives", see for instance Nancy Rose Hunt, "Domesticity and Colonialism in Belgian Africa: Usumbura's Foyer Social, 1946–1960," *Signs* 15 (1990).

spatial layout, the OCA neighborhoods differed significantly from the grid-pattern, commonly used as the template of the *cité indigène* because of considerations of efficiency and governmentality. In the OCA neighborhoods, a more diverse and visually stimulating landscape was created via an irregular pattern of main roads and dead-end streets, punctuated by open spaces creating gravitational points in the overall urban tissue, with rows of houses oriented in such a way that they took into consideration climatic conditions (protecting against the sun, while opening

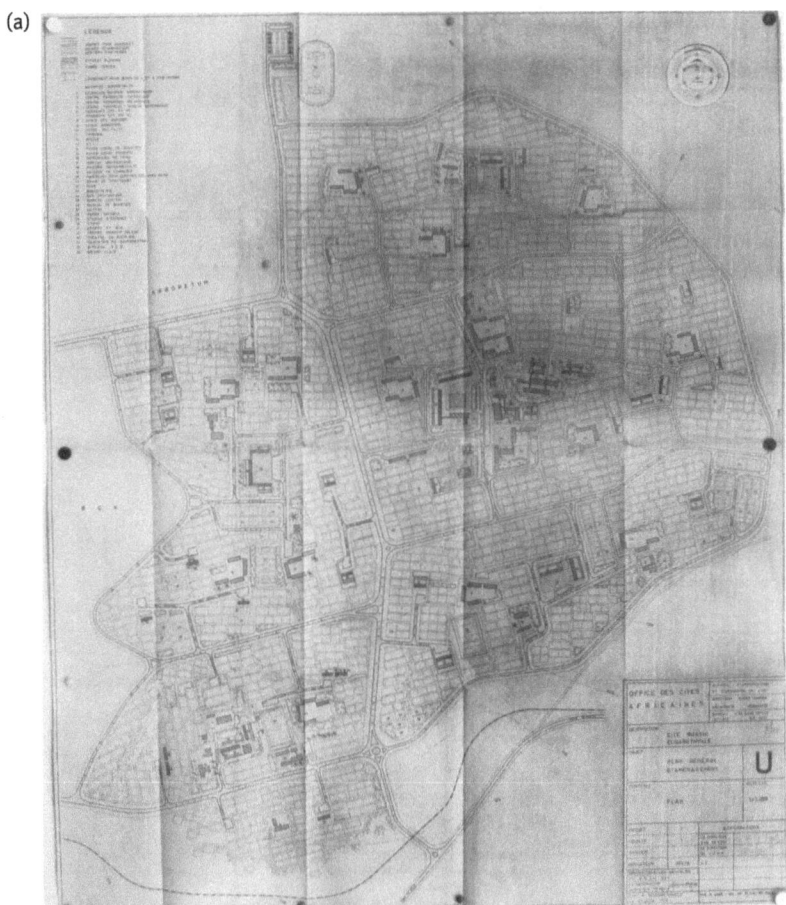

Figure 3.4a: "Ruashi/Elisabethville. Plan general d'aménagement." Overall masterplan for the Ruashi-neighborhood, Office des Cités Africaines, 1959.
Source: Africa Archives, Ministry of Foreign Affairs, Brussels; Fund OCA, Courtesy AA.

(b)

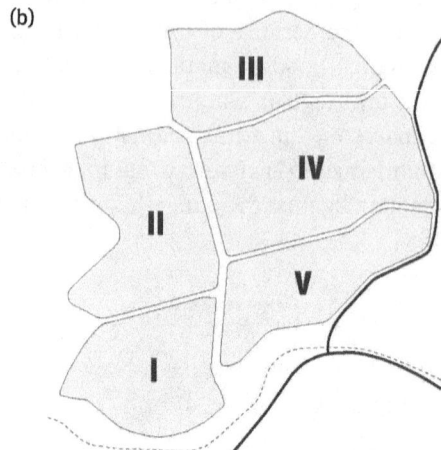

Figure 3.4b: Scheme of the division of the Ruashi neighborhood, designed for around 32,000 inhabitants, distributed into five sections of about 6,000 inhabitants each.
Source: scheme drawn by Céline Fenaux, based on archival material, 2010.

Figure 3.5: Fragment of the plan of the Ruashi neighborhood, indicating the public facilities and the main road infrastructure with the characteristic dead end streets.
Source: scheme drawn by Céline Fenaux, based on archival material, 2010.

Figure 3.6: The central market of Ruashi, designed by OCA architect J. Castel-Branco, ca. 1959. Source: photograph by Johan Lagae, 2006.

up to dominant breezes) as well as the characteristics of the site, such as hydrography and topography (Fig. 3.4a).[28]

Designing and building the Ruashi neighborhood proved a complex affair, however, with tensions between the central and local administration rising throughout the process. While Xavier Lejeune de Schiervel, the head of the OCA, tried to enforce general design guidelines to be applied all over the Congolese territory, the head of the OCA office in Lubumbashi, C. Porta, accused his colleagues in the mother country of being totally ignorant of local realities.[29] Major discussions occurred around the issue of density as well as on the introduction

---

28 In this respect, the OCA planners seemed to be also drawing lessons from the layout of the 1920s "garden city" neighborhoods in the periphery of Brussels, such as *Le Logis Floréal* which had gained international acclaim in its day. The low density of this "garden-city" model was countered by applying terraced houses and, if possible, *maisons à étage*, rather than single houses surrounded by individual gardens.
29 File 568, portfolio 96; file 569, portfolio 96; file 3012, portfolio 749, Inventory OCA dossiers, AA.

of new housing typologies, such as the *maison à étage*, a solution Porta feared would not be popular among Africans. The main office in Brussels, in turn, critiqued the local designers in Lubumbashi of treating the different sub-quarters as separate entities, fearing this would result in a loss of overall coherence.[30] Tellingly, when the first quarter was almost finished, the fifth was still in the phase of conception.

A Failed Housing Policy?

In a timeframe of eight years, OCA succeeded in constructing 40,000 houses, an achievement that was celebrated in colonial propaganda as an adequate response to the housing crisis. In 1957, official sources had reported that the OCA "builds one house every 15 minutes."[31] This substantial effort, however, did by far not match the actual needs. Ruashi was no exception, as in quantitative terms the number of houses planned was far too limited to tackle Lubumbashi's exploding population.[32] Moreover, in 1960 – the year that Congo gained its independence – the Ruashi neighborhood was still far from complete. Of the five sub-quarters initially planned, only the first was completely realized and two others were only partially built, while of the remaining two even the road network was not yet fully completed (Fig. 3.7).[33] Because of financial constraints, moreover, the public facilities were the first elements of the plan to be eliminated during construction.

Given the shortage of accommodation for Africans, it is remarkable that many of the OCA houses in Ruashi remained unoccupied, just as was the case in OCA neighborhoods in other cities.[34] The increase of building costs which

---

30 See for instance the correspondence between the Manager-Administrator of the OCA and the director in Lubumbashi. "Cité Ruashi à Elisabethville. Quartiers 3 et 4, 16 april 1957," File 3012, portfolio 749, inventory OCA dossiers, AA.
31 Statement from the 1957 annual report of OCA, mentioned in Bruno de Meulder, *Kuvuande Mbote*, 199.
32 In 1958, the city's population was 168,775 inhabitants, a number which almost doubled by 1970 to 318,000. Léon de Saint-Moulin, *Villes et organisation de l'espace en République Démocratique du Congo* (Paris: L'Harmattan, 2010), 127. For a more elaborate survey of the evolution of Lubumbashi's population, see Jean-Claude Bruneau and Marc Pain, eds., *Atlas de Lubumbashi* (Nanterre: Université de Paris X, 1990).
33 Céline Fenaux executed a detailed mapping of the existing physical landscape of Ruashi during a fieldwork trip in January-February 2010.
34 In 1955, the deplorable results were reported by presenting percentages of unoccupied houses in the OCA quarters of Kinshasa (36%), Stanleyville (40%), Bukavu (64%) and Usumbura (55%). Georges Moulaert, Comité du Congres Colonial National. Notes concernant le Rapport de la

Figure 3.7: Aerial photograph of the Ruashi neighborhood anno 2010, with an overlay of those fragments of the original masterplan, indicating those parts which were executed according to the initial design.
Source: montage by Céline Fenaux based on fieldwork observations, 2010.

had resulted from the use of durable materials, from the elaborate architectural design and from the provision of up-to-date domestic equipment, such as electricity or tap water, made the prices for which the houses could be sold or rented out too high for the majority of the African population and even for the emerging class of so-called "évolués". In his 1958 critical analysis of the urban conditions in Central African cities, geographer Jacques Denis provided another explanation for the limited success of the OCA housing policy: even if the OCA technicians had found "laudable solutions" in terms of urban planning, architecture, and funding, and even if their choice of adopting European standards

---

Commission pour l'étude de l'habitation du Congolais (July 1955). File 3012, portfolio 749, inventory OCA dossiers, AA.

in the domain of urban dwellings was "justified", they "hadn't paid enough attention to social and psychological issues" and should have prepared the public opinion for what was, in fact, a "revolution in African housing" in order to "soften its brutality."[35]

The OCA nevertheless had made a genuine effort of researching the dwelling needs and practices of its future inhabitants. Some of its housing types, for instance, were explicitly designed to allow inhabitants to respond to their evolving living conditions and dynamic patterns of occupancy and use. Not only did the OCA provide some types of mixed program dwellings (residence/commerce), it also elaborated the so-called "expanding house" or *la maison extensible*, a house that could grow in relation to the changing needs of the family (Fig. 3.8a, b).[36] This two-story house type was conceived so that it could accommodate a variety of scenarios of cohabitation, ranging from a family with up to eight children to a couple without children that could rent out rooms on the second story to five extra residents with neither having to alter fundamentally the internal structure of the house nor having to extend it with additional parts. The design allowed a response to such different scenarios and arrangements of living together with little to no modifications of the house itself in order to make sure that the overall architectural landscape of the OCA neighborhood would not be hampered in the future by the emergence of informal constructions. The development of the type of the *maison extensible* was, in other words, as much a question of aesthetics as it was of social and cultural sensitivity towards local dwelling practices.

Before proceeding to the actual construction of houses in Ruashi, different types were first tested out on an "experimental site" in the middle of the existing African quarter Kamalondo in order to grasp the reactions of the targeted inhabitants (Fig. 3.9).[37] While this demonstrated the unpopularity, particularly of the terraced and two-story housing types, all designs were nevertheless applied in Ruashi. The local government also undertook several initiatives to "educate" the African population in new dwelling practices, such as the publication of an informative brochure on the *maison modèle*, creating a fully furnished *maison témoin* that could be visited, and organizing a series of competitions honoring the most beautiful house/garden/interior of the *cité*. Deeply rooted in the paternalistic rationale underlying postwar colonial policies

---

35 Jacques Denis, *Le phénomène urbain en Afrique Centrale* (Namur: s.d. [1958]), 307.
36 Lejeune de Schiervel, *Les nouvelles cités congolaises*, 109–112.
37 Xavier Lejeune de Schiervel in a report sent to Emile Henvaux. "Rapport sur la direction d'Elisabethville," April 6, 1954, in: Inventory OCA dossiers, portfolio 96, file 566, AA. See also "Chantier expérimental au centre," August 5, 1954, file 1359, portfolio 270; file 3012, portfolio 749, inventory OCA dossiers, AA.

(a)

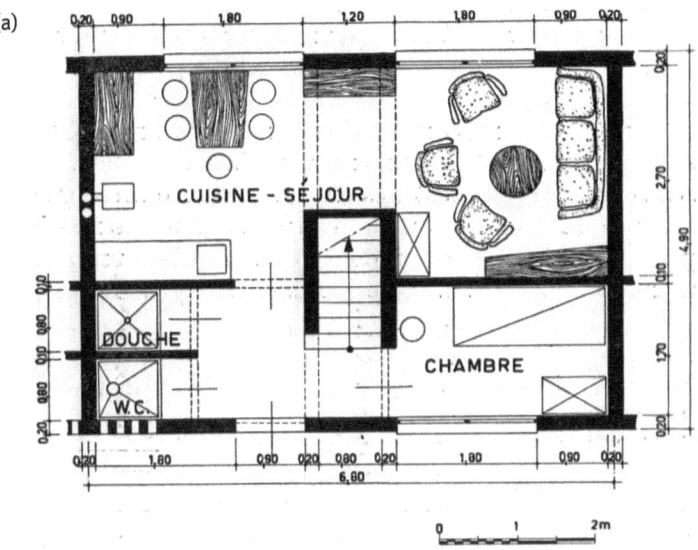

PLAN 22. — Maison à un étage, à occupation variable. Rez-de-chaussée.

Figure 3.8a: Plan of the ground floor of the *maison extensible-type*, with living unit, kitchen, one bedroom and sanitary facilities.
Source: Lejeune de Schiervel, Xavier. *Les nouvelles cités congolaises: L'architecture et le logement*, 1956, 111.

(b)

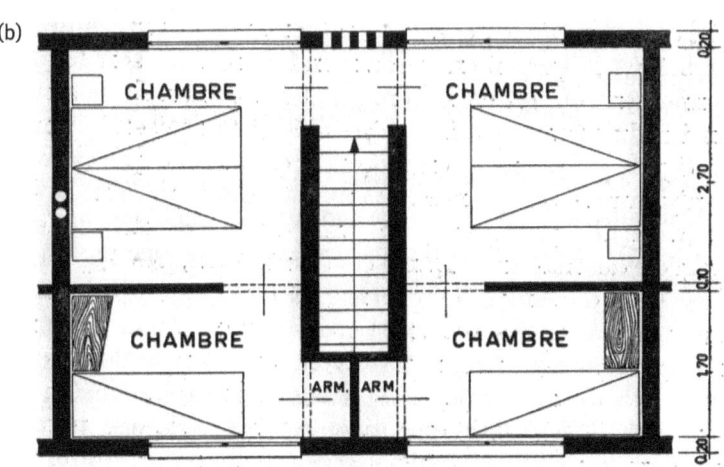

PLAN 21. — Maison à un étage, à occupation variable. Étage.

Figure 3.8b: Plan of the first floor of the *maison extensible*-type with two double bedrooms and two single bedrooms.
Source: Lejeune de Schiervel, Xavier. *Les nouvelles cités congolaises: L'architecture et le logement*, 1956, 110.

Figure 3.9: Two-story OCA houses erected in the "experimental site" in the *Kamalondo* neighborhood, situation anno 2010.
Source: photograph by Céline Fenaux, 2010.

in the Belgian Congo, such initiatives were also in tune with then current practices in the mother country that sought to educate the Belgian housewife in "modern living" via a variety of popularizing media targeting a broad audience (exhibitions of model houses and interiors, lectures, publications in newspapers and women's magazines etc.).[38]

A particular effort was made on behalf of the OCA to promote the *maison à étage*, as this was an essential instrument for reaching a sufficient density in the Ruashi neighborhood. Despite several initiatives, including conferences in the *foyers sociaux* that targeted a female Congolese audience, an exhibition, and special lectures on the topic in schools,[39] this particular housing type proved extremely unpopular because "Congolese felt cold on the first floor."[40] The number

---

[38] For a discussion of such initiatives in a metropolitan context, see Fredie Floré and Emiel de Kooning, "Post-war Model Homes: Introduction," *Journal of Architecture* 4 (2004).

[39] Files 3012 and 3019, portfolio 749, inventory OCA dossiers, AA.

[40] Letter of the director of the OCA in Lubumbashi to the central office of OCA in Brussels. "Construction de logements," 10 August 1959, file 419, portfolio 70, inventory OCA dossiers, AA. The fact that the housing designs followed the guidelines of "tropical modernism" and thus included architectonic solutions for enabling cross-ventilation was not appreciated by Congolese inhabitants as it created in their opinion a feeling of an uncomfortable draught. Interview with Jan Maes, a former OCA architect, April 1996.

of *maisons à étage* standing vacant after realization reached disturbing numbers by the end of the 1950s, leading local OCA officials to start negotiations with local enterprises to house their employees in these dwellings – an attempt that would, however, remain without much result.[41] If the housing policy of the OCA failed in a number of aspects, this was in large part due to the unwillingness of the Brussels-based OCA officials, architects, and planners who promoted general solutions to the problem of housing shortage based on abstract ideas of rationality and cost-efficiency rather than adapting to local specificities of which they were constantly informed by the local OCA branches operating on the ground.[42]

A Transformed Urban Landscape

The OCA houses were not merely intended to provide shelter for the booming African population in Congo's major urban centers. They were also a major element in a broader project of social engineering aimed at the "emancipation" of the African household that was defined in terms of a nuclear family. With the exception of the *maison extensible*, that in fact only formed a marginal typology in the OCA plans, the modest one-family dwelling typical in Belgium constituted the main template. Moreover, the kitchen was planned inside the house in order to "integrate" the Congolese woman more in the family life (Fig. 3.10). It would, as one contemporary observer put it, allow to have her children around her while cooking and stimulate her to eat together with the *chef de la famille*.[43] As such, the design of the generic OCA house was in tune with the policy of educating the Congolese housewife in the *foyer social* in order to turn her into a "devoted spouse."

It soon became clear, however, that this attempt at interiorizing the daily life was not very successful. The majority of inhabitants of the OCA neighborhood

---

41 An in-depth discussion of the measures to counter the fact that many OCA houses remained vacant is provided in Fenaux, L'Office des Cités Africaines, 217–221. This analysis is based on various files of the OCA fund in the AA (portfolio 749, files 3012, 2019; portfolio 70: 419; portfolio 96: 567).
42 It is tempting to draw a distinction here with the housing program in Casablanca run by the architect and planner Michel Ecochard around the same time, a program that seemed much more embedded in interdisciplinary research of local dwelling habits. See for instance Tom Avermaete, "Framing the Afropolis: Michel Ecochard and the African City for the Greatest Number," *Oase* 82 (2010).
43 Fernand Peigneux, "De l'habitation," *Bulletin de l'Union des Femmes Coloniales* 1 (1954). Peigneux also pointed out reasons for cost-efficiency.

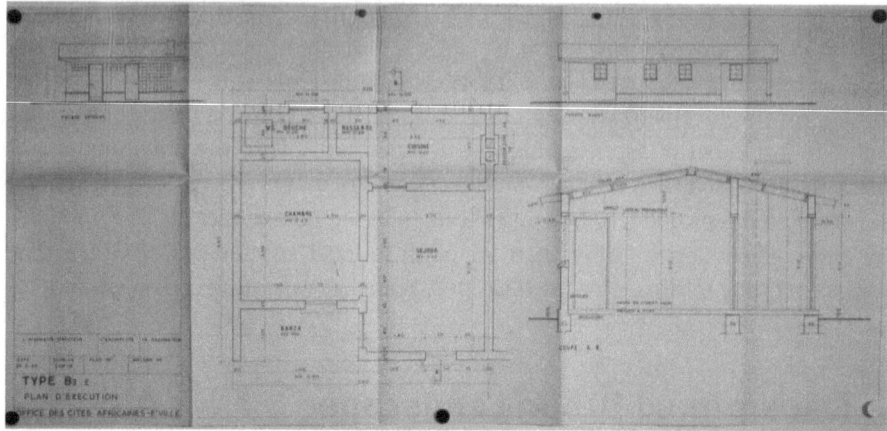

Figure 3.10: Architectural drawing of a single-story OCA house for Elisabethville/Lubumbashi, type B, 1954.
Source: Africa Archives, Ministry of Foreign Affairs, Brussels; Fund OCA, Courtesy AA.

continued to cook outside, in the open air, as this was an intrinsic part of African social life. On photographs commissioned by the OCA in the late 1950s, one can also see the first traces of an informal appropriation of the public spaces. In front of the two-story housing types with commercial shops on the ground floor, we actually see a number of women selling food on improvised stalls, while in other photographs some graffiti-like writings already appear on the colorful façades (Fig. 3.11a, 11b).[44] When, after independence, a new flux of migrants from the rural areas arrived in urban centers like Lubumbashi, the nuclear families living in the OCA houses were gradually being replaced or reshaped as extended families, defined by complex social relationships based on kinship and ethnicity. Hence, inhabitants were forced to adapt and transform the hardware of most of the houses and also started appropriating the open spaces of the neighborhood. Today, Ruashi presents a profoundly altered urban landscape, testifying of a long process of appropriation, adaptation, and transformation, a phenomenon that is also discernible in the OCA neighborhoods in other Congolese cities, in Kinshasa in particular.[45]

---

44 These photographs are kept in the form of color slides in the OCA fund, AA.
45 For Kinshasa, see Bruno de Meulder and Marie-Françoise Plissart, "Kinshasa, the Hereafter of Modern Architecture," in *Back from Utopia: The Challenge of the Modern Movement*, ed. Hubert-Jan Henket and Hilde Heynen (Rotterdam: 010 Publishers, 2002). Dirk Pauwels, "Souvenirs of Urbanism," in *Brakin: Brazzaville – Kinshasa: Visualizing the Visible*, ed. Wim Cuyvers (Baden: Lars Müller Publishers, 2006). For Kisangani, see Sally Lierman, "Office des Cités Africaines in

3 Ruashi, a Pessac in Congo? — 87

(a)

Figure 3.11a: Two-story housing with shops for commercial activities on the ground floor. Notice the informal infrastructure for selling food in the front, situation late 1950s.
Source: contemporary original color slide, AA, Ministry of Foreign Affairs, Brussels; Fund OCA, Courtesy AA.

(b)

Figure 3.11b: Two-story housing with shops for commercial activities on the ground floor and some storage facilities in the back. Notice the graffiti-like inscription *fantôme* ("ghost") on the side façade on the right, situation late 1950s.
Source: contemporary original color slide, AA, Ministry of Foreign Affairs, Brussels; Fund OCA, Courtesy, AA.

A detailed mapping of the transformed landscape of Ruashi was conducted during fieldwork in early 2010, documenting the altered built environments in photographs and drawings, and conducting interviews to gain an understanding of these transformations.[46] While several interviewees pointed out the orderly and clean character of the neighborhood when they first arrived, often decades ago, Ruashi's urban landscape now commonly evokes a strong sense of disorder and *bricolage*: "Ruashi no longer is clean, as it once used to be."[47] The mapping demonstrated a number of shared strategies of transformation, the most striking of which consists of enclosures that were put up around the houses and have significantly altered part of the streetscape of the OCA *cité*. (Fig. 3.12). Serving as a

Figure 3.12: Enclosures in various materials in front of two-story houses with commercial shops on the ground floor, situation anno 2006.
Source: photograph by Johan Lagae, 2006.

Kisangani: Een stedenbouwkundig onderzoek naar genese en toe-eigening van een woonwijk uit de jaren 1950 in Afrika" (Master diss., Ghent University, 2011).
46 During January and February 2010, a total of 35 interviews was conducted in Ruashi by Céline Fenaux in collaboration with Serge Songa Songa Mitwa, an assistant from the History Department of the University of Lubumbashi. Interviewees were selected in such a way as to obtain a varied sample of inhabitants by taking into consideration a distribution in space (interviewees came from the different sub-quarters), age, profession, and gender.
47 Madame M., a Congolese woman living in *quartier 1*, interviewed in Lubumbashi on 31 January 2010.

protective shield, such enclosures emerged mainly in the 1980s, an era of growing insecurity that has even reshaped Lubumbashi's city center into what now seems a completely privatized environment or a *ville bunkerisée*. Yet, such walls are never absolute boundaries but rather constitute liminal spaces allowing for different forms of negotiation and encounter.[48] Fieldwork demonstrated that the practice of constructing a small shop adjacent to the house is widespread, often in the form of a freestanding little, temporary shack, thus altering drastically the original structure of the OCA neighborhood unit model in which commercial activity was limited to the main market near the communal center and the submarkets on the level of each sub-quarter. Sometimes, the main structure of the OCA house itself has been changed, for instance, by filling in the so-called *barza*, a small outdoor space. Echoing the outdoor room of vernacular African houses where it constituted an important social space, the *barza* in the OCA houses were too small to be of any real use and have hence, not surprisingly, been adapted and often even extended with a complete extra room at the front of the house, accommodating sometimes complex arrangements of living together (Fig. 3.13). Such front rooms can serve commercial purposes with a semi-public character during the day, while at night they become part of the house again and serve as an extra bedroom. Another recurrent practice of transforming OCA houses consists of adding constructions to the back of the house, creating extra bedrooms or providing for better sanitary facilities. Apart from adding habitable space, such additions also fundamentally alter the status of the back garden, which often becomes an outdoor room that serves as the real heart of the home where people cook, wash, clean, play, rest, and socialize (Fig. 3.14).

A Pessac in Congo?

What do such transformations mean when reflecting on OCA's legacy in Congo? In a provocative analysis, Bruno de Meulder argued that the OCA *cités* quickly became seen as a "symbol of oppression" after independence, as they were associated with the paternalistic attitude of Belgian colonial policy and were thus infrastructures *par excellence* on which the discontent with the "petty apartheid" regime in Congolese cities was projected. In his opinion, it was no coincidence

---

[48] For a discussion of this phenomenon, see Johan Lagae, Sofie Boonen and Sam Lanckriet, "Navigating 'Off Radar': The Heritage of Liminal Spaces in the City Center of Colonial/Postcolonial Lubumbashi, DR Congo," in *Things Don't Really Exist Until You Give Them A Name: Unpacking Urban Heritage*, eds. Rachel Lee et al. (Dar es Salaam: Mkuki na Nyota, 2017), 86–93.

90 —— Sofie Boonen and Johan Lagae

Figure 3.13: Transformation of an OCA house with an extra room added to the front, situation anno 2010.
Source: photograph by Céline Fenaux, 2010.

Figure 3.14: Transformation of an OCA house with an additional facility added to the back side.
Source: photograph by Céline Fenaux, 2010.

that during the turbulent events linked to Congo's struggle for independence, buildings constructed by the OCA in various cities fell victim to looting and destruction.[49] Other historical research, especially by Congolese scholars, does not seem to corroborate such a reading.[50] Today, as our fieldwork revealed, Ruashi is considered one of the more attractive areas in Lubumbashi to live in because it offers a less dense and more comfortable environment than in other parts of the city. Moreover, the transformations we described above are not unique to the OCA *cités* but also emerged, for instance, in the workers' camps of the railway company in Lubumbashi in 2006–2007, when the infrastructure was given to its employees to compensate for years of delay in paying their salary.[51]

Should the transformations made to the OCA houses in Ruashi then be read, if not as a deliberate act of resistance against a patronizing colonial policy of social engineering, then at least as a proof of the failure of the imported Western model of the one-family house, as Jacques Denis already seemed to suggest in 1958?[52] For one thing, the sometimes radical transformations were surely not what the architects and planners of OCA had in mind, considering that even the type of *la maison extensible* was designed precisely to avoid the emergence of informal structures. We would like to offer a different reading here and argue that the spatial layout of the OCA *cités* and the architectural hardware of their houses actually offered inhabitants ample opportunities for changing their habitat and accommodating various arrangements of dwelling and occupation.[53]

---

49 De Meulder, *Kuvuande Mbote*, 204. See also his chapter in Tom Avermaete et al., *Wonen in welvaart*, 94–109.
50 No (strong) emphasis is put on the OCA *cités* in the context of Congo's struggle towards independence in the work of Congolese historians such as Isidore Ndaywel è Nziem, who wrote a general survey entitled *Histoire générale du Congo: De l'héritage ancien à la République Démocratique* (Paris: Duculot, 1998). Jean-Marie Mutamba Makombo Kitatshima, who authored an important study entitled *Du Congo belge au Congo indépendant 1940–1960: Emergence des "évolués" et génèse du nationalisme* (Kinshasa: IFEP, 1998); or Zana Etambala, who provided an account of the last years of colonial rule under the title *De teloorgang van een modelkolonie: Belgisch Congo 1958–1960* (Leuven: Acco, 2008).
51 Fieldwork observations in the *Camp Maramba* by Johan Lagae in 2005, 2006, and 2010. A similar transformation took place recently in the *Camp Kauka* in Kinshasa, also exactly at the moment the railway company, or *Office National du Transport* (ONATRA), ceded the houses to its agents (fieldwork observation by Johan Lagae, 2017).
52 Denis, *Le phénomène urbain en Afrique Centrale*, 302–310.
53 The same phenomenon is to be seen in the OCA *cités* of Kinshasa and Kisangani. What seems apparent, however, is that the extent and nature of the transformations do differ in the various cities, with Kinshasa standing out because of more radical changes made to the urban landscapes of the OCA *cités*.

It might be useful in this respect to bring to mind another, more well-known, case of a changed modern(ist) architectural landscape, the *Cité Frugès* in Pessac, near Bordeaux, which was built in 1925–1926 according to plans of Le Corbusier. Being one of the rare early projects in which Le Corbusier was able to test his innovative ideas on housing and urban planning, albeit still on a limited scale, this neighborhood has also become famous in architectural circles for the many transformations local inhabitants made in the course of time, thereby sometimes radically changing the architectural appearance that had been based on Le Corbusier's famous *cinq points*. Roof terraces, horizontal strip windows, and outdoor rooms all "fell victim" to different expectations of architect and inhabitants in terms of aesthetics, representation, and use. Confronted with this process, which led to some striking formal alterations of his initial architectural design, Le Corbusier is known to have reacted in a laconic way, stating that "*la vie a toujours raison*", "life is always right" and that it is "the architect who's wrong."[54]

In his now classic book entitled *Pessac de Le Corbusier: 1927–1967: Étude socio-architecturale*, published originally in 1969, Philippe Boudon studied in detail the process of profound physical transformation that the houses of Le Corbusier underwent, reflecting on what was to be learned from this *architecture habitée activement* ("actively lived-in architecture"). Rather than regretting the process of radical transformation, Boudon argued that the modifications done to the architecture represented an "in the end positive rather than a negative sequence of the original architectural concept."[55] His view parallels that of architectural critic Ada Louise Huxtable who, after having visited the *Cité Frugès* in 1981, wrote in *The New York Times* that "contrary to popular belief and the conventional wisdom, it works."[56] Pessac, Huxtable argued, was not "a testament to the miscarriage of modernism and the arrogance of its architects" but rather demonstrated that, despite "the loss of key elements of the Corbusian style," the settlement had "retained an impressive and recognizable integrity. Pessac was a very pleasant place to be. And these houses were clearly survivors." But, Huxtable added, "Pessac was a survivor precisely because of its architecture. Its strong identity absorbs almost anything." The

---

[54] An early reference to this statement of Le Corbusier is to be found in the seminal monograph by Charles Jencks, *Le Corbusier and the Tragic View of Architecture* (Cambridge, Mass.: Harvard University Press, 1973), 74. The origin of this by now well-known and widespread quote is Philippe Boudon's study of Pessac: Boudon, *Pessac de Le Corbusier*, 2.
[55] Boudon, *Pessac de Le Corbusier*, 167.
[56] Ada Louise Huxtable, "Le Corbusier's Housing Project: Flexible Enough to Endure." *The New York Times*, 15 May 1981. See Ada Louise Huxtable, *On Architecture: Collected Reflections on a Century of Change* (New York: Walker & Company, 2008), 160–165.

statement parallels the ones advanced by Boudon who wrote that the conclusion to be drawn from his study of the inhabitants' transformations was that the original architecture designed by Le Corbusier provided a clear "set of rules," or *règles du jeu*, which in terms of adaptation and transformation had proven to be "fruitful and full of opportunities."[57] Boudon went on to explain how this was mainly due to "standardization" and the particular relationship between closed and open forms, and between the inside and outside of the original architectural design.[58] We argue that the design of the Ruashi neighborhood, and in extension all OCA *cités*, offers a similar open-ended "set of rules," as the spacious urban layout as well as the basic infrastructure of the OCA neighborhood (buildings as well as streets, squares, green spaces etc.) provided room for maneuver for a future transformation which is lacking in other *cités indigènes* in Lubumbashi, such as Kamalondo, Kenya and Katuba, where densities are higher, space is much more cramped and the architecture less imaginative and open-ended. By documenting the kind of "actively lived-in architecture" of Ruashi, our research aims at taking seriously what we can define, in line with Henri Lefebvre, as a *praxis urbaine* (or "urban praxis") of the Congolese inhabitants.[59]

Such an enterprise is all the more important and timely, as the OCA legacy is gaining currency as an important "colonial built heritage" in the former Belgian Congo, as is demonstrated by publications coming out of the milieu of heritage experts, be they French or Belgian.[60] Defining the OCA *cités* as a "remarkable" example of modernist architecture in the Congo, heritage expert Yves Robert, for instance, wondered if their appropriation paved the way to a new form of *patrimonialité* (or "heritage practice"), adding that, as far as he was concerned, this was a question to which it is "too early to respond affirmatively."[61] While we do underwrite the importance of rediscovering and documenting the legacy of colonial architecture in the Democratic Republic of the Congo, such as the OCA *cités*, we remain reluctant of efforts to define it in

---

57 Boudon, *Pessac de Le Corbusier*, 169.
58 Boudon, *Pessac de Le Corbusier*, 169–170.
59 In his preface to Philippe Boudon's book on Pessac, Lefebvre explicitly situates this study at the crossroads of architecture and urbanism, and presents it, more particularly, as an innovative analysis of *praxis urbaine*. Boudon, *Pessac de Le Corbusier*, viii. For Lefebvre's ideas on *praxis urbaine* and its links with Pessac, see Lukasz Stanek, *Henri Lefebvre on Space: Architecture, Urban Research, and the Production of Theory* (Minneapolis: University of Minnesota Press, 2011), especially Chapter 2 and, more in particular, 89–93.
60 See for instance Marc Pabois, ed., *Lubumbashi: Capitale minière du Katanga 1910–2010: L'Architecture* (Lubumbashi: Espace Culturel Francophone de Lubumbashi, 2008).
61 Yves Robert, "L'œuvre moderniste remarquable de l'Office des Cités Africaines au Congo," *Les nouvelles du Patrimoine* 128 (2010).

terms of "heritage," let alone a "shared heritage."[62] The last thing Ruashi needs, we would claim, is the kind of heritage make-over deployed in Le Corbusier's Pessac, where most of the houses have been restored to their original state.[63] Cultural initiatives linked to urban heritage can act as important instruments of (re-)activating urban societies in a city like Lubumbashi.[64] But the issue at stake in re-assessing a neighborhood like Ruashi today does not reside in celebrating and fixing it in time as a remarkable and forgotten modernist legacy but rather in trying to understand the complexities of this "actively lived-in architecture" in order to address the challenges its current inhabitants face in their everyday struggle for life.

As such, our position aligns with what Viviana d'Auria and Hannah Leroux have recently argued for in a theme issue of the journal *Clara* that they dedicated to the theme of "*modernisme(s) approprié(s)*" in its double meaning of both an "appropriate modernism," well-attuned to the local context, and a modernism that is "appropriated" by its users.[65] In the editorial, they stress the need to analyze in detail the "encounter" between on the one hand "the residues of a utopic content that is intrinsically linked with the modernist project" and, on the other, "the appropriation of such places over time," as doing so can help us re-assess and gain a new understanding of "the urban phenomenon."[66] In other words, what they argue for is a form of writing narratives on buildings that not only takes into consideration the origins of the design (and the way architects and planners tried to engage with the specificities of the local conditions), but also, and perhaps more importantly, the moment when life takes over (*quand la vie prend le dessus*). Ruashi, as we have tried to demonstrate here, is a case in point to do exactly that.

---

62 Johan Lagae and Sofie Boonen, "Décoloniser l'espace (péri)urbain en République Démocratique du Congo: Le cas de Lubumbashi," in *Périurbains: Territoires, réseaux et temporalités*, ed. Jean-Baptiste Minnaert (Lyon: Ed. Lieux Dits, 2013).
63 See for instance Bernard Toulier, *Architecture et patrimoine du XXe siècle en France* (Paris: Editions du Patrimoine, 1999), 60–63.
64 A fine example of such initiative is the cultural event *Rencontres Picha*, a bi-annual festival on contemporary photography and video art organized by two young artists from Lubumbashi, Patrick Mudekereza and Sammy Baloji, the second edition of which took place in October 2010, see Simon Njami, ed., *Rencontres Picha: Biennale de Lubumbashi, 13–17 octobre 2010* (Paris: Filigraines édition, 2012), accessed October 17, 2017, online catalogue http://panicplatform.net/content/curated/Catalogue%20Picha%202010.pdf.
65 Viviana d'Auria and Hannah Leroux, "Modernisme(s) approprié(s)," *Clara* 4 (2017). The cases presented in this theme issue range from modernist projects in Buenos Aires, Cape Town, Caracas, Seoul, Lima, Cansado-Zouerate (Mauritania), Benin, Hanoi and Brussels.
66 Viviana d'Auria and Hannah Leroux, "Modernisme(s) approprié(s)."

References

Archival sources

The following files, held in the Africa Archives in Brussels, were consulted (these archives are now part of the State Archives, Brussels).
Portfolio GG.20.400 Fund Gouvernement Général.
Files 566, 567, 568, 569, portfolio 96 Fund Office des Cités Africaines.
Files 3012, 3019, portfolio 749 Fund Office des Cités Africaines.
File 1359, portfolio 270 Fund Office des Cités Africaines.
File 419, portfolio 70 Fund Office des Cités Africaines.
Color slide collection, Fund Office des Cités Africaines.

Secondary literature

Avermaete, Tom, et al., eds. *Wonen in Welvaart: Woningbouw en wooncultuur in Vlaanderen 1948–1973*. Antwerpen: deSingel, 2006.
Avermaete, Tom. "Framing the Afropolis: Michel Ecochard and the African City for the Greatest Number." *Oase* 82 (2010): 77–100.
Beeckmans, Luce, and Johan Lagae. "Kinshasa's Syndrome-planning in Historical Perspective: From Belgian Colonial Capital to Self-constructed Megalopolis." In *Urban Planning in Sub-Saharan Africa: Colonial and Post-Colonial Planning Cultures*, edited by Carlos Nunes Silva, 201–224. Abingdon: Routledge, 2015.
Boudon, Philippe. *Pessac de Le Corbusier: 1927–1967: Étude socio-architecturale*. Paris: Dunod, 1977.
Bruneau, Jean-Claude, and Marc Pain, eds. *Atlas de Lubumbashi*. Nanterre: Université de Paris X, Nanterre, 1990.
d'Auria, Viviana, and Hannah Leroux. "Modernisme(s) approprié(s)." *Clara* 4 (2017): 9–28.
De Meulder, Bruno. *De Kampen van Kongo: Arbeid, kapitaal en rasveredeling in de koloniale planning*. Amsterdam/Antwerpen: Meulenhoff/Kritak, 1996.
De Meulder, Bruno. *Kuvuanda Mbote: Een eeuw architectuur en stedenbouw in Kongo*. Antwerpen: Hautekiet/deSingel, 2000.
De Meulder, Bruno, and Marie-Françoise Plissart. "Kinshasa, the Hereafter of Modern Architecture." In *Back from Utopia: The Challenge of the Modern Movement*, edited by Hubert-Jan Henket and Hilde Heynen, 160–173. Rotterdam: 010 Publishers, 2002.
De Meulder, Bruno. "OCA (Office des Cités Africaines, 1952–1960) and the Urban Question in Central Africa." Accessed October 17, 2017. https://archnet.org/system/publications/contents/4922/original/DPC1635.pdf?1384787195.
Denis, Jacques. *Le phénomène urbain en Afrique Centrale*. Namur: FUNDP, n.d., 1958.
De Nys-Ketels, Simon. "Koloniaal beleid en stedelijke ruimte in een Congolese stad: De wijk Kenya in Lubumbashi, Congo." Master diss., Ghent University, 2011.
de Saint-Moulin, Léon. *Villes et organisation de l'espace en République Démocratique du Congo*. Paris: L'Harmattan, 2010.

Etambala, Zana. *De teloorgang van een modelkolonie: Belgisch Congo 1958–1960*. Leuven: Acco, 2008.
Fenaux, Céline. "L'Office des Cités Africaines in Lubumbashi. Ruashi: Architecturale analyse en studie van de toe-eigening van een Congolese wijk uit de jaren 1950." Master diss., Ghent University, 2010.
Fetter, Bruce. *The Creation of Elisabethville, 1910–1940*. Stanford: Hoover Institution Press, 1976.
Floré, Fredie, and Emiel De Kooning. "Post-war Model Homes: Introduction." *Journal of Architecture* 4 (2004): 411–412.
Grévisse, Ferdinand. *Le Centre Extra-Coutumier d'Elisabethville: Quelques aspects de la politique indigène du Haut-Katanga industriel*. Brussels: Institut Royal Colonial Belge, 1950.
Hins, R. "L'Urbanisme au Katanga." *Essor du Congo*, Special edition on the occasion of the international exposition of Elisabethville, 1931 [n.p.].
Hunt, Nancy Rose. "Domesticity and Colonialism in Belgian Africa: Usumbura's Foyer Social, 1946–1960." *Signs* 15 (1990): 447–474.
Huxtable, Ada Louise. "Le Corbusier's Housing Project: Flexible Enough to Endure." *The New York Times*, May 15, 1981 (reprinted as "Flexible enough to endure" in Huxtable, Ada Louise. *On Architecture: Collected Reflections on a Century of Change*, 160–165. New York: Walker & Company, 2008).
Lagae, Johan, Sofie Boonen, and Maarten Liefooghe. "Fissures dans le 'cordon sanitaire': Architecture hospitalière et ségrégation urbaine à Lubumbashi, 1920–1960." In *Lubumbashi: Cent d'ans d'histoire*, edited by Maurice Amuri Mpala-Lutebele, 247–261. Paris: L'Harmattan, 2013.
Lagae, Johan, and Sofie Boonen. "Décoloniser l'espace (péri)urbain en République Démocratique du Congo: Le cas de Lubumbashi." In *Périurbains: Territoires, réseaux et temporalités*, edited by Jean-Baptiste Minnaert, 141–151. Lyon: Ed. Lieux Dits, 2013.
Lagae, Johan, Sofie Boonen, and Sam Lanckriet. "Navigating 'Off Radar': The Heritage of Liminal Spaces in the City Center of Colonial/Postcolonial Lubumbashi, DR Congo." In *Things Don't Really Exist Until You Give Them A Name: Unpacking Urban Heritage*, edited by Rachel Lee, Diane Barber, Anne-Katrin Fenk, and Philipp Misselwitz, 86–93. Dar es Salaam: Mkuki na Nyota, 2017.
Lejeune de Schiervel, Xavier. *Les nouvelles cités congolaises: L'architecture et le logement*. Brussels: Académie Royale des Sciences coloniales, 1956.
Lierman, Sally. "Office des Cités Africaines in Kisangani: Een stedenbouwkundig onderzoek naar genese en toe-eigening van een woonwijk uit de jaren 1950 in Afrika." Master diss., Ghent University, 2011.
Ministère des Colonies, ed. *Plan décennal pour le Développement économique et social du Congo belge*. Brussels: Les Editions de Visscher, 1949.
Mulumba, Crispin. "Origines et évolution des institutions communales et urbaines au Congo." *Congo-Afrique* 29 (1968): 449–457.
Mumford, Eric. *The CIAM Discourse on Urbanism, 1928–1960*. Cambridge: MIT Press, 2000.
Mutamba Makombo Kitatshima, Jean-Marie. *Du Congo belge au Congo indépendant 1940–1960: Emergence des "évolués" et genèse du nationalisme*. Kinshasa: Publications de l'Institut de formation et d'études politiques, 1998.
Ndaywel è Nziem, Isidore. *Histoire générale du Congo de l'héritage ancien à la République Démocratique*. Paris: Duculot, 1998.

Nightingale, Carl. *Segregation: A Global History of Divided Cities*. Chicago: University of Chicago Press, 2012.
Pabois, Marc, ed. *Lubumbashi: Capitale minière du Katanga 1910–2010: L'Architecture*. Lubumbashi: Espace Culturel Francophone de Lubumbashi, 2008.
Pauwels, Dirk. "Souvenirs of Urbanism." In *Brakin: Brazzaville – Kinshasa: Visualizing the Visible*, edited by Wim Cuyvers, 245–263. Baden: Lars Müller Publishers, 2006.
Peigneux, Fernand. "De l'habitation." *Bulletin de l'Union des Femmes Coloniales* January 1954, 17.
Plumier, Georges J., ed. *Investir c'est prospérer: Les réalisations du Plan Décennal pour le Développement Economique et Social du Congo belge 1949–1959*. Brussels: Imifi, 1959.
Robert, Yves. "L'œuvre moderniste remarquable de l'Office des Cités Africaines au Congo." *Les nouvelles du Patrimoine* 128 (2010): 35–39.
Scaillon, Ernest. "La rénovation urbaine et l'unité de voisinage." *Rythme* 37 (1963): 10–12.
Toulier, Bernard. *Architecture et patrimoine du XXe siècle en France*. Paris: Editions du Patrimoine, 1999.
Van der Woud, Auke. *CIAM: Housing Town Planning*. Delft: Delft University Press, 1983.
Vantemsche, Guy. "Le Plan Décennal et la modernization du Congo belge (1949–1959)." In *La mémoire du Congo: Le temps colonial*, edited by Jean-Luc Vellut, 104–107. Gent/Tervuren: Snoeck/MRAC, 2005.

Martina Kopf
4 At Home with Nairobi's Working Poor: Reading Meja Mwangi's Urban Novels

Introduction

> The well-being of urban residents depends on access to a suitable place to live, in a healthy environment, and within reach of work opportunities and services. To ensure that adequate housing is available and that it can fulfil its potential roles in tackling poverty and increasing prosperity, *infrastructure, a flourishing urban economy, supportive social networks, and political voice are needed, as well as a house* (a dwelling and the land on which it sits).[1]

These statements, with which Carole Rakodi begins a comprehensive and revealing study on gendered inequalities in access to land and housing in cities of the Global South, essentially contain a utopia that is an unredeemed fiction for the vast majority of urban populations in the so-called developing world if measured against their real living and housing conditions. The core of this utopia is "adequate housing" and its "potential roles in tackling poverty and increasing prosperity." Apart from its central concern to make gender aspects of urban living clear, to create knowledge and awareness about inequality and to discuss effective means of overcoming these, Rakodi's report also offers an introduction to what housing means socially, economically, and symbolically: "Houses are not merely physical artefacts with practical functions and economic value. They also provide people with a sense of their own worth, enhance their sense of belonging, and empower them to act."[2]

It is interesting that in the list of factors that Rakodi defines as essential for the realization of this utopia, the material and actual living space, the "house", comes last. The "house" only makes sense in this utopia insofar as it stands and is perceived in a dynamic fabric of social, material, and political factors, as part of a network that points beyond the actual, individual living space and with which it is connected. It is also interesting that the study attaches a central role to the political voice in the implementation of the utopian potential of urban

---

[1] Carole Rakodi, "Addressing Gendered Inequalities in Housing," in *Gender, Asset Accumulation and Just Cities: Pathways to Transformation?*, ed. Caroline O. N. Moser (London: Routledge, 2015), 81, emphasis added.
[2] Rakodi, "Addressing Gendered Inequalities in Housing," 82.

Note: The work for this contribution was supported by the Austrian Science Fund (FWF) V 554 Richter Programme.

ə Open Access. © 2020 Martina Kopf, published by De Gruyter. This work is licensed under a Creative Commons Attribution-NonCommercial 4.0 International License.
https://doi.org/10.1515/9783110601183-004

living space. One factor which is curiously missing in this list, but which in a way builds a bridge between the material and social dimensions of housing and the political voice, is the production of knowledge on housing conditions and on ways to improve them. In other words, between the lived and experienced realities of urban living and the political voice, which ideally represents them adequately and speaks for their improvement, processes of knowledge formation and transfer inscribe themselves as part of which Rakodi's study itself can be seen.[3] Many normative assumptions exist about the living conditions of people of low income, who make up the vast majority in African larger cities. These assumptions are largely based on media representations of large "slum" areas in Asia, Africa and Latin America, and the myths they produce.[4] In popular European discourses on Africa, the "slum" has become the epitome of urban poverty. It stands for population explosion, urban mismanagement, poverty, crime, and insurmountable problems. Some of these normative assumptions are summarized and described in the report *The Seven Myths of "Slums."*[5] On the other hand, there are a number of efforts to break these myths, which are based on simplifying and stereotyping representations. In this article I take Rakodi's general observations on what housing means in processes of urban development as a starting point in reading two novels by the Kenyan writer Meja Mwangi, both published in the 1970s. Even though published four decades ago, these texts are still relevant in the way they tell stories of urban life from below.[6] Listening to

---

3 The study is based on a commissioned review, which the author, as she mentions in the endnote, prepared for the World Bank's follow-up to the 2012 World Development Report on *Gender, Equality and Development* published in 2014 as Carole Rakodi, "Expanding Women's Access to Land and Housing in Urban Areas," in *Women's Voice, Agency, and Participation Research Series* 8 (Washington, DC: World Bank Group, 2014). The annual World Development Reports inform and shape – or at least are meant to inform and shape – economic and social policies around the globe. We can describe this work as an utterance from the intersection of academic social research, political feminism, and the global governance of capitalist development. What comes across as a smooth overlapping of these three realms of knowing and speaking – in themselves further divided into a multitude of differing voices, subjectivities, and interests – circumscribes in fact a contested and loaded terrain of conflicting interests, players, and epistemologies.
4 Adam W. Parsons, *The Seven Myths of "Slums": Challenging Popular Prejudices about the World's Urban Poor* (Share the World's Resources (STWR), 2010).
5 Parsons, *The Seven Myths of "Slums."*
6 Both novels were recently re-edited in revised versions by the author. Meja Mwangi, *The Cockroach Dance* (HM Books Intl., 2013) and Meja Mwangi, *Down River Road* (HM Books Intl., 2014). This article does not provide the space to compare the original and the revised versions, although this would be an interesting study. In the revisions, Mwangi kind of "updated" the stories through inserting signifiers like mobile phones or substituting the venereal disease,

what these novels tell about houses in low-income neighborhoods in the Nairobi of the 1970s, and about the space people live in, I discuss ways in which housing in these novels emerges as a subject of narration. Furthermore, I am interested in how the novelistic representation connects to larger stories of urbanization and in what ways it contributes to understanding and reading processes of urbanization and urban development.[7] To that aim, Mwangi's novels will be brought into dialogue with studies and debates from the fields of development studies,[8] developmental journalism,[9] and urban anthropology.[10] In 2008, the Indian-Kenyan journalist and writer Rasna Warah published a collection of essays, most of them written by African writers, activists and intellectuals, entitled *Missionaries, Mercenaries and Misfits* to present an alternative view of the development industry in Africa. Warah herself introduces the compilation by describing her own discomfort as a member of the United Nations Human Settlements Program (UN-HABITAT), when she conducted interviews in Nairobi's largest slum settlement Kibera as part of a global slum analysis. In particular, she describes the situation with an interviewee, Mberita Katela, whose story was later published in a UN-HABITAT publication and taken up by the American author and urbanist Mike Davis for his book *Planet of Slums*.[11] The story, as Warah[12] explains, had thus been given credit to successfully represent the living conditions of urban poor. At

---

which befalls the customers of sex workers in *The Cockroach Dance*, through HIV. The fascinating thing about these revisions is that the basic plots, which remain the same, do not lose meaning in this transfer from the 1970s to the twenty-first century. Rather, they reveal that the social realities the novels portray do not make less sense today than they did 40 years ago.

7 This chapter was written in the course of a research project on concepts of development in postcolonial Kenyan writing, which I currently conduct at the University of Vienna, Department of African Studies. In this project, I investigate how Kenyan writers responded to political discourses on "development" and how they witnessed the international development industry in their writing on the one hand, while on the other hand I approach their works as a site of development theory, in the way it had been suggested by Adams and Mayes: "We can refer to concepts of 'development' for contemporary Africa drawn from the spheres of political economics and philosophy, as well as from literature itself." Anne V. Adams and Janis A. Mayes, "African Literature and Development: Mapping Intersections," in *Mapping Intersections: African Literature and Africa's Development*, ed. Anne V. Adams et al. (Trenton, NJ: Africa World Press, 1998), 4.

8 Rakodi, "Addressing Gendered Inequalities in Housing."

9 Rasna Warah, "Nairobi's Slums: Where Life for Women is Nasty, Brutish and Short," *Habitat Debate* 8/4 (2002): 16.

10 Nici Nelson, "Representations of Men and Women, City and Town in Kenyan Novels of the 1970s and 1980s," *African Languages and Cultures* 9/2 (1996).

11 Mike Davis, *Planet of Slums* (London: Verso, 2006).

12 Rasna Warah, "The Development Myth," in *Missionaries, Mercenaries and Misfits: An Anthology*, ed. Rasna Warah (Central Milton Keynes: Author House, 2008), 4.

the same time, this representation was from the outset marked by an ethical problem, which she describes as follows:

> I was sub-consciously doing what many people in the so-called development industry do: I was objectifying her, seeing her as part of a problem that needed to be solved so that she could be neatly compartmentalized into a 'target group' category. This allowed me to perceive her as being 'different' from me and bestowed on her an 'otherness' that clearly placed her as my inferior, worthy of my sympathy.

My argument here is that fiction and literary analysis are means of questioning and disrupting objectifying approaches towards people in low-income livelihoods. As I will show with regard to Mwangi's novels, they do so not only on the basis of sociological information they provide – since every piece of good fiction always works with and engages with the realm of facts – but also by the very means of literary writing, allowing the reader to witness processes of urbanization through (re)created voices and subjectivities commonly excluded from or objectified in knowledge production on urban development. In the words of Jini Kim Watson, "literary and cultural texts offer a unique window onto the rich worldviews of postcolonial subjects, too often constructed as mere objects of reform."[13]

Tracing Social and Economic Change Through City Novels: Meja Mwangi

In his book-length study on the emergence of the Nairobi city novel, Roger Kurtz understands and explains the city and the novel in postcolonial East Africa as products of the same processes of economic change.[14] His comprehensive discussion of Anglophone novels from the 1960s to the 1990s shows how challenges, problems, and perspectives of urbanization in post-independence Kenya have been continually reflected in the development of the urban novel as a genre. Reading the city through the novel and vice versa, he summarizes the most significant influences that characterize both as "the fundamental

---

[13] Jini Kim Watson, "'We Want You to Ask Us First': Development, International Aid and the Politics of Indebtedness," in *Negotiating Normativity: Postcolonial Appropriations, Contestations, and Transformations*, ed. Nikita Dhawan et al. (Switzerland: Springer International Publishing, 2016), 241.
[14] John Roger Kurtz, *Urban Obsessions, Urban Fears: The Postcolonial Kenyan Novel* (Trenton, NJ: Africa World Press, 1998).

experience of the colonial encounter, the political reality of the East-West superpower conflict and its aftermath, the economic constraints of international capital, and the underlying heritage of indigenous African traditions." These impacts "overlay, interweave and swirl together in fascinating and chaotic ways. City and novel are products of these realities and their interactions. City and novel – *the constructed environment and the creative environment* – at the same time influence and shape those interactions."[15]

One author who captured this conjunction of the constructed environment and the creative environment in his writing like few others before was Meja Mwangi with his early Nairobi trilogy *Kill Me Quick*,[16] *Going Down River Road*,[17] and *The Cockroach Dance*.[18] Mwangi strongly contributed to the popularization of Anglophone writing in East Africa in the 1970s and to moving it out of academic circles. His name is tightly connected with the postcolonial urban novel – "postcolonial" here understood not as a temporal, but as an analytical category for textual and narrative strategies moving beyond the legacies of cultural colonization[19] – and a new type of character described as the "Mwangian man", usually a young, urban, well-educated man who subsists on poorly paid jobs or tries to get his share of the unequally distributed wealth through criminal and criminalized action.[20] This character is the main focalizer in Mwangi's Nairobi trilogy, portraying lives in unstable and informal working and housing conditions at the margins of global and national capitalist market economies. For reasons of space, we put our focus on the latter two novels of the trilogy. What makes them particularly interesting here is that they both use houses as central signifiers and paradigms for different faces of urban development: the "Development House" in *Going Down River Road* and the "Dacca House" in *The Cockroach Dance*. The "Development House" in *Going Down River Road* is a twenty-five-story commercial building whose construction forms the plot of the novel. As a metaphor, it stands for the unreconciled division between labor and capitalist growth in

---

15 Kurtz, *Urban Obsessions*, 7–8, emphasis added.
16 Meja Mwangi, *Kill Me Quick* (London: Heinemann Educational, 1973).
17 Meja Mwangi, *Going Down River Road* (London; Nairobi; Ibadan; Lusaka: Heinemann, 1976).
18 Meja Mwangi, *The Cockroach Dance* (Nairobi: Longman, 1979). The novel was first published in 1979 by Longman, Nairobi. All quotations in this book chapter refer to the re-edition in the Longman African classics series, published in 1989.
19 Stuart Hall, "When Was 'The Post-Colonial'? Thinking at the Limit," in *The Postcolonial Question: Common Skies, Divided Horizons*, ed. Iain Chambers et al. (London: Routledge, 1996), 242–260.
20 Kurtz, *Urban Obsessions*. Tom Odhiambo, "Kenyan Popular Fiction in English and the Melodramas of the Underdog," *Research in African Literatures* 39/4 (2008).

Kenya after independence. Looking at capitalist development from the perspective of the construction workers, Mwangi creates "development" as a narrative space where class distinctions and unequal distribution of wealth and power become manifest. The construction site emerges as a microcosm which reflects hierarchies of class, "race", and gender in post-independence Nairobi.[21]

The "Dacca House" of *The Cockroach Dance*, in contrast, is a shabby and heavily overpriced residential house. The building is home to a crowd of people representing diverse faces and stories of urban survival in a rundown neighborhood in Nairobi. Through the novel, the story evokes the development of a private housing market for Africans moving to Nairobi in the 1960s and 1970s. Housing and living conditions at the lower ranks of the urban society had already been a major concern in *Going Down River Road*. In *The Cockroach Dance*, Mwangi moves this theme to the center of the novel, making also visible how closely interrelated these two stories – the story of post-independence capitalist development and the story of urban housing – have been.

Households Found Down River Road

Addressing gendered inequalities in access to land and housing in the Global South, Rakodi[22] takes issue with the category of the "household". Conventional analyses of the roles housing plays in livelihood strategies – thus her critique – focus on households, lacking interest in and understanding of the complex, diverse, and changing social relationships which become objectified and rendered invisible in the seemingly neutral concept of the "household". In fact, the author foregrounds her argument for a gender-sensitive approach in planning and evaluating measures of urban housing with an epistemological problem, captured in the sober statement: "Problems arise when the concept of a 'household' is taken to be unproblematic." She responds to that problem arguing that "[p]atterns of social relations within and beyond the households in which people live are key to both understanding gender inequalities in access to and control over real property and explaining the outcomes of urban policies and reforms."[23] Opening up the concept of the "household", her work challenges the assumption of universally practicable measures and abstract

---

21 Martina Kopf, "Encountering Development in East African Fiction," *The Journal of Commonwealth Literature* 54, no. 3 (2019).
22 Rakodi, "Addressing Gendered Inequalities in Housing," 82.
23 Rakodi, "Addressing Gendered Inequalities in Housing," 82.

solutions, creating instead a highly diversified narrative of access to and control over land and houses, varying enormously between households, cities, and countries.

If we want to take a non-normative look at patterns of social relations within and beyond households, it is instructive to turn to Meja Mwangi's novels. *Going Down River Road* covers a period of about two to three years during which Ben, the central character, changes place several times. There are a couple of diverse household constellations portrayed in the novel, and none of them fits into normative family schemes.

The first picture of Nairobi which the novel shows is a single room, modestly furnished with a bed, a baby's crib, a bedside table, a paraffin stove, and a transistor radio, in a residential house with toilets and a shower room shared by all tenants. It is, as we learn later, Wini's flat, located in Ngara, a lower middle-income neighborhood, two miles from the city center. Wini is a young woman who the protagonist Ben meets in a bar on the day of his release from a white-collar job. At the time, she lives in the flat with her four-year-old son, Baby, whom she gave birth to as a teenage mother at the age of 14. After Wini's friend, with whom she shared the room, got married, she finances the rent – as she openly admits to Ben – through relationships with men she meets in bars. These facts make her a whore in Ben's perception – through which the story is largely focalized. However, this does not prevent him from moving in with her and her son Baby a little later. Ben's moving occurs in parallel to his social decline from a former soldier and later employee of an insurance company, which he has to leave due to his involvement in an armed robbery, to a cheap contract worker on a construction site. The first household of which the novel draws a picture thus is managed and financed by an African woman in her early twenties, a mother who works as a secretary for a private company and attends further training in the evening to improve her position.

Ben contributes – as the novel suggests – nothing or in any case not enough to the household income. In fact, it is Wini who gives him accommodation and lodging and who supports him while he is in vain looking for a job.[24] The constellation lasts for about two years, during which Wini finances the rent not only with her income from the company, but also through occasional sex with the landlord and a relationship with her white superior. Ben only finds out about her arrangement with the landlord after Wini, pregnant by her superior, leaves him and her first son to marry the father of her second child. Only then, when he has to interact with the landlord on his own and tries to obtain

---

[24] Mwangi, *Going Down River Road*, 3.

postponement of rent, does he gain clarity about it and the sensitive reader becomes aware of Wini's previous distress. I say "the sensitive reader" because the novel offers little reason to empathize with the female protagonist. Rather, filtered through Ben's perception and his masculinist attitude, she embodies a morally at least ambiguous, if not ruthlessly upward, mobility.

Ocholla, Ben's friend and buddy at the construction site, lives in a shack. This becomes the subject of a short dialogue for the first time in the novel, when Ben, after one of the many evening boozes with Ocholla, thinks it is time to go home, and the latter replies that he no longer has a home because his shack was burned down by the City Council. Ocholla is a Luo worker, whose two wives with their children continue to live in the village. The two households – Ocholla's single shack and the polygamous household of his wives – remain connected through Ocholla's increasingly rare visits and through his wives' letters and their repeated demands to receive a share of his wage. After Wini's disappearance – explained only later through a letter left at the office for Ben to find, in which she asked him to bring her son to an orphanage and enclosed a check to provide for the costs – Ben and Baby continue to live in the one-room-flat until they are being evicted, ostensibly for renting without contract but more likely for the landlord to upgrade the room for higher rent. With Wini's check flushed down the toilet in an outburst of anger, Ben and Baby remain without shelter. After trying in vain to leave the crying child with an elderly woman who works as a vegetable hawker and lives next door, Ben takes the boy with him. With their nightly walk along the Nairobi River to the shanty town – as it is referred to in the novel – where Ocholla lives, and the lights of the distant downtown in their backs, the novel creates a powerful image of a silent exodus, signifying a further social decline.

After the loss of Wini's room, Ocholla's shack becomes the new home for the protagonist. The two men and the boy share the narrow, single space of the shack built on bare earth, described as follows: "The small hut is bare of furniture. Ocholla's few bits of clothing hang from nails on the walls. At one end near the smouldering fire is the crockery, a few tin mugs and utensils and a collection of bottles of various shapes and sizes. On the other side are the rags spread out to make a bed."[25]

Interestingly, in Mwangi's narration this male-only household becomes more of a home to the protagonist than any other household constellation in the novel, finding expression in shared warm meals of *Sukuma Wiki*[26] in the

---

25 Mwangi, *Going Down River Road*, 162.
26 Swahili expression for a leafy green vegetable and Kenyan staple diet, literally translated as "pushing the week".

evening, the child ultimately stopping to urinate on the sleeping mat at night, and the two men suspending their disastrous drinking tours – getting drunk on cheap, high-percentage alcohol outside the shack – and being with the boy instead, sleeping next to them.

The household constellation is short-lived. Its first, abrupt, end comes one morning when the health police knock on the door, ask the residents to immediately clear the shack and burn down the entire shanty town, allegedly for being built on land owned by the City Council. The evening of the same day, Ocholla and Ben rebuild a less solid version of the shack out of the remains. The second, permanent, end arrives when shortly after Ocholla's wives stand in front of the door, their small belongings and their children with them. They had been forced to leave the village after a drought and a cattle disease had taken all their livestock and supplies. The crisis their arrival means to the male-only household is vividly brought across in the following lines:

> Ben eats slowly, thoughtfully. He is not going to let anyone's family ruin his dinner. He tries not to look directly at the famished eyes all on his family meal. Then he starts to get embarrassed by all those little eyes glued to his plate. Finally he becomes infuriated, offensive. He dislikes them, almost hates them. They have no right to lock in on his hut like this, violate the peace and quiet. And did they have to come so many, all of them. Did they have to come at all? Bitches! Ocholla struggles on, determined not to let them run him down. He is clearly not allowing them to drag him into the urine-sodden family swamp. 'Don't tread on my bed,' Baby orders an emaciated child lost in the background gloom. The little girl has no idea that the rags she is standing on are Baby's territorial grounds and must not be trespassed upon.[27]

For a brief period, the shack of the size which was originally meant to shelter one man takes in the latter's workmate, a motherless child, one elder, and one younger woman with an unidentified number of children, among them three babies. The situation erupts into a conflict between the two very different and competing household constellations that cluster in the narrow square. For a period of three months they find an arrangement to coexist on the grounds that each party expects the other to leave. Both Ben and the two women put pressure on Ocholla, who is torn between the demands of his friend and those of his wives, but finally chooses his wives and children. At the end of the novel it is clear to Ben that he has to find a new place to live for himself and Wini's son, whom he now finances to attend school. That his living situation will improve socially in comparison to that of Ocholla and his family can be assumed from the different incomes that the two friends disclose to each other at the end:

---

[27] Mwangi, *Going Down River Road*, 185.

Ben, promoted to foreman, receives a wage increase of 50 Kenyan shillings, while that of Ocholla is only ten shillings, which, as he bitterly comments, makes about a tenth of what would make a meaningful family income.

What can we read from the novelistic representation of these constellations? On the level of content, the novel makes a statement on African lower income livelihoods in post-independent Nairobi which contains in a nutshell the following social diagnosis: first, none of the protagonists' formal wage work creates the income that would afford him or her decent housing. Secondly, housing means for the protagonists a source of constant stress and strain. On the one hand, this concerns the quality of living space – represented by smells, the lack and malfunctioning of sanitary services and narrowness – and on the other hand this concerns the precariousness and instability of housing, as a consequence of insecure tenancies, the illegalization of housing and the resulting threat of eviction. The third observation which can be drawn from the novel is that a "household" is not a stable but a fluid, dynamic category. Fourth, if we think of the peaceful image the novel draws of Ben's living in the shack with Ocholla and Baby, what makes a house a "home" is not only determined by material factors but by the quality of the social relationships between those who inhabit it.

Housing Madness: *The Cockroach Dance*

In *The Cockroach Dance* Mwangi moves the issue of housing to the center of the narrative. In fact, the novel has two central protagonists: Dusman Gonzaga, another version of the angry young, educated African man who struggles for a living in the economy of urban capitalist development, and "Dacca House", the block he lives in. Rather than the story of individuals, *The Cockroach Dance* sets out to narrate the story of an urban habitat, which right from the beginning of the novel is given a personality of its own. Even before the reader meets any of the novel's characters, she is introduced to the violence of the material structure which shapes and dominates their lives. The novel starts with a detailed and sensual account of what it feels, smells, and sounds like to wake up on an ordinary morning in an overcrowded one-story building, with one toilet and one shower shared among an estimated crowd of 200 tenants and a motor garage on the ground floor.

> There is no dawn in Dacca House. The new day arrives abruptly, unheralded, with a violence like that of a small earthquake, a sudden explosion that lasts all day. The tenants are all inveterate early risers. Most of them rise, almost before they have slept, in a vain attempt to beat the rush for the one cold shower in the block... The others, the numerous faceless

ones, turn their radios on full blast and go resolutely back to sleep until the queue outside the shower room has dwindled sufficiently to allow for a quick shower. Thus long before the rest of Grogan Road starts stirring from sleep, Dacca House is fully engaged in the helpless process of existing – frying pans locked horns with the perpetual odour issuing with an almost audible hiss from the overflowing garbage cans and the toilet out in the yard.[28]

The "Dacca House" of the novel offers a window into the history of urban settlement and of social and ethnic stratification at the shore of the Nairobi river. Originally, the fictional house was built by Kachra Samat, an Indian immigrant who came as a railway worker to Kenya during the reign of the British Empire. With other compatriots, he settled down on land granted to them by the colonial government and built the house as a one-floor building, with a drapery store selling Indian textiles on the ground floor and 15 rooms for his extensive family on the upper floor. Mwangi describes the building in great detail, its L-shape giving every room a door and a window opening into the yard, and connecting doors between all the rooms.[29] With increasing wealth and the removal of *de jure* racial segregation in independent Kenya, the Indian families moved to the formerly whites-only suburbs, leaving Grogan Road to a steadily growing African population. The neighborhood had in the meantime lost attraction to the wealthy, with the moving in of motor garages and the increasing pollution of the river through lack of canalization. Samat eventually sells the house to Tumbo Kubwa, meaning "big belly" in Swahili,[30] an African businessman who sees his chance in the residential needs of the quickly growing African population. The novel makes of this change of ownership an ardent critique of a rising African capitalist upper class in independent Kenya taking advantage of their entry into the urban housing market:

> Tumbo Kubwa was one of the first few Africans ever to open their eyes after the long slumber induced on the natives by colonialism. As soon as he realised that the winds of change and fortune were blowing hard, he unfurled his creased sails and struck out into the future of property investment. Roving on Grogan Road, his eyes landed on Kachra Samat's building. At once he saw the potential that lay behind the humble, cracked facade of Dacca House. Buried inside the mottled concrete walls were hundreds of thousands of easy shillings. All he had to do was get together his resources and borrow a little from the newly-formed, non-discriminatory credit companies.[31]

---

28 Mwangi, *The Cockroach Dance*, s.n.
29 Mwangi, *The Cockroach Dance*, 79.
30 As in many of his novels, Meja Mwangi names his novel characters ironically with Swahili expressions as a means of characterization.
31 Mwangi, *The Cockroach Dance*, 83.

Immediately after the bargain the new landlord expels the Indian tenants from the house and gets a handful of contract workers to remake the building. Once they finished their job, the original 15 rooms had been turned into 30 single rooms, with one shared toilet and shower in the courtyard, and the previous bathroom turned into a flat as well. Mwangi paints a vivid picture of the day a mass of new tenants move in, scrambling for the rooms.[32] Even before the renovations had been finished, the whole house was rented out, with some flats promised to more than one tenant. Without having done any advertisement, the new landlord leaves the place at the end of the day, making ten times the amount out of it the former proprietor had collected each month.

Besides evoking the history of African urban settlement in Nairobi, the "Dacca House" also represents the emergence of a particular modern African urban identity. This is achieved most vividly in a scene at a police station when Dusman is asked to identify himself during an interrogation:

'Home address?'
'Dacca House,' Dusman said.
They all looked up at him the inspector with a curious frown while the constable scowled angrily.
'Dacca what?' he yelled.
'House,' Dusman said calmly. . . .
'Home address.' The constable banged the desk with his fist so hard the station vibrated and the inspector looked down with disapproval.
The detective inspector had great self control.
. . .
'What he wants,' he said to Dusman, 'is your home address in the country.'
'I live in Dacca House,' Dusman said to him. 'I have no other home.'
. . .
'Where do your parents live?'
'They are dead.'
'Where did they live?'
'What does it matter where they lived,' Dusman said. 'My home is in Dacca House, Grogan Road. Haven't you guys ever heard of an urban African? I am one!'
. . .
The inspector looked him up and down and nodded to himself.
'What tribe are you?' he asked finally.
'It makes no difference,' Dusman said.
'Tribal origin?'
'What difference does it make?' Dusman asked. 'I have to be plotted out on a map like a bloody hill or a river?...'[33]

---

32 Mwangi, *The Cockroach Dance*, 85.
33 Mwangi, *The Cockroach Dance*, 335–336.

The dialogue is interesting on more than one level. We can read it as a sign of civil resistance against a power regime that survived from colonial rule to the postcolonial state. Just as *Going Down River Road* bears witness to colonial patterns of labor migration being continued as part of postcolonial capitalist development, this scene in *The Cockroach Dance* testifies to the continued restriction of urban space for Africans in the Nairobi of independence. In *Going Down River Road*, the living conditions of the workers – represented by Ocholla – are characterized by the illegalization and precarization of housing. Ocholla retains the status of a migrant in his own country, whose polygamous family continues to live in the country and is largely responsible for its own subsistence. Neither he nor the extended household of which he remains a part are meant to stay in the city beyond the limited period of his work contracts. In *The Cockroach Dance* Dusman reclaims that urban space as his home, thereby resisting the construction of African identity as primordially rooted in rural society and tribal culture.

Like in *Going Down River Road*, Mwangi focalizes the plot almost entirely through the eyes of the main character, Dusman Gonzaga. As readers, hence, we experience this story of urban housing through the eyes and senses of those who people the narrative. More than in the previous novel, in *The Cockroach Dance* Mwangi leaves the realistic narrative mode and works with hyperbole and satire. Dusman, the protagonist, works at the City Council and reads parking meters. Everything drives him mad: his job; the cockroaches that at night invade the shabby room he shares with Toto, a bank employee, and swarm in a choreography he tries to make sense of; the behavior of the other tenants; their efforts to organize a private life in the absurdly narrow and overcrowded space; their vain attempts of having a sexual life in some sort of intimacy. His madness culminates in his daily encounter with a tenant who everyone just calls "the Bathroom Man". The young man shares with his wife and a mentally disabled child the room that used to be the bathroom in the former house and was converted into a single flat by the landlord. The windowless room offers just enough space for the one bed the whole family sleeps in – brought into the room with utter effort – and is next to the block's only toilet. The violence inherent in the housing situation is reflected in the unsettling effect it produces on Dusman's mind. What his social environment increasingly declares him mad for, however, are not so much his violent outbursts of anger but the questions he asks. With these questions, which revolve around the existence of the tenants, Mwangi opens up a reflective space within the narration. This level of reflection is further enhanced by dialogues with a white psychiatrist, Dr. Bates, whom the protagonist pays regular visits at the instigation of his superior. Throughout the narration Dusman confronts the doctor with an epistemological problem, which is also a deeply humanist problem, caused by his living next door to the Bathroom Man and his family. Dusman repeatedly addresses the problem these inhuman living conditions pose to him as a daily witness:

> 'You ... you don't understand,' he [Dusman, MK] said gravely, 'You just don't understand.' Dusman was almost certain now. He would never get one honest answer to his numerous questions. Questions that had plagued him ever since he moved into Dacca House and met the Bathroom Man. Questions like – before he became the Bathroom Man, what was he? Who was he? And what would he become if he tired of, and quit being the Bathroom Man? Would he ever quit it? What was he really like behind that subdued black face of his? What did he say to his wife when they retreated into the bathroom when he loved her? [...] Did he kiss her, [...] promise to some day take her out of the lonely bathroom into the bigger rooms with the rest of the human race? What did he really say to her? Did he talk to her at all? Did he ever... play with his soft-brained off-spring? Did it ever ask, or even wonder why they lived alone in a bathroom by the smelly toilet?[34]

These questions could well be at the beginning of an anthropological or journalistic study on the living conditions of working poor in Nairobi. In the novel, however, they have a different function. First and foremost, they lead us away from reading the text exclusively as a source of information, as a simple description of a social reality. Instead, they open additional levels of meaning, inviting to be read in more than one way. Through these questions, the narrative makes those of whom it speaks subjects not only of their actions, but also of their knowledge of themselves and the conditions of their existence.

Let us turn again to the ethical problem Rasna Warah described when researching her study of housing conditions in Kibera. In a retrospective reflection she problematized the research situation which foregrounded her study:

> As I sat on one of two small stools in Mberita's tiny wattle, daub and tin shack – which was only marginally bigger than my bathroom at home – I found myself asking her the most intimate details about her life, questions that I myself would not have entertained: what she ate for breakfast, how many people she shared her shack with and, most important of all, where she defecated. Through this exercise, I found out that she shared one stinking pit latrine with some 100 of her neighbours and that the latrine was located less than 10 metres from her shack, which she shared with her daughter and two grandchildren.[35]

The article based on that interview had been published under the title "Nairobi's Slums: Where Life for Women is Nasty, Brutish, and Short."[36] With regard to the information it gives, this article is comparable to Mwangi's novels. It describes in

---

34 Mwangi, *The Cockroach Dance*, 137–138.
35 Warah, "The Development Myth," 3.
36 Warah, "Nairobi's Slums."

detail and seemingly comprehensible to the reader a typical daily routine in the life of a resident of Kibera, who maintains herself and her children through the trade of *sukuma wiki* and cigarettes. In her later critique of the generation of knowledge in the development industry she herself was part of when writing the article, Warah was going to trial with her work stricter than she had to. The article is brief, sober, and it speaks of the effort to present the living and working situation of a woman who lives and survives under extreme conditions based on the material facts in as much detail as possible. Other than Warah's self-criticism would suggest, the text shows nothing of a patronizing attitude and, on the contrary, portrays without judging. However, while her narrative represents a massive social, political, and human problem, the narration itself is apparently unproblematic. It leaves the reader with the impression that she had been given an adequate representation. What has disappeared from it is Mberita Katela as an acting, speaking, and thinking subject, as well as any awareness of the fact that her existence raises questions that lead and must lead to the limits of understanding. In other words, the text in UN-HABITAT, which had been received as a successful representation of urban poverty, did not offer the epistemological tools neither for the writer nor for the reader to meaningfully contain the ethical and epistemological problem which form necessarily part of the representation.

The novelistic dialogues between Dusman and Dr. Baker in *The Cockroach Dance* – all their seeming irony and absurdity notwithstanding – fulfil this function. In his sessions with Dr. Baker, Dusman repeatedly tries to explain what living in Dacca House means for the tenants. He tries to make meaning out of their experience and he tries to convey this meaning to the other – in this case represented by the white doctor – which is basically what fiction and narrative do: giving meaning to the realities people live with. From Dusman's perspective this conversation is from the outset limited by an imbalance: the doctor *thinks* he can understand Dusman's story from what he knows, while Dusman *knows* of the limits of the doctor's knowledge. The conversation forms a metatext to the actual plot by means of which the narration points to the incommensurability of the social reality it portrays. What returns in these dialogues is the communicative situation described by Warah above, which gives rise to the bulk of representations of marginalized people in canonical development literature.

All Households are Gendered

We started our reflection on how Mwangi's novels can contribute to understanding the housing conditions of Nairobi's working poor and to asking the right questions with Rakodi's report on gendered inequalities in urban housing. The question which inevitably arises from this starting point is how do the novels deal with gendered inequalities? One dimension that we have only touched on so far, but that is fundamental to any understanding of how social relations interfere with and shape urban housing, is the simple fact that – as Rakodi[37] states – all households are gendered. We can make the same observation for the novel: all novels are gendered. This is also and especially true of Mwangi's urban novels. The identities of his male protagonists – like Ben and Ocholla in *Going Down River Road* as well as Dusman and his roommate Toto in *The Cockroach Dance* – are strongly defined through their notions of masculinity and their macho attitude towards women.

In an interesting study Nici Nelson[38] – urban anthropologist and former consultant of development and aid agencies in East Africa with a focus on gender and development, urban livelihoods in the informal sector, marriage and households – compared Nairobi city novels of the 1970s, including Mwangi's texts, with the self-representations of low-income women in Mathare Valley. In her study, Nelson describes Mathare Valley as an "'informal sector' suburb", the women she interviewed made their living as "hawkers, street cleaners, barmaids, house servants, sex workers or beer brewers."[39]

In 1970s Kenya the discourse on women in the city was, as Nelson states, mainly defined by three stereotypes, showing the urban woman either as "wicked", as "competent" or as "betrayed".[40] She particularly takes issue with the stereotype of the "wicked woman", which represented urban women as corrupt, promiscuous, and self-centered. As Nelson notes, this was a widespread discourse at the time: "This [the 'wicked urban woman' representation, MK] was a very common representation of urban women in Kenya in this period. The letters to the editor of newspapers, the pronouncements of politicians and the discourses of ordinary so-called respectable people all created and recreated this stereotype."[41]

Nelson notes that popular discourse among the Mathare dwellers was similar to the discourse in media and fiction with regard to its dominating themes, namely gender relations and their transformation through urbanization and rural exodus. They differed, however, in their assessments of urban women. Her interviewees sharply rejected the "wicked urban woman" stereotype,

---
37 Rakodi, "Addressing Gendered Inequalities in Housing," 81.
38 Nelson, "Representations of Men and Women," 145–168.
39 Nelson, "Representations of Men and Women," 162.
40 Nelson, "Representations of Men and Women," 147–151.
41 Nelson, "Representations of Men and Women," 162.

which became most evident in differing assessments of commercialized sex: "They certainly defined urban women as hard-working, reliable, independent and strong. Sex work was cleared of all immoral connotations. It was referred to as 'selling from one's kiosk', a reference to owning a small shop. To put it another way, they were defining sex work as the commercialization of one of the reproductive roles of wives."[42]

Nelson explains the normative power of the "wicked urban woman" stereotype with the rapid social and economic changes that Kenya underwent during this period and with the fact that women in the cities increasingly became rivals to men in terms of jobs and income. According to her interpretation, Mwangi's novels nourished this stereotype in being heavily biased in their portrayal of women.

In fact, gender discourse in Mwangi's novels is more complex than Nelson's interpretation would suggest, and – what makes it particularly interesting with regard to the subject of urban housing – this discourse altered from the earlier novel *Going Down River Road* to its sequel *The Cockroach Dance*. If we compare the two texts with regard to their central female characters, we will notice that in *Going Down River Road* they have a voice and they are agents of change. This is especially true of Wini and Ocholla's wives. Wini is a strong and contradictory character who speaks in her own voice. Ocholla's wives, too, unfold a strong presence. They support each other, oppose the will of their husband, move to Nairobi on their own initiative, claim their space in the shack that Ocholla and Ben built for themselves and immediately take action to create their own income. Even though their representation is filtered through Ben and Ocholla's masculinist gaze, these literary portrayals reveal the initiative and agency of African women of lower income with which they countered the structural restrictions on their urban existence imposed by colonial and sexist legislation in Nairobi. The novel, biased as it may be, nevertheless includes a narrative of the particular struggle that women had to fight in order to stand their ground in poor urban livelihoods, which they did sometimes alongside with African men, sometimes in dependence and conflict with them, sometimes in open resistance.[43] In *The Cockroach Dance*, however, this narrative has almost disappeared, erased from the fictional plot. When it comes to the representation of female agency *The Cockroach Dance* falls behind Mwangi's earlier novel *Going Down River Road*.

---

42 Nelson, "Representations of Men and Women," 163.

43 These particular struggles of women have been increasingly acknowledged and brought to the fore through feminist research since the 1980s (see for instance White's book-length study on prostitution in colonial Nairobi). Luise White, *The Comforts of Home: Prostitution in Colonial Nairobi* (Chicago & London: The University of Chicago Press, 1990).

4 At Home with Nairobi's Working Poor: Reading Meja Mwangi's Urban Novels — 115

This is all the more remarkable since the later novel, when read against the wider history of urban settlement by the marginalized African population in post-independent Nairobi, captures moments of transition from individual suffering and discontent to collective struggle and resistance: The cure Dusman eventually finds for his madness is that he tries to initiate a rent boycott, and the novel has one of its major turning points when the Bathroom Man, the embodiment of silent endurance, decides to join the petition and puts his name under it. This act of self-representation is accompanied by the following dialogue:

> 'Where did you learn to write like that?' Dusman marvelled.
> 'I was an apprentice at a village polytechnic,' he said slightly uncomfortably.
> I will be damned, Dusman thought. Who could ever have guessed.
> 'They threw me out before the end of the course,' the Bathroom Man said.
> 'Why?'
> 'I made a girl pregnant.'
> Dusman looked up smiling, surprised.
> 'My wife,' the Bathroom Man said quickly.
> Having said more than he had ever said to a neighbour before in his life, the Bathroom Man was confused and a little embarrassed. But he was not afraid any more. He would never be afraid again. He returned Dusman's pen and without another word went back to his room.[44]

With the development of the Bathroom Man, the novel describes the coming into being of a political voice, which, as we remember, is one of the factors which Rakodi defines as essential for housing to fulfill its potential roles in tackling poverty and increasing prosperity. The novel accords this development, however, solely to the male subject; the agent of change is clearly and solely male. The female subject in the novel, the Bathroom Man's wife – although she plays a significant role throughout the narration – remains silent, without a voice of her own. Her story remains represented in her husband's narration, and at no point is she given a voice and a subjectivity for self-representation. This becomes most evident in the last scene, showing Dusman during an invitation for dinner with the couple, who finally succeeded in leaving the turned-into-rental-property, windowless bathroom behind and moving to a larger room in the same block:

> Too excited to eat herself, the woman served the men then shyly turned her attention to other things while they ate. She did not speak unless spoken to. She was a very pretty woman, more beautiful than she had appeared from outside the bathroom house. When Dusman finally belched and thanked her for the tastiest meal he had had for a long while, the woman's face lit up like a lamp and he was very happy both for her and her

---

44 Mwangi, *The Cockroach Dance*, 381.

husband. She was a full woman now, accomplished by the fact that she now had a house to live in, to clean and spend the day in, and to invite friends to. They were a genuinely happy couple.[45]

This social utopia – and it must be understood as a utopia, since even though the couple succeeded in moving to a better room, the general living conditions in the block give hardly reason to believe that it would make anyone happy to spend the day in – thus clearly marks a regression with regard to women's voices and subjectivities in the larger story of urban housing. To illustrate this, let us once again turn to the earlier novel, *Going Down River Road*, where Wini, right from the first chapter, is given a voice to speak and to represent her story, fragmented though, in dialogue with Ben:

> 'Where do you live?' Ben asked.
> 'Ngara. You?'
> 'In town.'
> 'Where in town?'
> 'River Road.' . . .
> 'Good house.'
> 'Not too bad,' he said, having in mind the roach epidemic and the blocked toilet.
> 'I would love to live in town,' she dropped.
> . . .
> 'Do you live alone?' he asked. She nodded.
> 'I used to live with a friend and split the rent. She got married.'
> 'And how do you pay the rent now?'
> 'From men. Men like you.'
> 'Do they pay a lot?'
> She smiled slyly.
> 'It depends.'
> 'On what?'
> 'On whether I like them or not.'[46]

This dialogue in a nightclub is followed by a night spent together in Ben's flat, after which Wini reveals to him that she is a mother. Again, the novelistic account allows her to give a version which subverts the stereotype of the "wicked urban woman", which Nelson identified in her study:

> 'You have a child?' he asked soberly.
> 'Four years old.'
> 'But you are hardly. . . it is unbelievable.'
> 'I was fourteen, still in school,' she said and shrugged. 'I was so scared having a baby.'
> . . .

---

45 Mwangi, *The Cockroach Dance*, 383.
46 Mwangi, *Going Down River Road*, 15.

'My boyfriend was not even interested,' she added, 'men are such brutes. He just ran off and never came back to see the fruit of his beautiful labour. He was so scared too. It is surprising how men are afraid of nothing until a baby threatens. You should have seen his face when I told him.'[47]

As it becomes evident in these brief passages, the devaluing portrayal of women pointed out by Nelson is counter-balanced by the self-representation of female characters. This self-representation, however, is getting weaker in the later novel. If we juxtapose the two main female characters – Wini in *Going Down River Road* and the Bathroom Man's wife in *The Cockroach Dance* – we notice how one speaks while the other remains silent and shy. Both were teenage mothers and each leads a life of utter harshness in the respective novel. The difference lies in the concept of a household which is conveyed through them. Wini embodies a self-determined and self-financed access to housing. The other, tellingly nameless woman is represented as a "housewife". The change in the novels' gender discourse thus bears witness to the adoption of a Western role model by an emerging African urban middle class, the married "housewife" who unites patriarchal values from her culture of origin and from Western modernity. While *Going Down River Road* is still relatively revealing about the struggles women from lower income groups have led in Nairobi's poor livelihoods, these struggles – and with them, female agency – are pushed to the margin in *The Cockroach Dance*. We find an echo of this struggle in the nameless sex workers, the "amazons" – as they are referred to in the novel – with whom Dusman and his roommate Toto literally lead physical fights. With the Bathroom Man's wife, however, a type of womanhood – the urban middle-class "housewife" – moves to the center of the narration that did not exist in the previous novel. In *The Cockroach Dance* we find a consolidation of gender roles linked to the desired consolidation of housing.

Conclusion

With this discussion of Meja Mwangi's Nairobi novels we intended to show the potentials of fiction to testify to the living and working conditions that characterize the daily struggle for the life and survival of the vast majority of men and women in African metropolises. Our focus was on the two novels *Going Down River Road* and *The Cockroach Dance* as two examples from African fiction, which tell the story of urban livelihoods from below. We analyzed the two

---

47 Mwangi, *Going Down River Road*, 24.

novels under three aspects: first, at the level of sociological information they provide, we described the household constellations reflected in *Going Down River Road*. Second, in the section "Housing Madness" our interest was in the particular modes of literary representation, and third, we took issue with the novels' discourse on gender. On the level of content, the novels open up the social dynamics of living space shared among the sexes and generations. Read as a source of knowledge the novels go beyond being mere reflections or documentations of social facts, however. As we showed with regard to their narrative strategies, they constitute creative responses to the social imbalances they witness. In Mwangi's novels, we encounter socially and economically marginalized people neither as a target group nor as objects of reform. We do not encounter them as part of a problem, nor does the narrative take a charitable or patronizing attitude towards them. Third, by means of feminist analysis, we have pointed out that although the novels break down normative approaches to low-income livelihoods on the one hand, they transport gender ideologies on the other hand through which they themselves generate gender stereotypes that ultimately determine unequal access to housing. In academic research, we can look at these stories in terms of "what" they tell about the history of urbanization. We can also look at them, however – as Nancy Rose Hunt suggests in her methodological approach to fiction as a source of knowledge in historical and social sciences – in terms of the questions they pose.[48]

If we look at African writing with an interest in urban development in mind, we will find an abundance of stories that runs through them, capturing how people have witnessed processes of urbanization. The story of housing is one key experience in that. With a look at the classics of twentieth-century African novels, reflections of urban housing range from the portrait of Igbo-neighborhoods in Lagos in the 1940s in Buchi Emecheta's *Joys of Motherhood*[49] to the racially segregated township in Dambudzo Marechera's *House of Hunger*[50] or Yvonne Vera's *Butterfly Burning*[51]; from urban homelessness in Marjorie Oludhe Macgoye's *Street Life*[52] up to the depiction of African migrants' livelihoods in Alexandria, Johannesburg in Binyavanga Wainaina's *One Day I Will Write About*

---

48 Nancy Rose Hunt, "Between Fiction and History: Modes of Writing Abortion in Africa," *Cahiers d'études africaines* 186 (2007).
49 Buchi Emecheta, *The Joys of Motherhood* (London: Heinemann, 1980).
50 Dambudzo Marechera, *House of Hunger: Short Stories* (London: Heinemann Educational, 1978).
51 Yvonne Vera, *Butterfly Burning* (Harare, Zimbabwe: Baobab Books, 1998).
52 Marjorie Oludhe Macgoye, *Street Life* (Nairobi: East African Educational Publishers, 1993).

This Place.[53] It is a story of urban housing narrated from inside perspectives, informed by autobiographical knowledge[54] and/or careful research.[55] Contrasting with the utter scarcity of material wealth and space, which housing in urban areas continues to mean for a vast majority of people, African writing offers an abundance of stories and cultural representations reflecting on the past and presence of urban living. Fiction and narrative provide a medium to "develop" individual and collective experiences, to uncover the resilience, creativities, and desires they contain and to translate them into knowledge. This richness of lived and reflected experience is currently gaining ground and importance through the digital transformation of African writing and the new opportunities for publishing it provides.[56]

References

Adams, Anne V., and Janis A. Mayes. "African Literature and Development: Mapping Intersections." In *Mapping Intersections: African Literature and Africa's Development*, edited by Anne V. Adams, and Janis A. Mayes, 1–11. Trenton, NJ: Africa World Press, 1998.
Adenekan, Shola. "Transnationalism and the Agenda of African Literature in a Digital Age." *Matatu* 45 (2014): 133–151.
Davis, Mike. *Planet of Slums*. London: Verso, 2006.
Emecheta, Buchi. *The Joys of Motherhood*. London: Heinemann, 1980.
Hall, Stuart. "When Was 'The Post-Colonial'? Thinking at the Limit." In *The Postcolonial Question: Common Skies, Divided Horizons*, edited by Iain Chambers, and Likia Curti, 242–260. London: Routledge, 1996.
Hunt, Nancy Rose. "Between Fiction and History: Modes of Writing Abortion in Africa." *Cahiers d'études africaines* 186 (2007): 2–25.
Kopf, Martina. "Encountering Development in East African Fiction." *The Journal of Commonwealth Literature* 54, no. 3 (2019): 223–368.
Kurtz, John Roger. *Urban Obsessions, Urban Fears: The Postcolonial Kenyan Novel*. Trenton, NJ: Africa World Press, 1998.
Macgoye, Marjorie Oludhe. *Street Life*. Nairobi: East African Educational Publishers, 1993.
Marechera, Dambudzo. *House of Hunger: Short Stories*. London: Heinemann Educational, 1978.
Moser, Caroline O. N., ed. *Gender, Asset Accumulation and Just Cities: Pathways to Transformation?* London: Routledge, 2015.
Mwangi, Meja. *Down River Road*. Columbus: Ohio HM Books Intl., 2014.

---

53 Binyavanga Wainaina, *One Day I Will Write About This Place* (London: Granta, 2011).
54 Marechera, *House of Hunger*; Wainaina, *One Day I Will Write About This Place*.
55 Vera, *Butterfly Burning*; Macgoye, *Street Life*.
56 Shola Adenekan, "Transnationalism and the Agenda of African Literature in a Digital Age," *Matatu* 45 (2014).

Mwangi, Meja. *The Cockroach Dance*. Columbus, Ohio: HM Books Intl., 2013.
Mwangi, Meja. *The Cockroach Dance*. Harlow: Longman, 1989.
Mwangi, Meja. *Going Down River Road*. London; Nairobi; Ibadan; Lusaka: Heinemann, 1976.
Mwangi, Meja. *Kill Me Quick*. London: Heinemann Educational, 1973.
Nelson, Nici. "Representations of Men and Women, City and Town in Kenyan Novels of the 1970s and 1980s." *African Languages and Cultures* 9/2 (1996): 145–168.
Odhiambo, Tom. "Kenyan Popular Fiction in English and the Melodramas of the Underdog." *Research in African Literatures* 39/4 (2008): 72–82.
Parsons, Adam W. *The Seven Myths of "Slums": Challenging Popular Prejudices about the World's Urban Poor*. London: Share the World's Resources (STWR), 2010.
Rakodi, Carole. "Addressing Gendered Inequalities in Housing." In *Gender, Asset Accumulation and Just Cities: Pathways to Transformation?*, edited by Caroline O. N. Moser, 81–99. London: Routledge, 2015.
Rakodi, Carole. "Expanding Women's Access to Land and Housing in Urban Areas." In *Women's Voice, Agency, and Participation Research Series* 8. Washington, DC: World Bank Group, 2014. http://documents.worldbank.org/curated/en/473001468323334380/Expanding-womens-access-to-land-and-housing-in-urban-areas.
Vera, Yvonne. *Butterfly Burning*. Harare: Baobab Books, 1998.
Wainaina, Binyavanga. *One Day I Will Write About This Place*. London: Granta, 2011.
Warah, Rasna, ed. *Missionaries, Mercenaries and Misfits: An Anthology*. Central Milton Keynes: Author House, 2008.
Warah, Rasna. "The Development Myth." In *Missionaries, Mercenaries and Misfits: An Anthology*, edited by Rasna Warah, 3–22. Central Milton Keynes: Author House, 2008.
Warah, Rasna. "Nairobi's Slums: Where Life for Women is Nasty, Brutish and Short." *Habitat Debate* 8/4 (2002): 16.
Watson, Jini Kim. "'We Want You to Ask Us First': Development, International Aid and the Politics of Indebtedness." In *Negotiating Normativity: Postcolonial Appropriations, Contestations, and Transformations*, edited by Nikita Dhawan, Ilona Elisabeth Fink, Johanna Leinius, and Rirhandu Mageza-Barthel, 241–53. Switzerland: Springer International Publishing, 2016.
White, Luise. *The Comforts of Home: Prostitution in Colonial Nairobi*. Chicago & London: The University of Chicago Press, 1990.
World Bank. *World Development Report 2012: Gender Equality and Development*. Washington DC: The International Bank for Reconstruction and Development/ The World Bank, 2011.

Donatien Dibwe dia Mwembu
5 La problématique de l'habitat dans la ville de Lubumbashi (Elisabethville), province du Katanga, 1910–1960

Gestion sécuritaire de l'espace

L'aménagement d'un espace géographique donné répond généralement aux exigences de sa gestion sécuritaire qui se veut une variable dynamique dans le temps et dans l'espace. La corrélation entre ces deux variables peut être justifiée par plusieurs indicateurs. La ville de Lubumbashi a hérité du système ségrégationniste sud-africain dans beaucoup de domaines, notamment en matière de logement.

Un exemple emprunté à la ville de Durban, peut nous édifier sur la ségrégation raciale et spatiale en vigueur dans les territoires urbains sud-africains à l'époque de l'apartheid. En effet, Hélène Mainet-Valleix note: "La législation d'apartheid divisait la population en quatre groupes racialement définis: les Blancs, les Noirs, les Métis et les Asiatiques. Chaque groupe était affecté à des quartiers spécifiques, la ville était, et demeure, découpée en quartiers ethniquement homogènes."[1] Les Blancs (14%) occupent la partie centrale de la ville, viennent ensuite les Métis (3%) et les Indiens (27%) et, enfin, les Noirs (56%) à la périphérie, dans les townships.[2] A l'origine de cette ségrégation raciale et spatiale se trouve le fameux "syndrome sanitaire" que brandissaient tous les pays colonisateurs, comme par exemple, la Grande Bretagne et la France. En outre, le *Native Urban Areas Act* de 1923 sera mis sur pied pour contrôler, freiner et ségréguer les Noirs qui accèdent au territoire urbain. La raison profonde de cette loi est donnée par Philip Bonner et Lauren Segal qui notent: "*The reason for passing the Act was so that the government could rid the urban areas of liquor sellers, criminals and the unemployed, thereby eradicating the promiscuous multiracial environment in which they lived and forcing the remaining African labour force on the Rand to live in townships and single sex compounds.*"[3]

---

[1] Hélène Mainet-Valleix, *Durban. Les Indiens, leurs territoires, leur identité* (Paris: IFAS-Karthala, 2002), 8.
[2] Mainet-Valleix, *Durban*, 8.
[3] Philip Bonner et Lauren Segal, *Soweto: A History* (Cape Town: Maskew Miller, Longman, 1998), 15.

122 —— Donatien Dibwe dia Mwembu

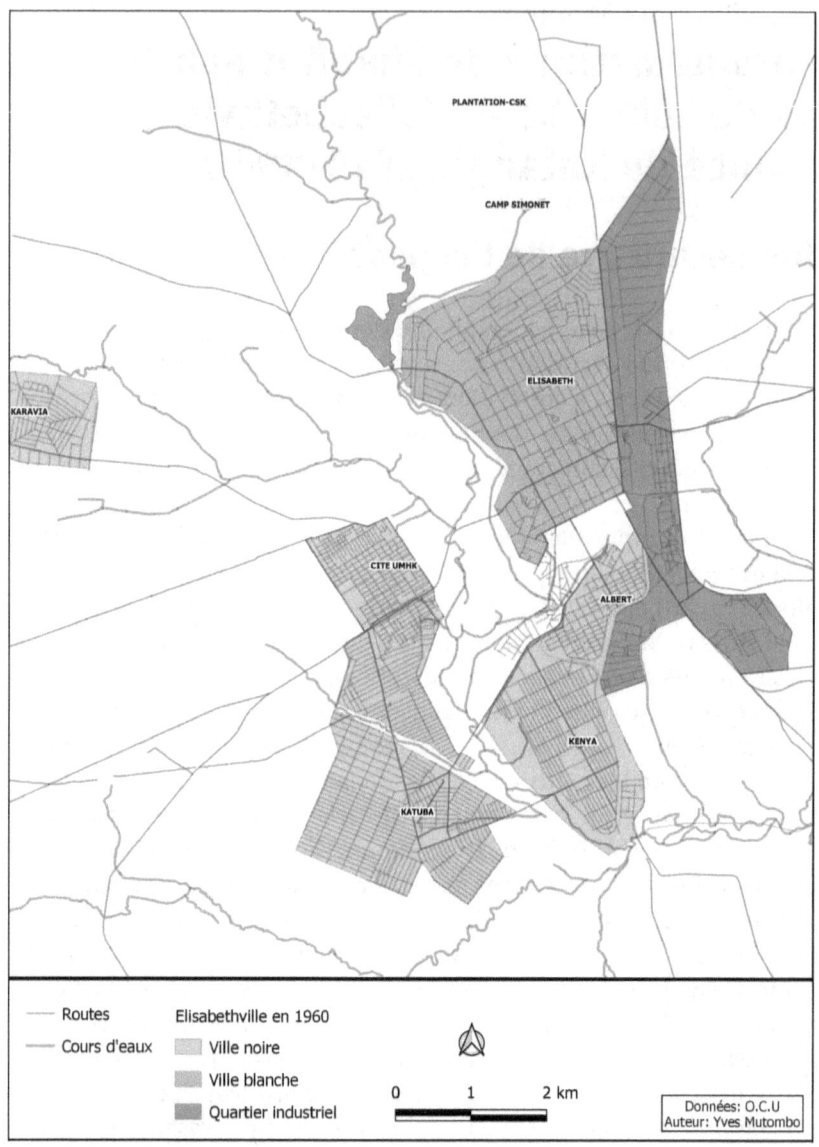

Figure 5.1: Carte de la ville d'Elisabethville (Lubumbashi) en 1960.
Source: Observatoire du Changement Urbain, La croissance spatiale de la ville de Lubumbashi, 1910–1973 (Lubumbashi, Université de Lubumbashi, 1973).

Le problème de la sécurité de la ville de Lubumbashi est aussi vieux que la ville elle–même. Mais la politique *ad hoc* a varié avec le temps. Au cours de la période coloniale, cette problématique était plurielle. Elle concernait différents secteurs de la vie quotidienne et était aussi fonction des circonstances du moment et du futur.

La ville était le bastion du Blanc et, le village, le monde du Noir. Le système du travail migrant, appliqué depuis la création de la ville jusque vers la fin des années 1920, trouve, entre autres, son origine dans cette idéologie. Après son contrat, le Noir devait rentrer dans son village d'origine, pour poursuivre ses activités agropastorales. Le fait que les femmes et les enfants étaient retenus dans le village était une sorte de prise d'otage, condition *sine qua non* pour le retour au village du mari parti en ville pour le travail.

La politique ségrégationniste a commencé avec la création d'Elisabethville. Mais l'identité de cette ville a varié avec le temps. De la ville "bastion" de l'homme blanc, Lubumbashi (Elisabethville) est passée à l'étape de la ville "multiraciale" avec la stabilisation de la main-d'œuvre africaine. L'idéologie de l'époque voulait voir les deux communautés blanche et noire vivre séparées. Ces changements identitaires ont eu des répercussions sur la gestion de l'habitat dans la ville de Lubumbashi durant toute la période coloniale. Nous allons voir comment a évolué cette politique basée sur la sécurisation des hommes et de leurs biens. Cette communication comprend trois volets essentiels: la ville blanche, la zone neutre et la ville noire.

Lubumbashi, barrière contre l'influence anglophone?

Lubumbashi est le chef-lieu de la province du Katanga, dans le sud-est de la République Démocratique du Congo. Située au 11°39′ de latitude sud, à une altitude variant entre 1220 et 1240 mètres, la ville de Lubumbashi couvre une superficie de 747 ha. Cependant, seuls 141,6 ha, soit 19%, sont urbanisés et comprennent six communes urbaines (Lubumbashi (1910), Kamalondo (1912), Kenya (1939), Ruashi (1956), Katuba (1950) et Kampemba (1972)) et une commune Annexe urbano-rurale (1957).

Elle est une ville sécuritaire sur le plan politique en ce sens qu'elle constituait une barrière contre l'avancée de l'influence anglaise en direction du nord. En fait, cette ville n'a pas constitué un frein à l'influence anglophone. D'abord, parce qu'à ses débuts, l'Union Minière du Haut-Katanga (UMHK) a été dirigée en grande partie par les Anglo-saxons qui occupèrent les hauts postes. Ensuite, la dépendance de l'UMHK vis-à-vis de l'Afrique australe était manifeste dans le recrutement de la main-d'œuvre africaine. Cette dernière était recrutée par la Robert Williams and Company au Mozambique, au Nyassaland et à la Rhodésie du nord. De plus, l'anglais et le français étaient parlés à Lubumbashi. Les premiers journaux qui ont commencé à paraître en 1911, une année après la fondation d'Elisabethville, comportaient des articles en anglais. Enfin, le kiswahili de Lubumbashi s'était lui-même enrichi de quelques emprunts anglais (kabati, armoire, provient de cupboard; blanketi, couverture, provient de blanket; nsopo, savon, provient de soap; nkopo, tasse, provient de cup; kuwina, gagner, provient du verbe to win; boyi, domestique, provient de boy etc.).

La fracturation spatiale à base raciale

L'ordonnance du Vice-Gouverneur Général n°11 du 23 mai 1917 créa la circonscription urbaine et en fixa les limites. Le premier plan d'aménagement de la ville exécuté en 1910 par le Colonel Emile Wangermée, alors Vice-Gouverneur général du Katanga, fut complété par le Gouverneur Général Lippens en 1921 en fonction de la ségrégation raciale. Par ordonnance du 18 mars 1932, la cité indigène devint le centre extra-coutumier. En 1941, Elisabethville obtint le statut de ville au sens juridique du terme au même moment que Léopoldville (actuelle ville de Kinshasa) et Jadotville (actuelle ville de Likasi). En 1957, on assista à une profonde réorganisation administrative de la ville qui comprenait désormais cinq communes dont quatre de l'ancien centre extra-coutumier et une englobant tous les quartiers blancs. Les premières élections communales organisées en 1957 virent pour la première fois des bourgmestres noirs à la tête des quatre communes africaines: Albert (qui deviendra Kamalondo en 1968), Kenya, Katuba et Ruashi. Seule la commune Elisabeth (qui deviendra Lubumbashi en 1968), bastion de la population blanche, était dirigée par un bourgmestre blanc.[4] Mais, jusqu'à la veille de l'indépendance, la ville de Lubumbashi (Elisabethville à l'époque) était divisée en deux quartiers communément appelés "ville blanche" et "ville noire".

---

4 En 1971, la commune de Lubumbashi, devenue très large, fut scindée en deux communes: Lubumbashi et Kampemba.

La ville blanche

La ville blanche abritait essentiellement les populations européennes, américaines et d'autres continents. Mais il y existait une discrimination entre les Blancs. Les "grands" (Belges, Anglais, Américains, Français, Allemands etc.) occupaient la partie centrale tandis que les "petits" Blancs (Grecs, Italiens, Portugais, Hindous etc.) habitaient la périphérie à cause des contacts permanents avec les Noirs que leur imposaient leurs activités économiques. Parmi les "grands" Blancs, il faut aussi noter la distinction entre les ouvriers, qui se réunissaient au cercle, les agents de l'UMHK, qui se réunissaient au mess et les responsable politiques et administratifs ainsi que les hauts responsables des entreprises qui se retrouvaient au cercle Albert 1er (actuel cercle Makutano). Augustin Ilunga Ndjoloko déclare que l'avenue Moëro constituait en quelque sorte une ligne de démarcation entre l'habitat des "grands" Blancs et celui des "petits" Blancs. Alors que l'hôtel Machris servait les Grecs, l'hôtel Belle Vue, à côté de la Banque commerciale du Congo, servait les Belges.[5]

Les Noirs n'étaient pas autorisés à circuler dans la ville blanche après les heures de service et surtout la nuit. Dans sa chanson intitulée "Kabwebwe Kitambala", Edouard Masengo Katiti se rappelle avoir passé une nuit au cachot pour avoir été surpris avec sa guitare, en dehors des heures de travail et sans autorisation, dans le quartier des Blancs. Kabwebwe Kitambala est le nom du brigadier noir qui l'avait arrêté et mis au cachot. Il le remercie parce qu'il lui avait donné ce dont il avait besoin pendant son séjour au cachot: boisson sucrée Coca Cola, limonade, de l'eau, etc.[6]

Les seuls Africains qu'on rencontrait dans la ville blanche étaient soit des travailleurs obligés alors de quitter ce quartier dès la fin de la journée de travail soit des domestiques prestant leurs services auprès des Blancs et qui y vivaient avec leurs familles restreintes, derrière la maison de leur patron, dans une petite maison de deux pièces (communément appelée boyerie) séparée de la maison du patron par une haie faite d'euphorbes ou de mur en briques cuites.

Les déclarations ci-après des domestiques d'Elisabethville mettent l'accent sur la promiscuité dans laquelle ils vivaient:

> Ce sont eux (Blancs) qui construisirent une maison à pièce unique destinée à un homme marié, de surcroît père d'une nombreuse famille. Quelle promiscuité avec des enfants des deux sexes! Quel homme, celui qui éprouve tant de peine que de gêne aussi bien au cou-

---

5 Dr Augustin Ilunga Ndjoloko, interview accordée à Lubumbashi, avril 1993.
6 Claude Mwilambwe, "Edouard Masengo Katiti," dans *Musique urbaine du Katanga. De Malaika à Santu Kimbangu*, éd. Bogumil Jewsiewicki (Paris: L'Harmattan, 2003), 122–123.

cher qu'au lever? Ce pauvre domestique confiné dans une unique pièce avec ses filles et fils dit, à son lever, à ceux de ses enfants qui ont atteint un certain âge: "Mesdemoiselles et Messieurs, s'il vous plaît, réveillez-vous et allez dehors, car je voudrais me changer". Alors toute la maisonnette s'ébranle parce que le père veut aller au service. Après, le père de famille appelle ses enfants: "Rentrez dans la maison s'il vous plaît", leur dit-il. Et la marmaille se rue dans la maison. Si d'aventure la mère, elle aussi, se réveille en ce moment, on revient au même rituel. Voilà notre calvaire de domestique! Même gêne quand on héberge un visiteur sous son toit. Rien de changé. Dans le même temps, le Blanc, lui, dispose de deux pièces supplémentaires qui auraient pu servir à son domestique, mais il les affecte à son poulailler ou en fait un clapier. La mauvaise foi des Européens était telle![7]

Sur le plan légal, les domestiques étaient admis à vivre dans les parcelles de leurs maîtres conformément à l'esprit de l'ordonnance n°3 du 6 février 1922 relative aux cités indigènes et aux camps de travailleurs dans les circonscriptions urbaines du Vice-Gouvernement Général du Katanga qui stipulait: "Les indigènes et les personnes d'un niveau moral équivalent, de résidence ou de passage dans une circonscription urbaine, sont tenus d'habiter la cité indigène. Toutefois, les personnes de couleur au service d'Européens pourront, à raison de deux serviteurs par maître, habiter le quartier européen avec leurs femmes et enfants."[8]

---

[7] Pierre Kasongo Pauni et Donatien Dibwe dia Mwembu, "Vocabulaire de ville Elisabethville, province du Katanga Oriental à Elisabethville rédigé par André Yav", dans *Lubumbashi 1910–2010. Mémoire d'une ville industrielle. Ukumbusho wa mukini wa komponi*, éd. Bogumil Jewsiewicki et al. (Paris: L'Harmattan, 2010), 45–46. Voici la version swahili: "28. Sababu waonjo waliwaza kumujengea mutu mweusi nyumba moja: moja/ yeye yule mutu: iko na bibi wake na watoto wake: wengine wanaume: na wengine wanawake/ sasa mutu huyu maskini mwenye bibi na watoto wake ni mwenye kuteswa pa kulala na pa kulamuka/ ni mutu gani? ni mutu maskini boy mwenye kulala mu ka chumba ka moja na watoto wake wanawake na wanaume/ yeye pa kwenda kukazi: sasa maskini boy pa kulamuka yeye anasema na watoto wake wote wale wenye kukomea asema: wamama na wababa muniwe kwanza razi/ mulamukemwende: ao mutoke kwanza inje/ mimi muzee wenu nataka kwanza kuvaa mavazi/ ni kweli: pale watoto wa mutu wanaanza kuibulula na kuogopaya kama baba anataka kuvalaende kazini/ watoto watatoka wote: baba ya bo ameyishavaa: njo ameita wanayeasema: wanawangu sasa muingieni: mimi baba yenu nimeyishavaa/ na tutoto sasa tunaanza tena kurudi nyumbani/ akiwa maman ayeamefikilia na kuamuka: ni namna moja tu: haiachane/ hiyi njo mateso ya sisi waboy/ pia ukipokelea mugeni: mugeni: ni namna moja tu: haibadirike hata kidogo/ 29. Tena ule muzungu yeye yipo na vyumba mbili/ ineneakuleta na mutumishi wake boy yote mbili/ yeye anatia moufungo wakewa makuku: na pia tululutwake yeye mwenyewe/ pale njo watu wa ulaya walikuwa na roho yao mubaya sana/".

[8] Ordonnance citée par Johan Lagae et Sofie Boonen, "Un regard africain sur une ville coloniale belge: architecture et urbanisme dans le "Vocabulaire de ville de Elisabethville" d'André Yav", dans *Lubumbashi 1910–2010. Mémoire d'une ville industrielle. Ukumbusho wa mukini wa komponi*, éd. Bogumil Jewsiewicki et al. (Paris: L'Harmattan, 2010), 115 (note 28).

La zone neutre

Avec la stabilisation de la main-d'œuvre africaine, Lubumbashi (Elisabethville), dont les concepteurs étaient les élèves fidèles du modèle sud-africain, fut une ville ségrégationniste à travers la création de deux quartiers blanc et noir, séparés, à partir des années 1920, par l'érection d'une barrière "naturelle", autrement appelée zone neutre ou encore "cordon sanitaire"[9] ou *no man's land*, large de plus ou moins 700 mètres. L'objectif, à l'époque, était de protéger, semble-t-il, la population blanche contre les maladies contagieuses en provenance de la ville "noire". En témoignent les deux extraits ci-dessous empruntés au procès-verbal du service de cadastre de 1951 et à R. Hins:

> La zone neutre, est une création médicale. Si les connaissances médicales et les découvertes en matière d'hygiène progressent sans cesse, il n'en reste pas moins, ainsi que le souligne le Médecin Provincial, que les diverses races humaines sont différemment sensibles vis-à-vis d'un même virus, qu'il faut des mesures de précaution qui n'ont pas pour but de protéger spécialement une race humaine déterminée vis-à-vis d'une autre, mais sont réciproques. Cette zone neutre peut d'ailleurs avoir d'autres justifications. Celle qui surgit de la considération des mesures de sécurité ne peut être perdue de vue.[10]

> La zone neutre, évite toute promiscuité entre le blanc et le noir. Elle sépare les deux cités par un espace pratiquement libre de 500 mètres au minimum, distance qui correspond à l'ampleur normale du vol du moustique transmettant la malaria. La zone neutre écarte donc la vie du noir de celle du blanc; elle met ce dernier à l'abri des foyers de malaria, des divertissements bruyants du noir et rend, en conséquence, les conditions d'existence de chaque race nettement indépendantes (...) c'est un véritable cordon sanitaire orienté, en conséquence, perpendiculairement aux vents dominants.[11]

Une série de bâtiments publics furent érigés le long des avenues "Limite Sud" (actuelle Likasi) et J.F. de Hemptinne (actuelle Sendwe) pour empêcher l'extension de la ville noire en direction de la ville blanche. Il s'agit des écoles pour enfants noirs (Collège Saint Boniface pour les garçons et Lycée Sacré Cœur pour les filles), du complexe hospitalier Prince Léopold (actuel Hôpital Général de Référence Jason Sendwe), de la prison de Kasombo (actuel site de l'Eglise Kimbanguiste), du bâtiment hébergeant aujourd'hui le ministère provincial de la Santé et les services de l'Inspection Provinciale de la Santé Publique, du bâtiment abritant la faculté de Médecine vétérinaire, du grand

---

[9] Jef van Bilsen, *Congo, 1945–1965. La fin d'une colonie* (Bruxelles: CRISP, 1994), 18.
[10] Procès-verbal de la réunion du comité urbain, Elisabethville, 13 décembre 1951, 5, Archives du Service de cadastre, Ville d'Elisabethville.
[11] R. Hins, cité par Lagae et Boonen, "Un regard africain sur une ville coloniale belge," 113.

laboratoire médical, de l'Eglise Méthodiste-Unie, du Home de Jeunes Filles et de l'Ecole Technique Don Bosco (actuel Institut Salama) et d'une bande verte. A en croire R. Hins, cette ceinture semblait sécuriser les Blancs contre les maladies, contre les morsures, par exemple, des moustiques en provenance de la ville noire qu'était le quartier Albert, l'actuelle commune Kamalondo.

Plus tard, la construction des quartiers commerciaux *Njanja* et *Bakowa* ont permis de filtrer les populations noires à destination de la ville blanche et de les en retenir éloignés, puisqu'elles trouvaient la quasi-totalité des produits dont elles avaient besoin dans ces espaces commerciaux. Cet apartheid à la belge persista jusqu'à la fin de la période coloniale.

Au sud-ouest de la ville blanche, une autre zone neutre, constituée de la rivière Lubumbashi, de la pépinière créée le long de la rive gauche de cette rivière, de la construction de l'hôpital pour la main-d'œuvre noire de l'UMHK et des usines de l'UMHK, séparait le quartier des ouvriers blancs (Makomeno) du camp de travailleurs de l'UMHK, actuelle Gécamines.

La politique ségrégationniste de zones "neutres" a été appliquée dans les autres villes minières du Katanga méridional, notamment Jadotville (Likasi) et Kolwezi. À Jadotville, la zone neutre, qui séparait le quartier blanc (Jadotville) du quartier noir (Kikula), était constituée par le chemin de fer Sakania-Tenke, l'hôpital pour Noirs (Daco), le camp de la police, la Basilique, le terrain de football et le cimetière de Sapins I. À Kolwezi, la zone neutre, qui séparait le quartier des Blancs du camp de travailleurs de l'UMHK, était composée de l'hôpital pour les travailleurs noirs de l'UMHK, du complexe omnisport Manika, de l'école protestante, de la carrière d'exploitation de l'UMHK. Du côté de la cité de Manika, la zone neutre était constituée du lac Kabongo, de la rivière qui s'y jette, du camp de travailleurs du BCK (actuelle SNCC) et de la gare du chemin de fer Dilolo-Sakania.

La ségrégation raciale à la mode dans les villes coloniales ne concernait pas uniquement l'habitat, mais aussi les espaces de socialisation, comme par exemple, les hôpitaux, les écoles, les magasins, les restaurants, les bars. Même les lieux de culte n'étaient pas en marge de cette réalité.

Nous résumons ici le débat sur la nécessité de disposer d'une zone des hôpitaux qui devait regrouper des hôpitaux pour Noirs et Blancs. L'emplacement choisi était l'espace qu'occupe aujourd'hui l'Hôpital Général de Référence Jason Sendwe. L'exposé des motifs a été le suivant:

> Nécessité de grouper les trois grandes constructions médicales à édifier à Elisabethville, à savoir: laboratoires, hôpital pour Européens, hôpital pour Congolais, en un seul et même complexe. Les raisons avancées en sont l'économie de matériel et de personnel pour les services communs: il n'est pas possible de doubler tous les spécialistes, il en est de même des appareils modernes. Du point de vue professionnel, la chose est absolument nécessaire et tout le corps médical consulté est unanime à ce sujet... Le groupement des 2 hôpitaux

5 La problématique de l'habitat dans la ville de Lubumbashi (Elisabethville) — 129

s'indique également pour des raisons politiques; il ne peut être question de faire une politique, basée sur la couleur de la peau.[12]

Le projet de regroupement des hôpitaux fut rejeté pour des raisons raciales voilées que nous reproduisons ci-dessous:

> Mais le problème d'ordre pratique se pose tout autrement lorsque le principe est appelé à se concrétiser dans la zone définie ci-dessus. Au cours de la réunion pré appelée, les objections suivantes ont été présentées:
> - Proximité de la gare et de voies de grand trafic: bruits etc.;
> - Déclivité du terrain;
> - Exiguïté du terrain empêchant tout agrandissement;
> - Caractère commercial et indigène du quartier où l'on veut situer les hôpitaux. Pas de place pour créer une zone de verdure pour le repos des malades;
> - Voisinage d'écoles dont celle des Sœurs et celle de la Mission Méthodiste, voisinage du Stade Léopold II et du Centre Extra-Coutumier;
> - Danger de contagion, le niveau d'hygiène des noirs étant ce qu'il est à l'heure actuelle.[13]

Le projet de construire une zone des hôpitaux a été rejeté pour l'hôpital des Blancs. Mais la construction de l'hôpital des Noirs n'a pas posé de problème. Cela veut dire que les objections avancées ne concernaient pas les Noirs, mais les Blancs. En d'autres termes, les Noirs pouvaient bien s'accommoder avec les bruits (1), avec le caractère commercial et indigène du quartier (4), avec le voisinage des écoles, du stade Léopold II et du centre extra-coutumier (5). La vraie raison de la séparation des hôpitaux demeure le problème d'hygiène (6). En effet, le même rapport rapporte:

> Il faut créer, en dépit de la conjugaison des bâtiments, et en dépit du personnel médical commun, des conditions qui permettent un isolément bactériologique et parasitologique complet des deux hôpitaux. Cette condition est primordiale en raison de la différence de sensibilité des diverses races humaines vis-à-vis d'un même virus. Ces mesures de précaution sont donc réciproques, et n'ont pas pour but de protéger une race humaine déterminée vis-à-vis d'une autre.[14]

---

12 Procès-verbal de la réunion du comité urbain, Elisabethville, 13 décembre 1951, 2, Archives du Service de Cadastre, Ville d'Elisabethville.
13 Procès-verbal de la réunion du comité urbain, Elisabethville, 13 décembre 1951, 2, Archives du Service de Cadastre, Ville d'Elisabethville.
14 Procès-verbal de la réunion du comité urbain, Elisabethville, 13 décembre 1951, 4, Archives du Service de Cadastre, Ville d'Elisabethville.

Une ville noire hétérogène

Cette juridiction, la ville noire donc, était considérée comme hétérogène dans la mesure où elle était composée de trois agglomérations différentes. Chaque quartier avait sa propre identité puisqu'il hébergeait des personnes qui exerçaient des fonctions différentes. On comptait ainsi deux camps de travailleurs, à savoir, le camp de travailleurs noirs de l'UMHK et celui des agents de la Compagnie du chemin de fer du Bas-Congo au Katanga (BCK). Enfin, il y avait la "cité indigène".

La cité "indigène"

La première agglomération fut le quartier Albert (actuelle commune Kamalondo). Elle a été appelée d'abord cité "indigène" en 1911 et ensuite centre extra-coutumier après la promulgation en 1933 du décret sur les circonscriptions indigènes. Le quartier Albert était habité exclusivement par des populations africaines noires. Aucun Blanc ne pouvait y habiter. Ce quartier noir hébergeait un amalgame de populations composées des agents et fonctionnaires de l'Etat colonial et des firmes importantes, des indépendants dont la plupart étaient des commerçants – et les camps de travailleurs noirs.

Avec le temps, et compte tenu de l'augmentation de la population africaine en fonction des besoins croissants en main-d'œuvre africaine, un nouveau quartier fut créé au sud du quartier Albert. Nous sommes en 1936. Cette nouvelle juridiction, appelée Nyasi (paille) puisque la toiture des maisons était en paille et brûlait à chaque passage des locomotives à vapeur, fut dénommée "bikopo" et, enfin, Kenya, en mémoire des soldats démobilisés de la Force Publique de retour dans ce quartier après la deuxième guerre mondiale.

Une dizaine d'années plus tard, et dans la même direction, fut créé le quartier Katuba, au début des années 1950. Katuba, comme Kenya allait héberger entre autres des vieux travailleurs de l'UMHK jugés dociles, bénéficiaires du fonds d'avance pour la construction de leurs maisons.

Au cours de la deuxième moitié des années 1950, le besoin de créer un autre quartier d'habitation pour Noirs se manifesta. La prolongation des activités économiques dans le quartier industriel exigeait la construction d'un quartier pour Noirs dans les environs immédiats pour éviter la traversée quotidienne de la ville blanche par des travailleurs Noirs. C'est dans ce contexte que le quartier Ruashi fut créé. Il devait servir de réserve de main-d'œuvre africaine pour le quartier industriel en plein développement et extension.

Les deux autres agglomérations étaient les camps de travailleurs de la compagnie du chemin de fer du BCK et de l'UMHK. Ces deux camps étaient exclusivement habités par les ouvriers noirs de ces entreprises et leurs familles. Il y avait un double souci dans cette ségrégation spatiale : celui d'abord de mettre la main-d'œuvre à l'abri de toutes influences extérieures susceptibles de la "corrompre" et de nuire ainsi à son rendement; celui, ensuite de renforcer son sentiment d'appartenir à une société à part, une "grande famille" disciplinée et saine. C'est ce double souci qui a amené l'UMHK et la compagnie du chemin de fer du BCK à construire les camps de leurs travailleurs à part, loin des centres extra-coutumiers, dont les habitants étaient considérés comme "indisciplinés". Ces camps étaient construits à côté de leurs lieux de travail (les Usines de Lubumbashi pour les travailleurs de l'UMHK et la Gare de chemin de fer pour les travailleurs de BCK) pour éviter les problèmes de transport, c'est-à-dire les longues distances à parcourir par les travailleurs.

Dans chaque camp de travailleurs, un chef de camp s'occupait du vécu quotidien de la population ouvrière et était épaulé par des policiers de l'entreprise (*malonda* pour l'UMHK), qui étaient en fait ses yeux et oreilles.

Le cas du camp de travailleurs de l'Union Minière du Haut-Katanga

Le camp de travailleurs l'UMHK (actuelle Gécamines) est né avec le recrutement de la main-d'œuvre africaine, conséquence du début de l'exploitation minière.

Le choix du site du camp de travailleurs de l'UMHK dépendait de plusieurs conditions, notamment la proximité des usines de Lubumbashi en vue de diminuer la distance entre le camp et le lieu de travail, ensuite, son érection à plus ou moins un kilomètre et demi du camp de travailleurs blancs (actuel quartier *Makomeno*) et, enfin, son emplacement sous les vents pour que les moustiques qui ont piqué les Noirs ne viennent pas piquer les Blancs. D'autres barrières furent érigées en vue d'éviter le rapprochement des deux camps: la construction de l'hôpital Sud pour les Africains, la rivière Lubumbashi qui, elle-même, constituait une barrière "naturelle" entre les deux camps et, enfin, les Usines de Lubumbashi et la centrale électrique.

L'histoire du camp de travailleurs de l'Union Minière du Haut-Katanga/ Gécamines-Lubumbashi était liée, à l'instar de l'histoire de tous les autres camps de travailleurs de cette entreprise, à l'exploitation minière et à la conjoncture économique et peut être subdivisée en deux grandes parties, en fonction de la politique même adoptée par les dirigeants de l'entreprise: la période du travail migrant et celle de la stabilisation de la main-d'œuvre.

La période du travail migrant (1910–1928): Au cours de cette période, les travailleurs noirs étaient engagés pour un contrat allant de trois à douze mois et étaient renvoyés dans leurs villages, poursuivre leurs activités champêtres. La ville était donc le bastion des Blancs comme les villages étaient le bastion des Noirs. Pour ce faire et étant donné la mobilité du camp, les maisons des travailleurs étaient rudimentaires et donc précaires. C'est, entre autres, pour cette raison que l'UMHK ne voulait pas construire des maisons confortables, en matériaux durables, pour ne pas augmenter le prix de revient moyen par ouvrier en cette période d'accumulation primitive du capital.

La loi congolaise détermine la surface de parquet et le cube d'air nécessaires par individu et exige certaines garanties pour assurer une bonne protection de l'occupant. Elle fixe aux constructions, suivant la nature des matériaux employés, une durée d'existence maximum. L'Union Minière a estimé qu'au moins pour les logements qui auront une longue durée, il était nécessaire de cimenter les parquets pour protéger l'occupant contre le *Kimputu*, insecte transmetteur de la fièvre récurrente, très répandu dans le sol poussiéreux des huttes des villages du Haut-Katanga.

De plus, toujours dans le but de satisfaire les goûts de sa main-d'œuvre noire et de la stabiliser tout en améliorant l'hygiène par la diminution des chances de propagation des maladies, la Société a jugé utile d'abandonner les logements grégaires, dénommés "blocs *Orenstein*" qu'elle avait construits dans les camps de Panda et de Lubumbashi. La superficie habitable était alors réduite à deux mètres carrés par habitant. De quatorze personnes, on passera à des huttes en briques cuites et ciment pour quatre personnes, puis pour trois personnes.

La période de stabilisation de la main-d'œuvre africaine (à partir de 1928): La (re)constitution des ménages ne pouvait être possible que dans un environnement physique favorable. Dans ce contexte, l'entreprise dut mettre sur pied des stratégies attractives efficaces d'encadrement des familles des travailleurs en vue de rendre attrayante la vie dans ses camps, d'apprivoiser et de soumettre les travailleurs et leurs familles.

Pour rendre le camp de travailleurs attrayant, il fallait répondre favorablement à certaines conditions: améliorer les conditions de travail, l'alimentation, les infrastructures socio-médicales, le logement.

Elle investit des capitaux colossaux pour améliorer les conditions de vie de ses travailleurs. Elle se mit d'abord à améliorer la qualité du logement. Les maisons en matériaux non durables, source de beaucoup de maladies, cédaient progressivement le pas aux maisons en matériaux durables en même temps que le logement grégaire, propre aux célibataires et favorable aux maladies contagieuses, était remplacé par le logement individuel.

L'administration coloniale s'investit également dans l'amélioration du logement par la promulgation d'une série d'ordonnances-lois dont l'objectif était non seulement de mettre fin à la promiscuité qui régnait dans les camps de travailleurs (hygiène industrielle), mais aussi d'exiger des entreprises une superficie de quatre mètres carrés par occupant dans les camps permanents.[15]

Au début de la stabilisation de la main-d'œuvre, l'UMHK adopta dans ses camps l'habitat par affinité ethnique ou tribale. La question tribale a aussi intéressé les entreprises minières et industrielles. C'est ainsi qu'au début de l'industrialisation, l'habitat séparé, par affinité ou par région de provenance fut mis en place non seulement à l'UMHK, mais aussi dans d'autres d'entreprises comme la Forminière ou Kilo-Moto, où les populations ouvrières étaient regroupées par "race".[16] La raison qui justifie la mise en application de cette politique avait eu pour fondement la sécurisation des populations sur le plan hygiénique.[17] Cette mesure sécuritaire était une sorte de mise en quarantaine des différentes populations installées dans la ville minière. Elle voulait à la fois limiter les dégâts causés par l'éclosion des épidémies meurtrières (certaines recrues étaient porteuses des germes de maladies contagieuses). La mortalité parmi les travailleurs était si forte que l'UMHK avait acquis la réputation d'être une "dévoreuse d'hommes", donc un instrument de dépopulation. En 1914, le taux de mortalité parmi les travailleurs a augmenté de 117 pourcent, et en 1918 de 201 pourcent. En 1926, il a atteint 53 pourcent. Ces taux de mortalité élevés étaient dus non seulement à l'éclosion des épidémies meurtrières telles la tuberculose pulmonaire, la pneumonie, les ulcères tropicaux, la dysenterie bacillaire, la fièvre typhoïde, la grippe espagnole (1918–1919), mais aussi aux nombreux accidents de travail qui frappaient une population ouvrière non familiarisée avec l'outil de travail. À cette époque, le Haut-Katanga industriel était considéré par les Africains rescapés comme le pays de la mort. Les nombreux cas de désertion observés parmi la population peuvent être à juste titre considérés comme une protestation

---

15 Province du Katanga, *Comité régional du Katanga* (Elisabethville: 1921), 79.
16 Jean-Luc Vellut, "Les bassins miniers de l'ancien Congo belge. Essai d'histoire économique et sociale (1900–1960)," *Les Cahiers du CEDAF* 7 (1981), 68.
17 Donatien Dibwe dia Mwembu, "Lubumbashi: histoire et mémoire d'une ville industrielle" dans *Villes d'Afrique. Explorations en histoire urbaine*, éd. Jean-Luc Vellut (Paris-Tervuren: L'Harmattan, 2007). Voir aussi l'ouvrage de René Mouchet et Arthur Pearson, *L'hygiène pratique des travailleurs noirs en Afrique tropicale* (Bruxelles: Goemaere, 1922).

silencieuse des travailleurs face aux conditions de vie et de travail effroyables à l'UMHK.

La deuxième raison importante était d'éviter de dépayser les nouvelles recrues. De ce fait, les nouvelles recrues admises dans les camps ne se sentaient pas seules et abandonnées; elles étaient encadrées par les anciens travailleurs de leur ethnie ou tribu et pouvaient ainsi garder intactes les coutumes et mentalités du milieu ancestral.[18] Enfin, il était tout aussi indispensable, aux yeux de l'employeur, d'étouffer la nostalgie qui rongeait l'esprit des travailleurs.

Mais cet habitat séparé ne facilitait pas l'existence et le développement d'un espace de socialisation des populations noires qui se considéraient comme ennemies entre elles. "Le tribalisme", note Jean-Luc Vellut, "joua un rôle important dans les stratégies des pouvoirs coloniaux. Dans un premier temps, les agglomérations, les chantiers, les camps, furent quadrillés suivant les ethnies (les "races", disait-on), sans qu'il soit possible de savoir si cette politique fut imposée par les travailleurs ou, au contraire, par les autorités."[19]

A la longue, cette politique sécuritaire a fini par engendrer un esprit de tribalisme qui a entraîné des rivalités et des querelles entre différentes populations ouvrières qui se considéraient comme ennemies et croyaient trouver leur sécurité dans la présence du Blanc. Le cas des disputes entre les Rwandais et les Luba du Kasai à Kipushi en 1931 est illustratif:[20]

> Les troubles les plus graves eurent lieu au mois d'août de la même année, à Kipushi, où se trouvait la mine la plus moderne de l'UMHK. Située à 30 kilomètres d'Elisabethville, la mine prince Léopold était son premier siège d'exploitation souterraine. En raison des qualifications supérieures exigées pour travailler dans une mine souterraine, les salaires des Noirs y étaient les plus élevés du Congo. Craignant de perdre leur emploi, les 1.500 Kasaiens et les 1.000 Rwandais de la mine se querellaient constamment. Un Kasaien ambitieux, Tshimanga André, décida de profiter des désordres pour affirmer sa position de meneur. Il organisa une émeute parmi ses camarades du Kasaï contre les Rwandais, puis offrit de restaurer la paix à condition que l'Union Minière le reconnaisse comme chef des Kasaiens de Kipushi. Les administrateurs découvrirent aisément la manœuvre, renvoyèrent Tshimanga à son village et rapatrièrent les Rwandais.[21]

Cet incident malheureux en pleine crise économique mondiale amena les colonisateurs à changer de politique sécuritaire. L'Union Minière dut alors abandonner,

---

18 Kazadi Munga, "La vie des travailleurs africains dans le Haut-Katanga industriel, (1906–1929)" (Mémoire de licence en histoire, Université Nationale du Zaïre, 1979), 81.
19 Vellut, "Les bassins miniers de l'ancien Congo belge," 68.
20 Bruce Fetter, "African Associations in Elisabethville, 1910–1935. Their origins and development," *Etudes d'Histoire Africaine* Vol. VI (1974).
21 Bruce Fetter, "L'Union Minière du Haut-Katanga, 1920–1940: la naissance d'une sous-culture totalitaire," *Les Cahiers du CEDAF* 6 (1973): 33.

au début des années 1930, la politique d'habitat par région de provenance et décida de mélanger des travailleurs aussi bien au camp que dans le milieu de travail. D'où le nom de *tshanga-tshanga* (mélangeur; *kutshanga* = mélanger) attribué au chef de camp. A partir de ce moment, les travailleurs ont commencé à avoir des amis en dehors des frontières ethniques respectives et à parler la même langue, le kiswahili. Ils vont prendre ensemble leur verre de *munkoyo*, de *tshibuku*, de *lutuku* ou, plus tard, de bière *Simba* au camp, à la cité ou au cercle récréatif en dehors des heures de service. Avec le temps, ils ont constitué des équipes de football, de basketball etc.

Ces populations vivant ensemble ont fini par créer une grande famille sociologique. On les appelait "*ba mu Union Minière, ba mu BCK, ba mu Cité* (Les gens de l'Union Minière, les gens de BCK, les gens de la Cité), etc." Et, dans les camps de travailleurs, les populations s'appelaient par "frère" ou "soeur" *ndugu na nyumba*, pour signifier voisin ou voisine de maison; *ndugu na kiwanza*, pour dire voisin ou voisine de parcelle, *ndugu na musalani*, pour dire voisin ou voisine des toilettes, *ndugu na balabala*, pour dire voisin ou voisine de route, de rue etc.[22]

Dans les camps de travailleurs, les grosses entreprises ont créé leur propre police. A l'Union Minière, par exemple, on les appelait *malonda*. Chaque rue, chaque avenue était sous la surveillance des *malonda*, véritables yeux et oreilles du chef de camp ou *tshanga-tshanga*. En effet, rien ne se passait au camp à l'insu des *malonda*. Ce sont ces derniers qui dénichaient les irréguliers dans les camps, détectaient les malades qui se cachaient et ne voulaient pas se rendre au dispensaire pour leurs soins médicaux, ce sont toujours eux qui dénichaient et amenaient les visiteurs au bureau du chef de camp et assistaient à leur départ ou leur retour au village; c'est encore eux qui tranchaient des différends entre les femmes au marché, à la borne fontaine etc.[23] Tout ce qui se passait dans les camps était connu et rapporté au chef de camp.

La stabilisation de la main-d'œuvre exigea de l'entreprise l'adoption d'une politique de logement compatible avec la politique nataliste. Le logement devait être désormais adapté à la taille de la famille du travailleur. Aussi pouvait-on lire ceci dans les documents d'archives:

> Des maisons spacieuses de 2, 3 et même 4 chambres sont réservées aux familles nombreuses; un type de maisons plus coquettes que les huttes ordinaires est réservé à la

---

[22] Donatien Dibwe dia Mwembu, *Histoire des conditions de vie des travailleurs de l'Union Minière du Haut-Katanga/Gécamines (1910–1999)* (Lubumbashi: Presses universitaires de Lubumbashi, 2001), 44.
[23] Fetter, "L'Union Minière du Haut-Katanga," 33.

main-d'œuvre spécialisée (M.O.I./S). Chacune de ces maisons possède son petit enclos bien fermé, donnant ainsi satisfaction au noir qui aime à se sentir chez lui. Il faut éviter dans les camps d'y réserver des secteurs groupant soit des MOI/S, soit les travailleurs d'une même équipe, soit des hommes originaires d'une même région; si pour ces derniers le groupement peut être toléré et parfois même conseillé au début de leur première arrivée au chantier européen, afin qu'ils ne se sentent pas isolés dans la foule des camps, il convient dès que leur acclimatement est fait, de les loger en dispersion dans les camps. Chez le Noir en effet, l'esprit de caste ou de race, excité par la sensation du nombre, est une cause trop fréquente de bagarres néfastes à la bonne renommée d'un camp auprès des indigènes.[24]

Mais la croissance démographique dans les camps de travailleurs était telle qu'on assista à la résurgence de la promiscuité après les années 1960 alors que la superficie habitable était en augmentation aussi. Elle passa de 4,96 mètres carrés en 1953 à 5,11 mètres carrés en 1954 et à 7,17 mètres carrés en 1960.[25] Vint ensuite la construction des maisons jumelées.

Vers la fin des années 1940, l'UMHK devient victime de sa politique de stabilisation de la main-d'œuvre: on observa une certaine inadéquation entre l'évolution de la population ouvrière et le nombre de logement dans le camp de travailleurs. Pour la première fois, l'UMHK se mit en contradiction avec sa politique de mettre ses travailleurs à l'écart de la population du centre extra-coutumier, CEC en sigle. Pour juguler la crise de logement; les dirigeants de l'UMHK décidèrent d'envoyer les travailleurs dociles au CEC.

À la fin des années 1950, on assista à la modernisation de certaines maisons. Dans les maisons "modernisées", il fallait augmenter sensiblement la surface habitable par l'adjonction de pièces supplémentaires en fonction de la croissance démographique. Mais les maisons "modernisées" n'ont pas résolu le problème dans ce sens que l'entreprise ne parvenait toujours pas à loger tous ses travailleurs. De plus, nombreuses étaient les maisons non modernisées qui gardaient leur aspect des années 1940. Toujours à la fin des années 1950, on assista aussi à la construction des nouveaux types de maisons pour les fonctionnaires de l'UMHK, appelés à devenir les futurs agents de maîtrise après l'indépendance.

C'est surtout à l'approche de l'indépendance que l'Union Minière commença la modernisation des logements des travailleurs. Il fallait doter les maisons d'un confort moyen s'accordant au standing de la nouvelle catégorie professionnelle qu'elle venait de créer à savoir la "fonction" (catégorie professionnelle

---

24 Aide-mémoire, fascicule II. Politique indigène, Elisabethville, 1942, 13, Service d'Afrique, Union Minière du Haut-Katanga, Lubumbashi.
25 Dibwe dia Mwembu, *Histoire des conditions de vie des travailleurs de l'Union Minière du Haut-Katanga/Gécamines (1910–1999)*, 32.

intermédiaire entre le statut de maîtrise et de cadre et celui d'agent d'exécution). De cette catégorie sortiront, au lendemain de l'indépendance, les premiers cadres africains appelés à remplacer les cadres européens.

Dans les camps de travailleurs qui n'avaient pas bénéficié de beaucoup de modifications et avaient conservé des habitations construites du temps où la plupart des travailleurs étaient encore non-mariés ou mariés sans familles nombreuses, la situation du logement contribua au cours des années 1960 à la désarticulation des structures familiales. La promiscuité qui s'y manifestait venait de ce déséquilibre qui ne cessait de s'accroître entre la taille des familles et les types de maisons en présence.[26] Dans la plupart des cas, les cuisines étaient transformées en chambre à coucher pour les grands garçons. La nuit venue, les salons faisaient à leur tour office de chambre à coucher pour les petits enfants.

A la fin de l'année 1958, les dirigeants de l'UMHK instaurèrent le statut "fonctions spéciales". Il s'agissait des agents africains "ayant réuni des conditions professionnelles, morales et sociales indispensables" auxquels l'UMHK avait confié des fonctions importantes. L'Union Minière venait de créer une classe intermédiaire entre le personnel blanc et le personnel noir. Cette promotion semble plus liée à des qualités de socialisation qu'à des qualités professionnelles tant le critère "conditions morales et sociales" s'avère important. Le statut "fonctions spéciales" constituait une étape vers l'africanisation des cadres appelés à occuper des postes de commandement et de responsabilité à l'accession du pays à l'indépendance. L'africanisation des postes de responsabilité a été graduelle. Il ne fallait pas que les Blancs et les Noirs exercent les mêmes fonctions. C'est pourquoi il s'agit en fait des tâches abandonnées par des Blancs qui furent confiées aux Noirs. Somme toute, ces agents furent les premiers noirs à accéder, au lendemain de l'indépendance du Congo, au statut d'agents de maîtrise, statut réservé aux Blancs pendant toute la période coloniale.[27] Après l'accession du pays à l'indépendance, la fonction spéciale était considérée comme une étape de transition vers la classe 3 car l'ouvrier appartenant à la classe "fonctions spéciales" était après six mois promu agent de maîtrise[28]. Dans les camps de travailleurs, des maisons spéciales

---

26 Rapport annuel, 1970, 43, Archives du Département de la Rémunération du Personnel/Gécamines. Lubumbashi.
27 Le nombre des travailleurs africains promus au statut de personnel de cadre est passé de 84 agents au 31 janvier 1960 à 98 au 1 janvier 1961, à 139 agents au 1 janvier 1962. Cf. Rapport annuel, 1970, 110, Archives du Département de la Rémunération du Personnel/Gécamines. Lubumbashi.
28 Au sein de l'entreprise, il y a deux catégories de personnel: le personnel cadre et le personnel d'exécution. Au lendemain de l'indépendance, les Africains accèdent au statut d'agents de cadre. La catégorie personnel d'exécution est subdivisée en classes 5 à 8 et classe 4. Cette dernière constitue en fait une étape intermédiaire entre le personnel d'exécution et le personnel de cadre. La classe 8 comprend les manœuvres et les manœuvres spécialisés. Ces travailleurs

leur furent construites qui comprenaient, un salon, une salle à manger, une cuisine, plusieurs chambres à coucher, une douche et des WC intérieurs et un robinet externe dans la parcelle.

Avec la promotion professionnelle, l'employeur voulait créer une nouvelle solidarité entre les travailleurs, fondée sur base de la profession en lieu et place de la solidarité fondée sur la tribu ou l'ethnie. Mais il faut reconnaître que c'est cette dernière qui l'a toujours emporté sur la première.

En guise de conclusion

La ville de Lubumbashi a été construite sur base du principe de la sécurisation sous toutes ses formes. Elle a connu deux étapes importantes dans la conception de son habitat. Une première fracture spatiale a été causée par la ségrégation raciale. Ainsi naquirent deux villes blanche et noire séparées par une ceinture de sécurité hygiénique. Cette situation a vécu le temps qu'a vécu la colonisation. La ville noire, bastion des seuls Africains noirs, a connu une fracture spatiale liée, elle aussi, à une certaine sécurité. Le souci de sécuriser ses travailleurs contre l'influence des autres Noirs habitant de la ville noire a amené l'UMHK à construire à part et près de ses usines son camp de travailleurs. Là, elle a exercé tout son paternalisme. Même dans le camp de travailleurs, le problème de sécurité a dicté le comportement des autorités de l'Union Minière du Haut-Katanga dans la construction des maisons et même dans la distribution de ces maisons à ses travailleurs, selon qu'ils étaient célibataires ou mariés, selon la taille de la famille de ses travailleurs, selon aussi leur statut professionnel. Les camps de travailleurs de l'Union Minière/Gécamines sont devenus pendant la période coloniale des lieux de socialisation des familles des agents de cette entreprise avec une nouvelle identité collective, celle de *"ba Union Minière"* (les gens de l'Union Minière) ou encore *"ba-toto ba Union Minière"* (enfants de l'Union Minière).

---

exécutent généralement des travaux simples, qui ne nécessitent pas de connaissance particulière. Les travailleurs semi-qualifiés appartiennent à la classe 7. Cette catégorie comprend des gens ayant fait au moins 6 années d'études primaires. Les travailleurs qualifiés font partie de la classe 6. Cette classe comprend des travailleurs de niveau A^3 ou assimilé. La classe 5 comprend la catégorie de travailleurs hautement qualifiés dont les travaux exigent non seulement une connaissance générale et approfondie du métier, mais aussi une formation professionnelle et des qualités requises. La classe 4 comprend généralement des travailleurs détenteurs d'un diplôme d'études secondaires ou l'équivalent ou des travailleurs hautement qualifiés. La classe 3 comprend les agents de maîtrise assimilés aux cadres de l'entreprise. Le personnel de cadre est détenteur d'un diplôme d'enseignement supérieur ou universitaire.

Références

Archives

Archives du Département de la Rémunération du Personnel/G.C.M.-L'SHI, Rapports annuels, Lubumbashi, 1965.
Archives du Département de la Rémunération du Personnel/G.C.M.-L'SHI, Rapports annuels, Lubumbashi, 1970.
Archives du Service de cadastre, Ville d'Elisabethville, Procès-verbal de la réunion du comité urbain, Elisabethville,13 décembre 1951.
Union Minière du Haut-Katanga, Service d'Afrique. "Aide-mémoire, fascicule II. Politique indigène." Document d'archives, Elisabethville, 1942.

Références

Bonner, Philip, and Lauren Segal. *Soweto: A History*. Cape Town: Maskew Miller, Longman, 1998.
Dibwe dia Mwembu, Donatien. "Lubumbashi: histoire et mémoire d'une ville industrielle." Dans *Villes d'Afrique. Explorations en histoire urbaine*, édité par Jean-Luc Vellut, 131–144. Paris-Tervuren: L'Harmattan, 2007.
Dibwe dia Mwembu, Donatien. *Histoire des conditions de vie des travailleurs de l'Union Minière du Haut-Katanga/Gécamines (1910–1999)*. Lubumbashi: Presses Universitaires de Lubumbashi, 2001.
Fetter, Bruce. "African Associations in Elisabethville, 1910–1935. Their origins and development." *Etudes d'Histoire Africaine*, vol. VI (1974): 205–23.
Fetter, Bruce. "L'Union Minière du Haut-Katanga, 1920–1940: la naissance d'une sous-culture totalitaire." *Les Cahiers du CEDAF* 6 (1973): 1–40.
Kasongo Pauni, Pierre, et Donatien Dibwe dia Mwembu. "Vocabulaire de ville de Elisabethville, province du Katanga Oriental à Elisabethville", d'André Yav, dans *Lubumbashi 1910–2010. Mémoire d'une ville industrielle. Ukumbusho wa mukini wa komponi*, édité par Bogumil Jewsiewicki, Donatien Dibwe dia Mwembu, et Giordano Rosario, 33–71. Paris: L'Harmattan, 2010.
Lagae, Johan, et Sofie Boonen. "Un regard africain sur une ville coloniale belge: architecture et urbanisme dans le "Vocabulaire de ville de Elisabethville", d'André Yav". Dans *Lubumbashi 1910–2010. Mémoire d'une ville industrielle. Ukumbusho wa mukini wa komponi*, édité par Bogumil Jewsiewicki, Donatien Dibwe dia Mwembu, et Giordano Rosario, 107–24. Paris: L'Harmattan, 2010.
Mainet-Valleix, Hélène. *Durban. Les Indiens, leurs territoires, leur identité*. Paris: IFAS–Karthala, 2002.
Mouchet, René, et Arthur Pearson. *L'hygiène pratique des travailleurs noirs en Afrique tropicale*. Bruxelles: Goemaere, 1922.
Munga, Kazadi. "La vie des travailleurs africains dans le Haut-Katanga industriel (1906–1929)." Mémoire de licence en histoire, Lubumbashi, Université Nationale du Zaïre, 1979.

Mwilambwe, Claude. "Edouard Masengo Katiti." Dans *Musique urbaine du Katanga. De Malaika à Santu Kimbangu*, édité par Bogumil Jewsiewicki, 122–23. Paris: L'Harmattan, 2003.

Province du Katanga. *Comité régional du Katanga*. Elisabethville: 1921.

Van Bilsen, Jef. *Congo, 1945–1965. La fin d'une colonie*. Bruxelles: CRISP, 1994.

Vellut, Jean-Luc. "Les bassins miniers de l'ancien Congo belge. Essai d'histoire économique et sociale (1900–1960)." *Les Cahiers du CEDAF* 7 (1981): 1–70.

Daniela Waldburger
6 House, Home, Health and Hygiene – Social Engineering of Workers in Elisabethville/ Lubumbashi (1940s to 1960s) Through the Lens of Language Usage

Introduction

After the foundation of Elisabethville (nowadays Lubumbashi) in 1910, one of the most important players in the mining sector in Katanga was the *Union Minière du Haut-Katanga* (UMHK). Especially after in the 1930s, the International Labor Organization (ILO) was putting pressure on the UMHK to abandon forced labor and the UMHK had to search for a solution to secure its high demand for a permanent workforce. The company's strategy was to implement a huge project of social engineering, including a new employment policy called "stabilization". To foster this new strategy, in 1925 the UMHK founded a specialized department, the *Département Main d'Oeuvre Indigène*. Besides the provision of schools, hospitals, leisure facilities and, of course, housing for UMHK workers, the company and its owner, the Belgian colonial state, relentlessly pursued their ideas of cleanliness and hygiene. Hygiene was immanently linked to health and both aspects were monitored by authorities at different levels. On a larger scale, the Belgians' concern for hygiene and health was visible in their policy of segregation in the city[1] with different neighborhoods for the different city dwellers and a neutral zone (*cordon sanitaire*) in-between.[2] On a smaller scale, the house became one of the core objects of the Belgians' concern for hygiene. The provided housing was therefore not only a tool of social engineering but – as the analyzed discourse on concrete measures reveals – a constant topic in debates often linked with concerns of health and hygiene.[3]

---

[1] The segregation of a city was not a unique strategy of the Belgians but an approach taken also by the British and French colonial states.
[2] See also Dibwe dia Mwembu in this publication.
[3] For a discussion of the sanitation syndrome see e.g. Maynard W. Swanson, "The Sanitation Syndrome: Bubonic Plague and Urban Native Policy in the Cape Colony, 1900–1909," *The Journal of African History* 18, 3 (1977).

∂ Open Access. © 2020 Daniela Waldburger, published by De Gruyter. This work is licensed under a Creative Commons Attribution-NonCommercial 4.0 International License.
https://doi.org/10.1515/9783110601183-006

The Belgian colonial state and the UMHK planned houses for the workers that reproduced the colonizers' ideas of family and home in every sense. The house and its interior design defined the ideal size of a family and the distribution of duties within the household.[4] The worker's wife was supposed to secure a healthy and hygienic house to ascertain the productivity of the husband. She thus played a central role and became an addressee of the UMHK's different measures and channels of communication.

Writing about the ideal house for the staff of the colonial state in the Congo, Lagae[5] points out that:

> [H]ygiene remained a key issue in the discussions on the colonial house in Congo throughout the colonial period. To a large extent, nor architects neither engineers but doctors controlled the debate. The central argument of the hygienist discourse on the colonial house was simple: healthy living conditions generate a good health, and thus increase the efficiency and working capacities of the colonial.

In this paper[6] I will illustrate the UMHK's "civilizing" measures based on four interconnected topics (i.e. house, home, hygiene, and health) by analyzing the language usage through a variety of texts in which the respective authors argue for their specific position. By doing so, I put the discourse on these topics in focus. I follow Bendel-Larcher's definition of discourse.[7] She states that discourse is a social process of understanding how to interpret and shape the world and that a discourse is modeled by the material reality (such as body painting, clothes, architecture or urban planning) and therefore takes effect on it through social practices. Discourse manifests itself in concrete texts that represent the knowledge and reasoning of a particular time. If we want to investigate why

---

[4] For a discussion on the definition of social engineering see Etzemüller (2010). He hints at the organization of space as one of the central domains of social engineering (he refers e.g. to Ebenezer Howard's plan of the garden city) and specifies that city planners not only planned on larger scales (e.g. cities) but also on smaller ratios such as an apartment or a house. He discusses the example of a "functional" apartment, where spatial segregation prevents undesirable behavior, such as the blending of areas for sleeping, cooking and personal hygiene. Mixing these spatial domains was considered problematic from an ethical and hygienic viewpoint. Thomas Etzemüller, "Social Engineering, Version: 1:0," *Docupedia-Zeitgeschichte* (11.2.2010): 7–8, accessed November 20, 2018.

[5] Johan Lagae, "In Search of a 'comme chez soi.' The Ideal Colonial House in Congo, 1885–1960," in *Itinéraires croisés de la modernité Congo belge, 1920–1950*, ed. Jean-Luc Vellut (Paris & Tervuren: L'Harmattan, 2001), 242.

[6] This paper was written within the scope of the Austrian Science Fund granted project "Employment-tied Housing in (post)colonial Africa" (Project no. P29566-G28, Department of African Studies, University of Vienna). For further information see: housing.univie.ac.at

[7] Sylvia Bendel-Larcher, *Linguistische Diskursanalyse* (Tübingen: Narr, 2015), 16.

certain ideologies prevail at a given time, we must first reveal the ideological background based on texts.[8] Texts, of course, contain several topics. In my contribution, I will highlight parts of texts that approach the same topic(s). The fragments of discourse that share a topic are threads of a discourse. The discourse level is the social locus from where a statement is made (in spoken or written form). These levels are closely intertwined with the discourse position, a term that refers to the ideological locus of the speaking person, group or medium.

In my analysis, I aim to reveal the perceptions of house, home, health, and hygiene via its discursive realization to gain a better understanding about the discourse positions of the actors involved in the process of social engineering. All involved actors (the colonial state, the company, but also the workers) participated in the negotiation processes on what was relevant at a specific moment in time.

For this paper, the textural cores (i.e. material reality) for my analysis are, firstly, official publications of the Belgian colonial state such as *À chacun sa maison*.[9] Such publications offer an insight into the ideologies prevalent at the time of Belgium's colonial policy that formed the basis for the UMHK's strategies and decisions. Therefore, the second source of texts is from the company: the company-owned journal *Mwana Shaba*[10] and the minutes of different of UMHK[11] board meetings from the corresponding years.

Communication, including negotiation processes, was based on the very trivial fact that those communicating needed to make sure that they would be understood. The choice of French was obvious for UMHK minutes, as these

---

[8] For a comprehensive overview on discourse analysis see e.g. Bendel-Larcher, *Linguistische Diskursanalyse*. Siegfried Jäger, *Kritische Diskursanalyse: Eine Einführung* (Münster: Unrast, 2012), 80, 83. Walter Schicho, "Diskursanalyse" in *Qualitative Methoden in der Entwicklungsforschung*, ed. Petra Dannecker and Birgit Englert (Wien: Mandelbaum, 2014), 135.
[9] Editions du Bureau de l'Information pour Indigènes (INFIND), Service des A.I.M.O. du Gouvernement Général, *À chacun sa maison* (Kalina, 1953).
[10] Accessed at the Library of Contemporary History in the Royal Museum for Central Africa, Tervuren, Belgium. *Mwana Shaba* is the Swahili term to describe a copper worker and, as the journal's name reveals, the potential readers were the workers of UMHK's copper mines. This journal contains information about the company, pages for distraction, riddles, information on lifestyle, reports about other countries, letters to the editors, information about the political situation etc. *Mwana Shaba* was published on a monthly basis and was written in French and Swahili. The journal reached a readership of approximately 28,000 workers, plus respective family members living in the same household.
[11] In the state archives in Brussels, Archives générales du Royaume 2 – Dépôt Joseph Cuvelier, the minutes of the different boards are available, from the foundation of UMHK in 1906 until the company became *Gécamines* in 1966 and later UMICORE.

documents were intended for internal use and communication with the metropolis Brussels.¹² But French was – in combination with Swahili – also the language chosen for publications of the Belgian colonial state such as *À chacun sa maison*.

Even though in primary education the colonial authorities generally gave preference to the use of African rather than European languages, they promoted French[13] with regard to "secondary education [which] was always, and in all locations, organized around French as the sole medium of instruction, except in most technical schools and in teacher training schools."[14] The colonial state could therefore proceed from the assumption that the Congolese readership had proficiency in French; moreover, Meeuwis describes how the Congolese demanded education in French, as they did not want to be inhibited from upward social mobility by a language barrier. However, the workers of the mines were not necessarily highly proficient in their colonizers' language, as not all of them received formal education. Moreover, workers were recruited from diverse regions of the Congo and thus brought their different languages to Elisabethville. Swahili (the language also strongly promoted by the missionaries) represented the *lingua franca* in the mining camps and later became the first language in the region.[15]

The languages used in *Mwana Shaba* were French and – to a lesser degree – Swahili. The editors often advertised information bilingually as will be shown further below. The UMHK's language policy for *Mwana Shaba* reflects their wish to be understood – hence, their choice of Swahili – but also their aim to educate their workers. Also, in the minutes of the meetings of the Department of the UMHK *Service d'Afrique*,[16] it was explicitly stated that French and Swahili should be used for *Mwana Shaba*.

---

[12] For a comprehensive overview of the Belgians' controversial subject of the role of Dutch and French in the metropolis, but also in the colony, see Michael Meeuwis, "Bilingual Inequality: Linguistic Rights and Disenfranchisement in Late Belgian Colonization," *Journal of Pragmatics* 43 (2011).
[13] Meeuwis, "Bilingual Inequality."
[14] Meeuwis, "Bilingual Inequality," 1280.
[15] Aurélia Ferrari, Marcel Kalunga and Georges Mulumbwa, *Le Swahili de Lubumbashi* (Paris: Karthala, 2014), 107. Daniela Waldburger, "Swahili in Eastern Congo: Status, Role and Attitudes," in *Pluricentric Languages and Non-Dominant Varieties Worldwide*, ed. Rudolf Muhr (Frankfurt am Main; Bern; Bruxelles; New York; Oxford; Warszawa; Wien: Peter Lang, 2016), 149.
[16] Rapport Annuel 1959, Union Minière du Haut-Katanga – Services d'Afrique, Département M.O.I., AGR 2, n°658, 57.

In the following, I will first provide some background information on the (urban) history of Lubumbashi (Elisabethville) and the UMHK in order to then discuss the UMHK's mission of social engineering by illustrating the themes of house, home, health and hygiene based on the above-mentioned text types that were produced by the involved actors. The colonial endeavor of social engineering is thus looked at through the lens of linguistic representation of power strategies. I argue that the Belgian colonial state and the UMHK acted on the basis of paternalism to control and stabilize the workforce. The provision of housing was one of their means of surveillance. The company's decisions in favor of specific house types and of the disposition of interior design were discussed from a technical perspective, but they deceitfully imposed an ideologically biased understanding of domesticity on the workers and their families.

Lubumbashi (Former Elisabethville) and the Union Minière du Haut-Katanga

Elisabethville was founded in 1910 by the Belgian Government two years after it had taken over the colony from King Leopold II.[17] Belgium chose this location because of its geo-political importance. The Belgian Government wanted to control the British influence from Northern Rhodesia and South Africa which went hand-in-glove with the railroad construction in the region. The railroad became Katanga's first and main link to the outside world until the late 1920s.[18] The site was chosen because of its proximity to the already existing copper mine of *Etoile du Congo* and the copper-ore smelting oven installed by the UMHK on the nearby Lubumbashi River but also to keep an eye on the English-speaking Europeans who were already developing mines as well the railroad in the Copperbelt.[19]

The first European quarter of Elisabethville was planned as early as 1910. One year later, an African quarter was formed, but it lay separate from the European quarter with a distance of 170 meters. This so-called *zone neutre* was

---

[17] For a comprehensive overview of the history of Elisabethville see e.g. Bruce Fetter, *The Creation of Elisabethville, 1910–1940* (Stanford: Hoover Institution Press, 1976).
[18] Johan Lagae and Sofie Boonen, "A City Constructed by 'des gens d'ailleurs': Urban Development and Migration Policies in Colonial Lubumbashi, 1910–1930," *Comparativ: Zeitschrift für Globalgeschichte und vergleichende Gesellschaftsforschung* 25, no. 4 (2015): 52.
[19] Fetter, *The Creation of Elisabethville*, 3.

not unique for Elisabethville but typical for colonial urban planning elsewhere and reflected the colonial state's concerns of sanitation and hygiene.[20]

In the center of the mining area in Katanga, one of the most significant players was the UMHK. This company was founded in 1906 and for about 100 years, it was the most important mining company of the Congo. Hence, the history of the UMHK and the history of Lubumbashi/Elisabethville were closely linked, as the following quote also illustrates:

> [T]he town lived according to the rhythm of the Union Minière/Gecamines which regulated the lives of its personnel from birth to death: the company housed and fed them, sent missions to the country side to seek spouses for the worker, educated their children, planned their leisure and so on. (Dibwe 2001) A proverb stated that 'the Union Minière [or alternatively: salaried work] is the father and the mother' (Union Minière [kaji] njo baba, njo mama).[21]

The city and work were inseparable, as Dibwe dia Mwembu describes.[22] He stresses that in order to stay in Elisabethville (and later Lubumbashi)[23] a person needed a contract of employment. The formal sector reigned supreme. The informal was excluded, absent or pretended to be unknown. Work had deeply influenced the urban mentality, and the public image of the city even influenced the neighboring territory of Northern Rhodesia in a positive manner.

To maintain a profitable mining sector, the UMHK not only needed to recruit but also to accommodate a rapidly increasing number of workers. The company did so by creating workers' camps for bachelors in close proximity to their mines

---

20 Lagae and Boonen, "A City Constructed by 'des gens d'ailleurs'," 56–57. For Lubumbashi in the 1920s Lagae states: "While both hospitals were erected outside the grid of the ville européenne, the hospital for Africans was located within the so-called zone neutre, the cordon sanitaire introduced in the early 1920s as a buffer zone between the ville européenne and the first native town, the commune Kamalondo. [...] The hospital for the white community was built on the opposite side, at the largest possible distance from where lived the majority of the native population." Johan Lagae, "Towards a Rough Guide for Lubumbashi, Congo: Rethinking 'shared built heritage' in a former Belgian colony," http://bk.home.tudelft.nl/fileadmin/Faculteit/BK/Actueel/Symposia_en_congressen/African_Perspectives/Programme/African_Architectures/doc/APD_wp_5_lagae_paper.pdf, accessed July 3, 2018.
21 Pierre Petit and Georges Mulumbwa Mutambwa, "'LA CRISE': Lexicon and the Ethos of the Second Economy in Lubumbashi," *Africa* 75, no. 4 (2005): 470.
22 Donatien Dibwe dia Mwembu, "Lubumbashi: histoire et mémoire d'une ville industrielle," in *Villes d'Afrique: explorations en histoire urbaines*, ed. Jean-Luc Vellut (Paris: L'Harmattan, 2007), 138.
23 In 1966, the city's name was changed from Elisabethville to Lubumbashi.

in the early years. But very soon, the UMHK also started to build houses for workers and their families. On 9 December 1941, the mining workers in Elisabethville went on strike as a culmination point of a longer wave of protest.[24] Their main goal was to demand higher wages to meet rising living costs. While the workers assembled, the situation got out of control and at least 20 workers died. The strike and the subsequent uncertainty took place in the middle of the Second World War when the copper industry crucially mattered as a backbone of Belgium's economic strength. At that time the stabilization of workforce was highly important to the UMHK: "The strike wave of 1941 clearly shows that the around 17,000 workers were not content with the working and living conditions in *Union Minière*'s mines and compounds. The company portrayed itself as a considerate employer and displayed photos and films of smiling workers, clean hospitals, and happy families."[25] It is against this backdrop that the project of social engineering started.

Social Engineering and Stabilization

The project of social engineering was played out by the UMHK on different layers. Not only were the work and the housing situation of workers controlled but equally so education or leisure activities. In 1956, the UMHK produced a series of films celebrating its fiftieth anniversary. One of these films, entitled *En Cinquante Ans*[26] (*In 50 Years*), portrayed the workers' lives, the benefits of being an UMHK employee, however, not work itself. The housing facilities provided were displayed, as well as all the advantages from healthcare to courses offered to workers and their wives. One particular scene portrayed a family sitting around a table in their home. A tablecloth protected the table, some

---

24 For further details see e.g. Donatien Dibwe dia Mwembu, *Histoire des conditions de vie de travailleurs de l'Union Mininère du Haut-Katanga/Gécamines (1910–1999)* (Lubumbashi: Presses universitaires de Lubumbashi, 2001). Julia Seibert, "'Wind of Change': Worker's Unrest and the Transformation of Colonial Capital in Katanga – Belgian Congo," in *Work and Culture in a Globalized World: From Africa to Latin America*, ed. Babacar Fall, Ineke Phaf-Rheinberger and Andreas Eckert (Berlin & Paris: Karthala, 2015).
Julia Seibert, *In die globale Wirtschaft gezwungen: Arbeit und kolonialer Kapitalismus im Kongo (1885–1960)* (Frankfurt: Campus, 2016).
25 Seibert, "Wind of Change," 263.
26 *En Cinquante Ans*, accessed June 23, 2018, https://www.youtube.com/watch?v=9z4GtyCvlCg&sns=em.

flowers were arranged in the middle, the head of the family was sitting at the end of the table, and all members of the family were gathered to enjoy the meal with fork and knife. They enjoyed the food cooked by the wife and were combining the best of what in the film is called the "art" of European cuisine with the "traditional" cuisine. Not only the workers but also the workers' wives were supposed to attend different types of courses, from childcare to shoe shining. The UMHK covered all possible aspects of life and conditioned the workers and their families according to the Belgian ideal of middle-class life. Typical Sundays were accurately described to be very similar to the Sundays in Europe with going for a walk and meeting friends. The scene ended with a shot of a table outside in the garden with several persons sitting around a table that was covered by a tablecloth and glasses perfectly laid out on the table. Using the medium of film, the UMHK made propaganda not only for the workplace but also for the very life they offered their workers, thereby presenting the company's perception of a family life. At its very center were the house and domesticity.

The UMHK tried to stabilize the workforce by ensuring that workers stayed healthy and were emotionally balanced. The film mentions that 80 percent of the workers then (1956) were married. A married man was considered to be even-tempered and taken well care of. Hunt points out that the Belgian authorities as well as missionaries were concerned about the demographic pattern in their colony, with men outnumbering women.[27] Therefore, the hint in the film to the nearly balanced ratio between men and women shows the UMHK's awareness of this topic and their pride of the achieved demographic pattern.

The alleged balanced ratio between men and women in workers' camps as presented in the film differed from the situation outside the camps. In the camps, married women were presented to have a stronger position especially compared to the unmarried women in the city where "[c]olonial commentators thought women in the cities were floundering, disoriented, vulnerable, and corruptible due to idleness, excessive leisure, and a void of custom. The notion that the moral authority of customary culture did not extend to urban centers was ubiquitous in Belgian colonial discourse."[28]

Moreover, the UMHK was fighting against customary culture and especially tried to suppress bigamy, as the annual reports of the *Département Main d'Oeuvre*

---

[27] Nancy Rose Hunt, "Domesticity and Colonialism in Belgian Africa: Usumbura's Foyer Social, 1946–1960," *Signs: Journal of Women in Culture and Society* 15, no. 31 (1990): 451.
[28] Hunt, "Domesticity and Colonialism in Belgian Africa," 451.

Indigène reveal. A section on *parasitism* appeared each year. In 1948, for instance, the UMHK stated that they would continue to fight against bigamy:[29]

Nous avons continué notre campagne contre la bigamie et divers cas spéciaux montrant à quels résultats peut conduire la bigamie ont été exposés aux C.I.E. Certains travailleurs ont encore essayé de prendre en défaut notre vigilance. Il existe certainement encore dans nos camps des cas de bigamie, déjà anciens, contre lesquels la réaction sera plus difficile et où, actuellement, la seule attitude possible est d'ignorer la seconde femme. Ce n'est que petit à petit, par une inlassable propagande éducative que nous pourrons définitivement éliminer ces situations anormales. Il faut aussi espérer que le Gouvernement donnera suite au voeu[sic] exprimé par le Conseil de Gouvernement – Session 1948 – de voir interdire progressivement la polygamie dans les centres extra-coutumiers.[30]	We continued our campaign against bigamy, and various special cases showing to which results bigamy can lead were exposed to C.I.E. Some workers have again tried to defect our vigilance. There are certainly still cases of bigamy in our camps, old ones, against which the reaction will be more difficult and where, at present, the only possible attitude is to ignore the second woman. It is only little by little, by a tireless educational propaganda that we can once for all eliminate these abnormal situations. It is also hoped that the Government will respond to the wish expressed by the Governing Council – Session 1948 – to progressively ban polygamy in extra-customary centers.

Bigamy is described with the adjective "abnormal." The UMHK's concern had thus an ethical background, as the existence of several wives was not in line with the idea of the nuclear family, but bigamy also constituted a financial problem. Workers acknowledged the – according to Europeans' perspective – illegitimate children and demanded the same rights with respect to housing, education, and food rations, for these children and their mothers as they were granted for the official wife and children. In the annual report of 1947, the UMHK's financial concerns were explicitly verbalized: *"Enfin, au moment où des charges sociales de plus en plus lourdes viennent grever le budget des employeurs de main d'oeuvre indigène, il importe que soit nettement défini le Statut de la famille indigène."*[31]

The UMHK's decisions and strategies in the project of social engineering mirrored the Belgian colonial state's ideas of development for the colony. In 1949, the Belgian colonial Government introduced a 10-year plan for the

---

29 Rapport Annuel 1948, Union Minière du Haut-Katanga – Services d'Afrique, Département M.O.I., AGR 2, n°654–03043, 18.
30 All translations are by the author.
31 "Finally, when increasingly heavy social charges are burdening the budget of employers of native labor, it is important that the status of the indigenous family is clearly defined." Rapport Annuel 1947, Union Minière du Haut-Katanga – Services d'Afrique, Département M.O.I., AGR 2, n°654-03042, 21.

economic and social development of the Congo,[32] which included important infrastructure projects, such as public buildings and housing facilities for the Congolese.[33] One of the proposed plans was the so-called *Système Grévisse*. Ferdinand Grévisse was a district officer of that time who published a study about so-called "native quarters" in Lubumbashi. In his view, Africans should be motivated to build the houses themselves, of course under strict supervision and under consideration of a long list of constraints.[34] The idea of the *Système Grévisse* was that the colonial state builds the foundation to ensure the right size and exact location of the house on a parcel of land, but that its future inhabitants should build the houses themselves from the material provided by the government at a good price. Ideally, this would minimize the costs, as no construction company was involved and many pre-fabricated parts such as windows, doors, and roofs would be used. For Grévisse[35] himself, the social component was equally important. He argued that such a scheme would lead to the stabilization of the lives of urban Africans and it would be easier to incorporate them in the colonial administration.[36] The director of human resources of the *Département Main d'Oeuvre Indigène*, Dr. L. Mottoule, defined the company's stabilization policy in 1946 as "*l'emploi de tous les moyens normaux propres à amener le travailleur noir à aimer le travail et à y rester attaché le plus long possible.*"[37] The policy included a number of measures aimed at binding the workers to the UMHK in the long term.[38] Brausch points out that the stabilization was successful: "This paternalistic policy, which so irritates the champions of social freedom, produced nevertheless a remarkable stabilisation of labour and encouraged the establishment of workers' settlements with a fairly good demographic equilibrium."[39]

---

[32] Ministère des Colonies, *Plan décennal pour le Développement économique et social du Congo belge* (Brussels: Editions de Visscher, 1949).
[33] Johan Lagae, "Modern Living in the Congo: The 1958 Colonial Housing Exhibit and Postwar Domestic Practices in the Belgian Colony," *The Journal of Architecture* 9, no. 4 (2004): 479.
[34] Alice Chapelier, *Elisabethville – essai de géographie urbaine* (Brussels, 1957), 47–49, 65.
[35] Ferdinand Grévisse, *Le Centre Extra-Coutumier d'Elisabethville: quelques aspects de la politique indigène du Haut-Katanga industriel* (Brussels: Institut Royal Colonial Belge, 1951).
[36] See also Boonen and Lagae in this publication.
[37] "The use of all the normal means necessary to bring the black worker to love the work and to remain attached to it as long as possible." L. Mottoule, *Politique sociale de l'Union Minière du Haut-Katanga pour sa main d'oeuvre indigène* (Brussels, 1946). Citation in: *Union Minière du Haut Katanga* 1906–1956, N.N., (1956), 242.
[38] Seibert, "Wind of Change," 261.
[39] Georges Brausch, *Belgian Administration in the Congo* (Oxford: Oxford University Press, 1961), 13.

The stabilization came at the price of a constant surveillance of the UMHK workers. As pointed out in *Mwana Shaba*,⁴⁰ workers were requested to always carry the plastic identity and working card with their picture, which was a document that indicated the workplace and job title of the worker, and a family register booklet. *Mwana Shaba* published this notification in French and Swahili to ensure that everybody would understand the ordinance.

As work was the element linking the colonial state, the UMHK and the employees, it is worth looking at the perception of the concept of work. Dibwe dia Mwembu discusses three different stages of a temporal perception of work (*kazi* in Swahili) by workers of which the second is relevant for the time focus of this paper. While approximately up to the 1940s *kazi* was considered slavery, after World War II the perception of *kazi* gained a very positive connotation equaling *kazi ni maisha mzuri* (work means a good life).⁴¹ This experience of having a good life was due to the appreciation workers experienced when the UMHK needed their workforce and thus provided them with rich social services and amenities. Fabian discusses the meaning of the word *kazi* (work) on a semantic level:

> In Katanga Swahili the noun *kazi* may cover a wide range of activities, moods, attitudes, and attributes. [...] In some expressions a specific denotation may be due to idiomatic usage, e.g. in the often heard *kaziyako* "that's your business, it's up to you, go to hell." It may also be achieved through a context-specific contrast such as in the opposition between *furaha* and *kazi* [...]. But the overwhelming majority of expressions in which *kazi* has a specified meaning is based on complexes formed with the connective particle {a}, especially those which function as characterizations. These may signify a trade or profession: *kazi ya mwalimu* "being a teacher;" a type of employment: *kazi ya Union Minière* "being employed by the Union Minière;" a degree of exertion, effort: *kazi ya nguvu* "hard work." Similarly we find that most verbal expressions are complex, combining a verb with the noun *kazi* and often adding further specifications through the connective {a}. Examples are *kufanya kazi ya chauffeur* or *kutumika kazi ya chauffeur* "to work as a driver."⁴²

Why is the perception relevant here? I argue that, when focusing on the analyzed time period, work was experienced as the source of a good life, that the house was one, if not the central, element of this experience of the good life. The life of a worker was defined by work itself, while the status of the position was relevant for the allocation of housing in general, and the type of house in

---

40 *Mwana Shaba*, no. 123, 15 April 1966, 15.
41 Donatien Dibwe dia Mwembu, "La Perception du kazi (travail salarié) par les travailleurs de la Gécamines (1910–2010)," in *La Société congolaise face à la modernité (1700–2010): mélanges eurafricains offerts à Jean-Luc Vellut*, ed. Mathieu Zana Etambala and Pamphile Mabiala Mantuba-Ngoma (Paris & Tervuren: L'Harmattan, 2017), 163–167.
42 Johannes Fabian, "Kazi: Conceptualizations of Labor in a Charismatic Movement among Swahili-Speaking Workers," *Cahiers d'études africaines* 13, no. 50 (1973): 304–305.

particular. In the "slavery" phase of work, housing for workers basically was a shelter and workers were housed in poor conditions. However, after the Second World War, work was more and more linked to reputation and social security, and this materialized in the house itself. Moreover, the house offered many possibilities to shape the everyday life of Congolese workers and their families. In other words, the house (i.e. the home) was a main target for social engineering. In the following, I will extract fragments of discourse in some publications by the UMHK and the Belgian government, which refer to house, home, health, and hygiene to demonstrate the linguistic strategies of persuasion of workers by the UMHK and the Belgian government.

Voices of the Belgian Colonial State and the UMHK

Paternalism

Against the backdrop of the 10-year plan for the development of the Congo, let us first have a look at the publication *À chacun sa maison* first published in 1953. The Belgian colonial state's Office for the Information of the Native People published and distributed this brochure for free. It was written in order to motivate the Congolese to build their houses along the lines of Grévisse's philosophy.

The preface of the brochure explicitly stated that, "*nous avons voulu aider le plus grand nombre d'entre vous à faire de ce rêve une réalité.*"[43] The "we" was the Belgian colonial state while the "you" were the Congolese. This opposition of "we", the Belgians, and "you", the Congolese, was often combined with the paternalistic approach of the Belgians, like in the following sentence which also appeared in the preface:

Nous exprimons le souhait que, si vous lisez aujourd'hui cette brochure sous un toit étranger, vous ayez dans quelques mois le plaisir de la relire confortablement installé dans la maison attrayante que le conseils et instructions données plus loin vous auront permis de bâtir.	We express the wish that, if you read this brochure today under a foreign roof, you will have the pleasure of rereading it in a few months comfortably installed in the nice house that the advices and instructions given later will have allowed you to build.

With this wording the Congolese were not attributed an active role; they were presented as beneficiaries of the colonial state's welfare. Jean Jadot, a well-known engineer working for the Belgian colonial state, explicitly referred to the welfare

---

43 "We wanted to help as many of you as possible make this dream become true."

thought as follows: *"N'oublions jamais que la seule justification de notre action coloniale, c'est le bien que nous faisons aux populations indigènes."*⁴⁴

Also, Grévisse used the paternalistic style when he pointed to the urgency of achieving hygienic standards to protect the population from consequences of poor hygiene and cited a medical report:

Dès la fin de 1912 se posent à la cité indigène de très sérieux problèmes d'hygiène. Les habitants se ravitaillent en eau dans un dembo. Cette eau est polluée par les baigneurs, les lavandières et les animaux divaguant. A ce moment, un premier rapport médical souligne l'urgente nécessité de prendre des mesures pour protéger 'la population si cruellement décimée jusqu'à présent.'	As early as the end of 1912, the native city faced a very serious problems of hygiene. The inhabitants refuel water in a *dembo*. This water is polluted by swimmers, washing women and wandering animals. Right now, a first medical report underlines the urgent need to take measures to protect 'the population so cruelly decimated so far.'

But not only the Belgian colonial state but also the UMHK positioned the workers in the same beneficiary role and, in addition, often criticized them. As shown above, this occurred in the company's campaign against *parasitism*. The voice of the UMHK is available through the administrative and technocratic language style in the minutes of the different kind of board meetings. As far as workers' demands are concerned, they were (only) presented in form of a bullet list, without comments, which therefore does not reveal anything about the company's point of view on those demands. The company's mindset regarding the workers becomes visible in the comments on evening courses for the workers. In the annual report of 1950, the courses for general education were introduced as following:⁴⁵

Donne aux illettrés et semi-lettrés l'occasion d'augmenter leur bagage en lecture Kiswahili, calcul, dessin, et notions de français parlé. Prépare aux Cours de Perfectionnement Professionnel. Fonctionne régulièrement dans certains sièges, moins bien dans d'autres. Le Noir ne considère que l'intérêt immédiat. Sa grande ambition est de connaître le français, signe extérieur de civilisation. Calcul, mesure, dessin, langue maternelle, lui semblent superflus.	Give the illiterate and semi-literate an opportunity to increase their proficiency in reading Kiswahili, calculation, drawing, and notions of spoken French. Prepare for professional development courses. Work regularly in some places, less well in others. The black considers only the immediate interest. His great ambition is to know French, an outward sign of civilization. Calculation, measurement, drawing, mother tongue, seem superfluous to him.

---

44 "Let us never forget that the only justification for our colonial action is the good we are doing to the native people." Citation in: André-Bernard Ergo, *Congo Belge – La colonie assassinée* (Paris: L'Harmattan, 2009), preface.
45 Rapport Annuel 1950, Union Miniére du Haut-Katanga – Services d'Afrique, Département M.O.I., AGR 2, n°655–03046.

On House, Home, Health and Hygiene

With the following sentence, readers were introduced to *À chacun sa maison*:

*Qui n'a rêvé d'être propriétaire d'une **jolie maison**, d'avoir à soi **un vrai foyer** où se retrouvent chaque jour **l'époux dévoué, la femme aimante et de beaux enfants pleins de santé**?* (emphasis added)	Who is not dreaming of being the owner of a **nice house**, having a real home where every day **a self-sacrificing wife, the loving woman and handsome healthy children** are waiting?

The introduction to this brochure, dedicated to technical aspects on how to construct houses, started with a presentation of the house, which was characterized as being the place of the "real home." What was presented was the idea of what a home should be, rather than the house as a materialized object itself. Home and house were thus discursively linked.[46] In addition, children were described as healthy, and health and hygiene were closely connected as will be presented later.

The brochure burst with advice which was visually identifiable by boxes, with capital letters. Young, newly wed husbands were also among the potential readers:

JEUNE MARIE! *N'oublie jamais, en choisissant le plan de ta maison, que tu es appelé à devenir père d'une famille peut-être nombreuse. Il est moins coûteux de construire grand dès le début que faire des agrandissements plus tard!* (15)	YOUNG HUSBAND! Never forget, by choosing the plan of your house, you are encouraged to become the father of a potentially large family. It is less costly build big from the beginning than to make enlargements later!

This idea of a home and the provision of sufficient space for all members of the family was repeated over and over in similar words and phrases. The Belgian colonial state's concern for enough space for the family – as it becomes clearer in a section about the ventilation of the house – was not linked with their idea of comfort for the inhabitants but rather with the concern for hygiene. What the "neutral zone" was for the city, "sufficient space" was for the house. Hygiene was thus one of the main fragments in the discourse on house and home, not only in this brochure but also for the colonial state. The discourse fragments of technical and constructional aspects of the interior were not only linked with

---

46 In Swahili the expression for "at home" *nyumbani* stems from the noun for "house", *nyumba*, which gets a locative-suffix – *ni*. In Swahili therefore, there is no lexical difference of "at/in the house" and "home".

questions of domesticity but also with the colonizers' ideas to control hygiene and health.

The idea of the so-called evolution was another aspect prominently featured in the publication. The introduction of the brochure offered an overview of the Belgians' assumption about the history of the house in the Congo and opened with a reference to what the Belgians considered the simplest form of a traditional Congolese house. A picture of a cave illustrated what was described as not comfortable.[47] Several pages were then dedicated to the different types of houses. It was a demonstration of the evolution of housing types with increasing influence by European houses. Finally, the ideal house for a Congolese was presented under the name *maison de pisé influencée par l'architecture européenne*[48] (clay house influenced by European architecture). The house was praised for being appealing and the reader learnt that adding some changes to the traditional house would be sufficient so that – without investing a lot more money – the house would become *plus saine et plus agréable* (a healthier and more pleasant home). Again, a box with bold and capital letters concluded this section and referred to health:

CIVILISATION implique MAISONS SAINES ET CONFORTABLES	CIVILIZATION implies HEALTHY AND COMFORTABLE HOUSES

---

47 In "Vocabulary of Elisabethville" Yav describes the housing situation of domestic servants in the years after King Leopold's death. In contrast to the Belgians' assumptions (Congolese are happy with caves etc.), the domestic servants in Elisabethville complained early about the unsuitable housing situation offered by their employers. For instance, "as far as sleeping goes they failed us by building for us those outhouses which have remained the same up to now.", "They were big trouble, those many Whites when they lived in Termite Hills [Termite Hills was the first white settlement in Elisabethville, DW]. Then we boys lived in true misery.", "Because they thought [it good] to build for the black man just a one-room-house. [But] this man had his wife and his children some of them male, some of them female. When he goes to work, the poor boy, when he wakes up, he says to all his grown-up children: Mothers and fathers, you must excuse me. Get up and leave, or go first outside. Me, your old man, I want to put on my clothes first. Truly, then the man's children began to file out, out of respect because their father wanted to get dressed so he could go to work.", "And should this White man have two rooms, enough to give both to his employee, the boy, he puts a lock on it [to make it] his chicken coop or rabbit hutch." Johannes Fabian, *History from Below: The "Vocabulary of Elisabethville" by André Yav, Text, Translations, and Interpretive Essay* (Amsterdam & Philadelphia: John Benjamins, 1990), 71, 75.

48 "*Mais l'existence des habitants des cavernes ne devait guère être confortable, comme le laisse supposer la photo ci-dessous.*", 5. Editions du Bureau de l'Information pour Indigénes (INFIND), Service des A.I.M.O. du Gouvernement Général, À chacun sa maison (Kalina, 1953), 5.

Another publication which gave significant importance to the concept of health and hygiene was the UMHK's journal *Mwana Shaba*. In that sense, the persuasive intention of the company to socially engineer the workers remained a continuous feature in the colonial as well as the postcolonial era.[49]

In an article from 1967, *Mwana Shaba*[50] offered a brief outline of workers' housing in Lubumbashi. Photographs showing the old and new refurbished houses illustrated the text. This article appeared when the shortage of housing had again become a serious problem. An interview with Mr. Mulunda, head of the Housing Service Department, complemented the descriptive part of the text. The voice was given to an individual explaining the measures that were taken to improve the situation. He answered the question of his interviewer who wanted to know about the used materials for the new houses for the workers:

Elles répondent toutes aux exigences de l'hygiène et du confort. Dans les nouveaux quartiers, vous trouverez toutes les maisons pourvues de distribution d'eau, d'une douche et de l'éclairage électrique. [...] Avec un peu de persévérance, les travailleurs peuvent aménager un jardin coquet et bien fleuri.	They all meet the requirements of hygiene and comfort. In the new neighborhoods, you will find all houses provided with water supply, a bathroom and electric lighting. [...] With a little endurance, workers can develop a pretty flower garden.

Once again, the focus lays explicitly on hygiene (and comfort), with explanations of what that meant in terms of technical equipment. Evidently, the editors did not take it for granted that workers generally showed enough effort, otherwise they would not have added this complement. Workers were constantly assessed as unable to anticipate.

But already years before, in 1949, in the annual report of UMHK's *Département Main d'Oeuvre Indigène* the company had expressed its lack of understanding that workers did not possess *"le mobilier que l'on pourrait raisonnablement s'attendre à trouver chez eux."*[51] The company stressed that workers would indeed have had enough money and that the situation could only be explained by the workers' lack of discipline:

---

[49] By 1966 *Gécamines* was the successor to the UMHK and by then a state-controlled company, but *Mwana Shaba* was still published.
[50] *Mwana Shaba*, no. 147, 15 October 1967, 2–4.
[51] "Furniture that we could reasonably expect to find at home." Rapport Annuel 1949, Union Minière du Haut-Katanga – Services d'Afrique, Département M.O.I., AGR 2, n°655-03045, 23.

Nous ne pouvons, pour expliquer cet état de choses, que répéter les raisons que nous invoquions dans notre Rapport de 1948, c'est à dire notre refus de vendre à crédit et l'imprévoyance di noir qui ne sait pas s'imposer la discipline de l'économie. Nous sommes cependant tentés d'y ajouter l'influence du jeu et l'abus des boissons qui prennent de plus en plus d'extension.	To explain this situation, we can only repeat the reasons we invoked in our 1948 report, that is, our refusal grant credit [to buy the furniture] and the improvidence of the black who is unable to show thrifty discipline. We are, however, tempted to add the influence of gambling and the abuse of drinks that are becoming more and more extensive.

The company linked the alleged lack of discipline in financial issues with a lack of discipline in other domains, such as the lack of willingness to buy adequate furniture. The worker was presented as attracted by gambling and alcohol – two leisure activities that led to spending money in the presumedly wrong way. Hence, the lack of discipline was discursively linked with the lack of furniture, the materialized object of what constituted a home. A year later, furniture was again an issue mentioned in the annual report. The UMHK had tried to sell simple and cheap furniture to the workers but failed:[52]

Le Département a renoncé à intervenir pour procurer aux travailleurs, du mobilier simple et peu coûteux. Cette initiative n'a pas rencontré le succès qu' on attendait. Il se confirme que l'amélioration du confort dont s'entoure le travailleur, ne peut résulter que d'une lente mais persistante action éducative.	The Department has refrained from intervening to provide workers with simple and inexpensive furniture. This initiative did not meet the expected success. It seems that the improvement of the comfort of which the worker surrounds himself can only result from a slow but persistent educational action.

Interestingly though, in the annual report from 1960, the members of the *Département Main d'Oeuvre Indigène* explicitly claimed that the company should sell furniture to workers.[53] Furniture was a recurring topic throughout the years without significant changes regarding the point of views of the company or the workers. The UMHK tried to sell furniture, stopped again, tried again, while workers expressed their concerns as regards prices that were considered too high. In the end, the UMHK had the workers pegged as lacking financial discipline.

---

[52] Rapport Annuel 1950, Union Minière du Haut-Katanga – Services d'Afrique, Département M.O.I., AGR 2, n°655-03046, 12.
[53] Rapport Annuel 1960, Union Minière du Haut-Katanga – Services d'Afrique, Département M.O.I., AGR 2, n°636, 88.

Another topic with which housing was discursively linked was technical facets. In the annual report of 1947, the UMHK uttered a very brief idea of the ideal family home under the section "housing" which usually discussed more technical issues:[54]

Des logements de 2, 3 et même 4 pièces sont réservés aux familles nombreuses. Outre les pièces d'habitation proprement dites, il existe une cuisine. Les derniers types de logement, adoptés en 1946, sont conçu de telle façon qu'on pourra plus tard y ajouter un "living-room" spacieux, doté d'une cuisinière en fonte où la ménagère pourra préparer les repas en saison froide, la cuisine se faisant en saison chaude dans une annexe, le fournil de chez nous. Si on obtient, grâce à ce living où se réunira la famille, que la femme y prépare les repas, y vive avec son mari et ses enfants et, dernière mais difficile étape, que les repas y soient pris en commun, un pas énorme sera réalisé vers l'évolution de la femme indigène et la constitution de familles suivant la conception européenne.	Houses of 2, 3 or even 4 rooms are reserved for big families. If not mentioned otherwise, there exists a kitchen. The latest type of houses (adopted in 1946) were planned so that one can later add a spacious living-room, equipped with a cooking range made of cast iron where the housewife can prepare the meals in the cold season, while in the warm season meals are prepared in an annex [...]. If, thanks to this living room, we achieve that the family sits together, that the woman prepares the meals there, that she lives there together with her husband and their children, and – the last and most difficult step – that the meals are partaken of together, then a huge step for the evolution of the native woman as well as the constitution of the family according to the European concept will be realized.

Like in the above discussed brochure, *À chacun sa maison*, the house – in this case the kitchen and the living room – was not only referred to in technical terms. These two rooms represented the location of an idea, namely the Europeans' ideology of the ideal family and the role of the woman as the responsible one for the preparation of the meals to be shared in the living room. The kitchen and the living room served as a place to project ideas of social engineering. The ideal home was the place where the worker ideally spent his leisure time with his wife and children, with furniture he was able to afford because he withdrew from gambling and drinking alcohol.

Mwana Shaba also had a section dedicated to *le vrai savoir vivre* (the real art of living). Workers were able to read about lifestyle questions such as how to eat with a fork and knife or new technologies, such as how to make or receive a phone call and the corresponding social behavior. Under the section *Votre Page Madame (Your Page Madam)*, a section dedicated to the wives of the

---

[54] Rapport Annuel 1947, Union Minière du Haut-Katanga – Services d'Afrique, Département M.O.I., AGR 2, n°654-03042, 29.

workers, a picture of a flower arrangement was introduced by the following words:⁵⁵

Garnissez votre intérieur, rendez-le accueillant.	Garnish your interior, make it welcoming.
Fleurissez-le, et votre mari, le soir, sera heureux après sa journée de travail de retrouver son beau foyer, et d'y rester...	adore it with flowers, and in the evening your husband will be happy after his day's work to find his beautiful home, and stay there...

The flower bouquet was not only presented as a home decoration but first and foremost as a tool for emphasizing after-work domesticity of the husband. The imperative form chosen to address the housewife further attributed to her the power and responsibility to help condition a productive worker. Flower arrangements in the Belgian Congo were promoted by missionaries' ideas of domesticity⁵⁶ and were later popularized by *foyers sociaux* (social homes) which were "Belgian domestic training institutions for African women, founded for married women living in colonial urban centers. Some women were learning to cook, mend, iron, and wash clothes, and how to wean their infants and decorate their homes, and a selected few were being trained to work (for pay) as auxiliary aids or monitors in the classroom."⁵⁷ Thus, workers were useful to the colony as labor force, while women were ensuring the reproduction of the labor force.⁵⁸ The knowledge of household tasks such as arranging flowers was therefore only one of the many reflections of colonial attempts of social engineering of the Congolese.⁵⁹

Votre page madame offered a wide variety of topics considered important for women by the editors, from ideas about hairstyle to the importance of handbags or recipes for the loving husband. These "civilizing" ideas of how a woman should be and of how she should behave were often linked – to the UMHK's idea of hygiene, from proper nails for proper women to the proper way of childcare. Another example within the same domain of hygiene and health referred to the big cleaning of the house (*le grand nettoyage*) which was published in the very

---

55 *Mwana Shaba*, no. 13, Dec. 1964.
56 See Hunt, "Domesticity and Colonialism in Belgian Africa." Nancy Rose Hunt, *A Colonial Lexicon of Birth Ritual, Medicalization, and Mobility in the Congo* (Durham, NC: Duke University Press, 1999), 83, 153, 249, 254; Peter Lambertz, *Seekers and Things: Spiritual Movements and Aesthetic Difference in Kinshasa* (Oxford/New York: Berghahn, 2018), 99.
57 Hunt, "Domesticity and Colonialism in Belgian Africa," 447.
58 Hunt, "Domesticity and Colonialism in Belgian Africa," 451.
59 Lambertz points out in Chapter 3 of his monograph that flower arrangements were a totally new concept for the Congolese. Flowers were associated with plants and plants were used for traditional medicine and not as a decorative object. Lambertz, Peter. Seekers and Things: Spiritual Movements and Aesthetic Difference in Kinshasa. Oxford and New York: Berghahn, 2018.

first issue of *Mwana Shaba* in 1965. In a highly detailed manner, every step of a big cleaning was described. Readers learnt, for instance, that the woman was expected to make use of a wet cleaning rag, know how to scrub the clothes and many more details. As a term, however, "the big cleaning" also referred to general suggestions. It was deemed inappropriate if children slept in dirty clothes. They were supposed to be clean and to sleep in a clean bed. Moreover, it was lectured that insects must either not enter a house or be relentlessly dispelled. The article ended with the notification that UMHK's *service d'hygiène* would regularly enter the house to disinfect the rooms. Insects, more particularly anopheles mosquitos, represented not only a threat to an individual's health but constituted a major threat to the productivity of the UMHK worker.

Voices of UMHK's Workers

In 1947, the UMHK established the *Conseil indigène d'entreprise* whose members were selected by the workers themselves. The company listened to the demands and suggestions of these members, as these representatives of the workers attended the company meetings.

The annual reports of the UMHK's *Département Main d'Oeuvre Indigène* reveal the company's view on housing issues in many subcategories linked to the workforce, such as numbers of workers, legal aspects, pension schemes, infrastructure, the organization of leisure activities, housing etc. Among the topics discussed and recorded in writing are also the lists of demands by the *Conseil indigène d'entreprise* directed at the company. As these demands were written down by a member of this board, they do not represent the direct voices of the workers but at least offer an understanding of the workers' concerns and opinions.

In the following, the claims by the members of the *Conseil indigène d'entreprise*, as reported in the annual reports from 1947 to 1965,[60] shall illustrate that the demands were very diverse; they illustrate the link between house, home, health, and hygiene and that the house was part of the infrastructure provided. The workers expressed, among other things, concerns that schools were progressively closed, a path to have access to the cemetery, permission of mothers to stay with a child who is hospitalized, a bicycles parking area close to the

---

60 See primary sources: Rapports Annuels 1947–1965, Union Minière du Haut-Katanga – Services d'Afrique, Département M.O.I., AGR 2.

workplace, the reopening of the canteens in the *Cité*,[61] signs for toilets in the *Cité* indicating *femmes* (women) and *hommes* (men) etc. Most demands by the workers in the minutes of these annual reports touched on themes linked to work, health issues (e.g. hospitals), social activities and, more generally, the life in the *Cité* as well as the services provided – from food distribution to films projected during the movie nights and pension schemes.

The workers' demands related (besides work issues themselves, such as working hours, safety regulations etc.) to houses as well as the infrastructural environment. One category around which the demands concentrated was the provision of electricity. Electrification was generally urgently demanded and, over the years, dissatisfied workers repeatedly demanded electric light in each room of the house. Some of the requests were very detailed and included the wish for quicker replacement of broken electric bulbs or an increase of the hours with illumination. Another issue raised concerning infrastructure was water. On the one hand, workers demanded that the company distributed water containers to the houses, while on the other hand they explicitly expressed their desire to have running water in all houses. Equally, the shortage of water was repeatedly raised, as was the bad quality of water or problems with water pressure. Furthermore, health, hygiene, and disinfection were equally important to the workers. They asked for the distribution of disinfectant or a better quality of the insect control drugs. The provision of litter bins was likewise claimed.

As regards the houses, the toilet, a basic object linked to hygiene, was a topic of permanent request, as the council kept raising the demand for provision of toilets in all houses. Individual toilets, showers and sinks were requested as well as the fact that toilets should adjoin the houses. Other issues linked to the house concerned the demand for floors made of concrete (including in the old houses), the repair of houses, a wooden balcony and a *cusinière bantoue* (i.e. a simpler charcoal stove), more wood for cooking and heating or sinks situated also outside the house. Generally, the council claimed access to bigger and more modern houses during several years, with a special emphasis on bigger houses for big families and/or houses with bigger windows and interior doors. The doors represent by far the most frequently discussed subject matter among the house-related complaints. Workers requested the installation of interior doors in the houses during several years or asked that the process of the installation of the interior doors should be speeded up. Other laments referred to the quality and the type of doors. Requests for specific doors were

---

61 The term *Cité* refers to the area in Elisabethville where workers were accommodated by the UMHK.

doors to separate the dining room from the living room, dividing walls between shower and toilet or to have a second exterior door. Other physical structure related requests also popped up, such as the size and quality of windows or the quality of the paint and chalk used for the interior; workers equally asked for a projecting roof to store charcoal and new or renovated kitchens.

The main concerns remained the same over many years: water, electricity, and doors. Repeated requests for doors that could be locked from the inside might allude to the workers' need to gain some privacy. The workers' concerns also increasingly reflected health and hygiene issues, as mosquito nets, disinfection drugs, and the waste problem started becoming topics. Starting as of the 1960s, the demands changed and were more frequently linked with their wish for more comfort, like having more rooms, getting more modern kitchens, and services such as public phones nearby.

This long list of demands by the workers is the only information we can filter out of the annual reports about their concerns, even though, as mentioned above, the demands were minuted by the UMHK. There are no sources that reveal how the negotiation process actually unfolded, how the members of *Conseil indigène d'entreprise* argued for their claims or the counterarguments the company put forward. While the UMHK's viewpoints in the discussion with the *Conseil indigène d'entreprise* were sometimes well documented, the workers' ideological locus was silenced, as their voice is reduced to a bullet list of technical topics in the annual reports.

Conclusions

The UMHK's policy of stabilization was a way to control all aspects of the workers' lives from birth to death. The company took care of housing for the workers, provided food, health care, leisure activities etc. The UMHK and the Belgian colonial state conditioned the workers in every sense. As has been shown above, the Belgian colonial state and the UMHK acted with a paternalistic attitude that intruded on nearly every domain of the workers' everyday life. The paternalistic approach is manifested in the constant "othering" of the Congolese. The UMHK saw its "other" – the workers – mainly as beneficiaries in need of guidance. In addition, publications by the UMHK (like *Mwana Shaba* or the issues mentioned in the annual reports) and by the Belgians presupposed that the Congolese needed to be educated or that they lacked discipline. The provision of housing was one of UMHK's major means of surveillance.

The ideological locus of the Belgian colonial state and the UMHK is identifiable in the topics and the fragments of discourse they chose to combine in their discussion on housing issues. Not only in official state propaganda publications but also in annual reports by the UMHK, the discourse fragment of "house" (i.e. the material provided) was constantly coupled with several other fragments which equally intersect: firstly, with "home" as the location of domesticity, the place of wife and children; secondly, with "health" as a standard to be ensured in the house, guaranteeing that the husband stayed a profitable employee (the family's health was, for the same reasons, likewise important); thirdly, with "hygiene" as the basis for health which became an issue of general importance.

The ideological locus of the workers cannot be identified, but based on the topics they submitted, we do at least get an idea of their concerns and demands as has been shown on the basis of the minutes of the UMHK meetings with the *Conseil indigène d'entreprise*. Against this backdrop, it can be assessed that the workers' notion of a healthy and hygienic house largely corresponded with the social notions and cultural paradigms of the Belgian colonial state and the UMHK. Workers' requests did not differ from what workers would have requested in the metropolis. Smaller differences, such as the demand for the "Bantu kitchen", might have existed.

As has been discussed, the Belgians and the UMHK linked the concept of the house to their policy of social engineering. Thus, the Belgian colonial state's advice for the construction of houses, along with the UMHK's arguments and decisions for specific types of houses, as well as other issues regarding workers' housing, did not merely represent a discourse on technical measures – even though interior design, for instance, was discussed in technical terms (e.g. the ideal location of the stove in the kitchen). The technical discourse imposed the Belgian colonial state's and the UMHK's ideologically biased understanding of domesticity on the workers and their families.

References

Archival Sources

State archives in Brussels, Belgium, Archives générales du Royaume 2 – Dépôt Joseph Cuvelier, Première série (AGR 2)

N°634 Union Minière du Haut-Katanga – Services d'Afrique, Département M.O.I.: Rapport Annuel, 1958.

N°635 Union Minière du Haut-Katanga – Services d'Afrique, Département M.O.I.: Rapport Annuel, 1959.

N°636 Union Minière du Haut-Katanga – Services d'Afrique, Département M.O.I.: Rapport Annuel, 1960.
N°637 Union Minière du Haut-Katanga – Services d'Afrique, Département M.O.I.: Rapport Annuel, 1961.
N°638 Union Minière du Haut-Katanga – Services d'Afrique, Département M.O.I.: Rapport Annuel, 1962.
N°639 Union Minière du Haut-Katanga – Services d'Afrique, Département M.O.I.: Rapport Annuel, 1963.
N°640 Union Minière du Haut-Katanga – Services d'Afrique, Département M.O.I.: Rapport Annuel, 1964.
N°654-03042 Union Minière du Haut-Katanga – Services d'Afrique, Département M.O.I.: Rapport Annuel, 1947.
N°654-03043 Union Minière du Haut-Katanga – Services d'Afrique, Département M.O.I.: Rapport Annuel, 1948.
N°655-03045 Union Minière du Haut-Katanga – Services d'Afrique, Département M.O.I.: Rapport Annuel, 1949.
N°655-03046 Union Minière du Haut-Katanga – Services d'Afrique, Département M.O.I.: Rapport Annuel, 1950.
N°656-03049 Union Minière du Haut-Katanga – Services d'Afrique, Département M.O.I.: Rapport Annuel, 1952.
N°657-03051 Union Minière du Haut-Katanga – Services d'Afrique, Département M.O.I.: Rapport Annuel, 1954.
N°657-03052 Union Minière du Haut-Katanga – Services d'Afrique, Département M.O.I.: Rapport Annuel, 1955.
N°657-03053 Union Minière du Haut-Katanga – Services d'Afrique, Département M.O.I.: Rapport Annuel, 1956.
N°657-03054 Union Minière du Haut-Katanga – Services d'Afrique, Département M.O.I.: Rapport Annuel, 1957.
N°658 Union Minère du Haut-Katanga – Services d'Afrique, Département M.O.I.: Rapport Annuel, 1959.

Library of Contemporary History, Royal Museum for Central Africa, Tervuren, Belgium

Mwana Shaba, no. 13, December 1964.
Mwana Shaba, no. 1, January 1965.
Mwana Shaba, no. 10, October 1965.
Mwana Shaba, no. 123, 15 April 1966.
Mwana Shaba, no. 147, 15 October 1967.

Secondary literature

Bendel-Larcher, Sylvia. *Linguistische Diskursanalyse*. Tübingen: Narr, 2015.
Brausch, Georges. *Belgian Administration in the Congo*. Oxford: Oxford University Press, 1961.
Chapelier, Alice. *Elisabethville – essai de géographie urbaine*. Brussels, 1957.

Dibwe dia Mwembu, Donatien. *Histoire des conditions de vie de travailleurs de l'Union Minière du Haut-Katanga/Gécamines (1910–1999)*. Lubumbashi: Presses universitaires de Lubumbashi, 2001.
Dibwe dia Mwembu, Donatien. *Bana Shaba abandonnés par leur père: Structures de l'autorité et histoire sociale de la famille ouvrière au Katanga (1910–1997)*. Paris: L'Harmattan, 2001.
Dibwe dia Mwembu, Donatien. "Lubumbashi: histoire et mémoire d'une ville industrielle." In *Villes d'Afrique: explorations en histoire urbaines*, edited by Jean-Luc Vellut, 131–144. Paris: L'Harmattan, 2007.
Dibwe dia Mwembu, Donatien. "La Perception du kazi (travail salarié) par les travailleurs de la Gécamines (1910–2010)." In *La Société congolaise face à la modernité (1700–2010): mélanges eurafricains offerts à Jean-Luc Vellut*, edited by Mathieu Zana Etambala and Pamphile Mabiala Mantuba-Ngoma, 161–176. Paris & Tervuren: L'Harmattan, 2017.
Éditions du Bureau de l'Information pour Indigènes (INFIND), Service des A.I.M.O. du Gouvernement Général. *Á chacun sa maison*. Kalina, 1953.
Ergo, André-Bernard. *Congo Belge – La colonie assassinée*. Paris: L'Harmattan, 2009.
Etzemüller, Thomas. "Social Engineering, Version: 1:0." *Docupedia-Zeitgeschichte* 7–8 (11.2.2010). https://docupedia.de/zg/Social_engineering?oldid=75535. Accessed November 20, 2018.
Fabian, Johannes. "Kazi: Conceptualizations of Labor in a Charismatic Movement among Swahili-Speaking Workers." *Cahiers d'études africaines* 13, no. 50 (1973): 293–325.
Fabian, Johannes. *History from Below: The "Vocabulary of Elisabethville" by André Yav, Text, Translations, and Interpretive Essay*. Amsterdam & Philadelphia: John Benjamins, 1990.
Ferrari, Aurélia, Marcel Kalunga, and Georges Mulumbwa. *Le Swahili de Lubumbashi*. Paris: Karthala, 2014.
Fetter, Bruce. *The Creation of Elisabethville, 1910–1940*. Stanford: Hoover Institution Press, 1976.
Grévisse, Ferdinand. *Le Centre Extra-Coutumier d'Elisabethville: quelques aspects de la politique indigène du Haut-Katanga industriel*. Brussels: Institut Royal Colonial Belge, 1951.
Hunt, Nancy Rose. "Domesticity and Colonialism in Belgian Africa: Usumbura's Foyer Social, 1946–1960." *Signs: Journal of Women in Culture and Society* 15, no. 31 (1990): 447–474.
Hunt, Nancy Rose. *A Colonial Lexicon of Birth Ritual, Medicalization, and Mobility in the Congo*. Durham, NC: Duke University Press, 1999.
Jäger, Siegfried. *Kritische Diskursanalyse: Eine Einführung*. Münster: Unrast, 2012.
Lagae, Johan. "In Search of a 'comme chez soi'. The Ideal Colonial House in Congo, 1885–1960." In *Itinéraires croisés de la modernité Congo belge, 1920–1950*, edited by Jean-Luc Vellut, 239–282. Paris & Tervuren: L'Harmattan, 2001.
Lagae, Johan. "Modern Living in the Congo: The 1958 Colonial Housing Exhibit and Postwar Domestic Practices in the Belgian Colony." *The Journal of Architecture* 9, no. 4, (2004): 477–94.
Lagae, Johan. "Towards a Rough Guide for Lubumbashi, Congo. Rethinking "Shared Built Heritage" in a Former Belgian Colony." http://bk.home.tudelft.nl/fileadmin/Faculteit/BK/Actueel/Symposia_en_congressen/African_Perpectives/Programme/African_Architectures/doc/APD_wp_5_lagae_paper.pdf. Accessed July 3, 2018.
Lagae, Johan, and Sofie Boonen. "A City Constructed by 'des gens d'ailleurs': Urban Development and Migration Policies in Colonial Lubumbashi, 1910–1930." *Comparativ: Zeitschrift für Globalgeschichte und vergleichende Gesellschaftsforschung* 25, no. 4 (2015): 51–69.

Lambertz, Peter. *Seekers and Things: Spiritual Movements and Aesthetic Difference in Kinshasa*. Oxford and New York: Berghahn, 2018.
Meeuwis, Michael. "Bilingual Inequality: Linguistic Rights and Disenfranchisement in Late Belgian Colonization." *Journal of Pragmatics* 43 (2011): 1279–1287.
Ministère des Colonies. *Plan décennal pour le Développement économique et social du Congo belge*. Brussels: Editions de Visscher, 1949.
Petit, Pierre, and Georges Mulumbwa Mutambwa. "'LA CRISE': Lexicon and the Ethos of the Second Economy in Lubumbashi." *Africa* 75, no. 4 (2005): 467–487.
Schicho, Walter. "Diskursanalyse." In *Qualitative Methoden in der Entwicklungsforschung*, edited by Petra Dannecker, and Birgit Englert, 127–512. Wien: Mandelbaum, 2014.
Seibert, Julia. "'Wind of Change': Worker's Unrest and the Transformation of Colonial Capital in Katanga – Belgian Congo." In *Work and Culture in a Globalized World: From Africa to Latin America*, edited by Babacar Fall, Ineke Phaf-Rheinberger, and Andreas Eckert, 253–271. Berlin & Paris: Karthala, 2015.
Seibert, Julia. *In die globale Wirtschaft gezwungen: Arbeit und kolonialer Kapitalismus im Kongo (1885–1960)*. Frankfurt: Campus, 2016.
Swanson, Maynard W. "The Sanitation Syndrome: Bubonic Plague and Urban Native Policy in the Cape Colony, 1900–1909." *The Journal of African History* 18, no. 3 (1977): 387–410.
Waldburger, Daniela. "Swahili in Eastern Congo: Status, Role and Attitudes." In *Pluricentric Languages and Non-Dominant Varieties Worldwide*, edited by Rudolf Muhr, 149–163. Frankfurt am Main; Bern; Bruxelles; New York; Oxford; Warszawa; Wien: Peter Lang, 2016.

Ambe Njoh and Liora Bigon
7 Spatio-physical Power and Social Control Strategies of the Colonial State in Africa: The Case of CDC Workers' Camps in Cameroon

Introduction

Among the many indelible imprints of European colonialism on the landscape of African countries are company towns. Defined as settlements built, owned and operated by corporations or individual investors, company towns have been influential in countries undergoing rapid economic development.[1] As an instrument of "economic pioneering", these towns played a major role in opening up previously unexploited regions in Europe and North America from the eighteenth to the early nineteenth century.[2] In Africa, these towns were built and used by colonial authorities not only to open up previously unexploited areas but also as instruments of power and social engineering. In the first instance, company towns, and especially workers' camps, were employed to articulate the power of colonial authorities in built space.[3] In the second instance, company towns and the concomitant lifestyle-change they engendered were used as a conduit for transmitting Eurocentric ideals of work and general conduct to the worker. Despite their presence as a conspicuous feature of the landscape, company towns remain a largely ignored topic in academic discourse in Cameroon and other erstwhile colonial states. Consequently, many questions about company towns are yet to be answered. What is their form and function in developing countries? In what ways did/do they contribute to the realization of colonial/postcolonial development goals? This chapter seeks to address these questions. In particular, it employs workers' camps and company towns of the Cameroon Development Corporation (CDC) to show how such facilities were, and continue to serve as, tools of power and social control in a developing country.

---

1 John D. Porteous, "The Nature of the Company Town," *Transactions of the Institute of British Geographers* 51 (1970).
2 Porteous, "The Nature of the Company Town." James B. Allen, *The Company Town in the American West* (Norman, Oklahoma: Oklahoma University Press, 1966).
3 Ambe J. Njoh, *Planning Power: Town Planning and Social Control in Colonial Africa* (London/New York: University College London Press, 2007).

Open Access. © 2020 Ambe Njoh and Liora Bigon, published by De Gruyter. This work is licensed under a Creative Commons Attribution-NonCommercial 4.0 International License.
https://doi.org/10.1515/9783110601183-007

This contribution takes off in the next section with an overview of the power theoretical framework. This is followed with a brief history and description of CDC employee housing as an important feature of built space in Cameroon. A subsequent section analyzes company towns as an instrument for the articulation of power and maintenance of social order in the built environment of colonial and postcolonial Cameroon. The chapter ends with a discussion of the future of company towns as well as some suggestions for further research on the subject.

Power in Urban Planning Discourse

One factor that appears to have eluded the attention of analysts for a long time is the importance of physical space in the articulation of power in social intercourse. This situation significantly changed once urban planning critics began challenging the view of planning as a neutral tool designed to promote spatial order and conceived of planning as a tool of power and social control.[4] A foremost social critic, Michel Foucault in *Discipline and Punish*, characterized planning as a tool for expressing negative institutional oppression.[5] On this score, he referred to Jeremy Bentham's 1791 plan for the *Panopticon*. The *Panopticon* was an elaborate plan for an incarceration facility.[6] Its most conspicuous features included a semi-circular structure, a centrally-located inspection ledge which was circumscribed by cells, a shrewdly designed lighting system, and a set of wooden blinds. This latter feature would ensure that the prison guards could see, but could not be seen by, the inmates. This design would be effective in impressing upon the inmates that they are under the constant watch of the

---

[4] Ambe J. Njoh and Liora Bigon, "The Toponymic Inscription Problematic in Urban Sub-Saharan Africa: From Colonial to Postcolonial Times," *Journal of Asian and African Studies* 50 (2013). Ambe J. Njoh, "Urban Planning as a Tool of Power in Africa," *Planning Perspectives* 24 (2009). Nicola Cooper, "Urban Planning and Architecture in Colonial Indochina," *French Cultural Studies* 11 (2000). Kim Dovey, *Framing Places Mediating Power in Built Form* (New York and London: Routledge, 1999). Zeynep Çelik, *Urban Forms and Colonial Confrontations: Algiers under French Rule* (Berkeley and London: University of California Press, 1997). Gwendolyn Wright, *The Politics of Design in French Colonialism Urbanism* (Chicago, IL: University of Chicago Press, 1992). Anthony D. King, "Exporting Planning: The Colonial and Neo-colonial Experience," in *Shaping an Urban World*, ed. Gordon E. Cherry (New York: St. Martin's Press, 1980). Janet. L. Abu-Lughod, *Rabat: Urban Apartheid in Morocco* (Princeton, NJ: Princeton University Press, 1980).

[5] Michel Foucault, "The Politics of Health in the Eighteenth Century," in *Michel Foucault, Power Knowledge: Selected Interviews and other Writings, 1972–1977*, ed. Colin Gordon (Brighton: Harvester Press, 1980), 166–182.

[6] Foucault, "The Politics of Health."

prison guards. This would ensure that inmates behave according to the dictates of the powers. In this case, physical objects – including the set of wooden blinds, the centrally-located inspection ledge and semi-circular structure – would contribute to making the inmates behave in ways they would ordinarily not, or perform tasks in a manner they would not otherwise.

The articulation of power in urban space can be seen as an extension of the use of physical objects to discipline as in the case of inmates in facilities such as the *Panopticon*. It is in this light that strategies to manipulate space can be characterized as tools of power.[7] Dovey has identified five different ways, including force, coercion, seduction, manipulation, and segregation, in which urban planning has been employed to articulate such power.[8] Force in built space entails the use of physical structures designed to confine individuals within a certain locale. Coercion alludes to the latent use of force wherein there is a threat but not the actual use of force. This type of force finds expression in built space through the use of buildings of grandiose scale and/or embellished with superfluous décor. Such buildings are often designed to advertise the resourcefulness of their owners. Seduction refers to tactics and strategies promoting an idea, artefact or way of life. Efforts on the part of colonizers to acculturate and assimilate the colonized typically involved seduction. Segregation entails the construction of boundaries or pathways for the purpose of separating or compartmentalizing built space along racial, socio-economic, or other lines. Efforts to segregate human settlements along racial lines by authorities in colonial Africa are illustrative.[9] Concomitant with this is often an effort to impose a socially constructed hierarchical structure on the affected groups. In colonial East and Southern Africa, human settlements were divided into three hierarchically arranged zones to accommodate Europeans, colored people comprising mainly people of Indian descent, and members of the native population.[10]

Colonialism and Plantation Agriculture in Cameroon

Cameroon was initially colonized by the Germans (1884–1916). However, Bismarck, the German Chancellor, had extended imperial protection to the

---

[7] Njoh, "Urban Planning." Cooper, "Urban Planning." Çelik, *Urban Forms*.
[8] Dovey, *Framing Places*.
[9] Njoh, "Urban Planning." Liora Bigon, "Bubonic Plague, Colonial Ideologies, and Urban Planning Policies: Dakar, Lagos, and Kumasi," Planning Perspectives 31 (2016).
[10] Njoh, "Urban Planning."

territory in 1882, two years before the formal onset of the colonial era. The Germans were attracted to Cameroon mainly by the country's agricultural potential.[11] Consequently, soon after the formal annexation of the territory on 12 July 1884, German colonial authorities proceeded speedily to convert the land around Mount Cameroon into German Crown land. By 1885, according to some accounts, the German colonial government under Von Puttkamer had confiscated approximately 400 square miles of land in said area.[12] This resulted in the displacement of thousands of Bakweri people – that is, natives of the Mount Cameroon region. In fact, the German colonial land confiscation plan included a provision that encamped most of the displaced persons in reservations (*Reservate*).

The encampment of members of the indigenous population, whom colonial authorities pejoratively called "natives", in reserves was not the only scheme concocted by German colonial authorities to free land for plantation agriculture. Another scheme designed to accomplish this objective entailed drastically reducing the quantity of land available to members of the indigenous population. This scheme was effectively implemented in Tiko.[13] During the German colonial era, Tiko, then known as Keka, was a small fishing village on the Atlantic Coast at the foot of Mount Cameroon. A number of soil tests conducted by the German colonial government in 1892 attested to Tiko's suitability for plantation agriculture.[14] The revelation heightened the German colonial government's desire to procure the land for agro-plantation development purposes. The government's strategy to realize this desire entailed conducting a census. The census, which was completed in 1908, revealed that Tiko contained 50 adult males.[15] In 1911, the colonial government crafted a plan that dedicated 300 hectares to Tiko's population on the basis of six hectares per adult male or family. Within the broader scope of this scheme, the German colonial government declared all of the land outside of the aforementioned 300 hectares in the region as "vacant/unoccupied". Also designated as property of the German Crown, the "vacant/unoccupied" land was placed at the disposal of private agro-plantation companies in 1912. Two private German companies – the African Fruit Company and Holforth Company – were among the first to establish farms in the Tiko area. These two firms joined others, such as Woerman

---

11 Njoh, *Planning Power*.
12 Charley K. Meek, *Land Tenure and Land Administration in Nigeria and the Cameroons* (London: H.M.S.O. Colonial Office, 1957).
13 Njoh, "Urban Planning." Ambe J. Njoh, "Development Implications of Colonial Land and Human Settlement Schemes in Cameroon," *Habitat International* 26 (2002).
14 Njoh, "Development Implications."
15 Njoh, "Urban Planning," 196.

and Jantzen und Thormalen, that were already operating agro-plantations in the Mount Cameroon region.[16]

One of the nagging problems encountered by agricultural firms related to the scarcity of workers. This problem was compounded by the unwillingness of members of the indigenous population to work for the Germans whose land grabbing and other proclivities they vehemently detested.[17] As a result, the firms resorted to recruiting workers from the hinterland. This triggered yet another problem – that of retaining workers in places geographically far-removed from their places of birth. As part of efforts to address this problem, plantation operators decided to develop living facilities for their workers. This marked the beginning of employment-tied housing schemes in the territory.

German colonial rule in Cameroon came to an abrupt end in 1918 as an outcome of World War I. With the departure of the Germans, Cameroon became a Mandate Territory of the League of Nations, forerunner to the United Nations. The League moved to divide the territory into two unequal parts of four-fifths and one-fifth. The larger portion was placed under the colonial control of France while the smaller part – Northern and Southern Cameroons – was placed under the British. The German plantations were located in Southern Cameroons and remained under the management of German entrepreneurs as Custodian of Enemy Property subsequent to the end of World War I.[18] This arrangement continued until the outbreak of World War II in 1939. At this point, the Nigerian Government, through which the British colonial authorities administered the Cameroons, bought the plantations.

In 1946, the British colonial government in Nigeria enacted two important measures that significantly changed the status of the plantations. These measures comprised mainly two ordinances, Ordinance No. 38 and Ordinance No. 39.[19] Ordinance No. 38 of 1946 empowered the colonial Governor to acquire and use the land for the common good of the indigenous population of Southern Cameroons. Ordinance No. 39 of 1946 created the Cameroon Development Corporation (CDC) as a statutory body to assume control of the erstwhile German agro-plantations. The CDC assumed formal control of these plantations, which were mainly located on the southern and southwestern slopes of Mount Cameroon, on 1 January 1947.

---

16 Njoh, "Urban Planning." Meek, *Land Tenure*.
17 Meek, *Land Tenure*.
18 Meek, *Land Tenure*.
19 Meek, *Land Tenure*.

CDC Workers' Camps

The birth of the Cameroon Development Corporation (CDC) coincided with a time when colonial powers in Africa were under pressure to afford the colonial project a humane face. Consequently, colonial powers embarked on programs and projects to improve social conditions in the colony. In Cameroon, colonial authorities implemented these programs as part of the British Colonial Development and Welfare Act of the 1940s. In this regard, and as Meek noted, the CDC adopted an ambitious program designed to provide "up-to-date accommodation for its resident labour force of some 20,000 men."[20] Thus, the corporation's initial welfare-related initiative included the provisioning of the following:
- Workers' housing, a project that required a capital outlay of £2,250,000;
- Facilities for universal primary education for children of its employees;
- Medical facilities, including health posts, dispensaries, and well-equipped hospitals.

The CDC operated four categories of worker housing, corresponding with the following classifications of workers:[21]
- Laborer housing, comprising multi-units of one room (2.70 m × 2.70 m), a kitchen (1.50 m × 2.00 m), and communal toilet facilities (latrines);
- Junior clerical staff housing, comprising single, duplex, triplex, and sometimes multi-units of one bedroom, one living room, a kitchen, and communal latrines;
- Intermediate staff housing, comprising one-bedroom self-contained duplex units;
- Senior staff quarters, comprising well-furnished three- and sometimes four-bedroom bungalows, each of which was equipped with a bar, a large kitchen, a two-car garage, servants' quarters, a large garden, and an orchard as well as lawns that were catered for by company laborers. In a few cases, senior staff housing units were enclosed within a fence and a gate manned by armed guards.

The term *company town* as used here is intended to capture the entire assemblage of housing units of all the categories described above, including the concomitant facilities such as company stores, club houses, health, recreation, and education facilities. The narrower term *camp* is used to refer to a locale containing mainly

---

20 Meek, *Land Tenure*, 368.
21 Njoh, "Urban Planning."

(low-income) workers' housing units without the concomitant facilities. However, it is worth noting that facilities such as the club houses and certain recreational facilities such as golf courses and tennis courts have usually been reserved for the senior cadre. Housing units for members of this group of workers have typically been far-removed from areas housing other classes of employees. During the heydays of the colonial era, these units were reserved for European employees of the corporation. The units have typically been set on spacious parcels of land complete with lawns and gardens that until today are cared for by CDC laborers. Borrowing from Porteous, we identify the following as constituting five of the main features of CDC company towns: spatial segregation, gridiron physical layout, uniformity of style, spatial isolation, and physical expression of economic enterprise.[22]

Spatial segregation. This entails the distribution of housing units either by the socioeconomic class or race of their occupants. Racial segregation in these towns was the norm during the colonial era. At the time, the managers and other senior staff of the CDC were exclusively of European extraction, and their residential facilities were physically far-removed from those of the African employees. In addition, they were typically perched atop higher elevations overlooking these quarters.

The company towns of CDC have, in effect, been comprised of three distinct living quarters that can be respectively designated as laborers' quarters (Fig. 7.1 and 7.2), junior clerical staff quarters, intermediate staff quarters (Fig. 7.3) and senior staff quarters (Fig. 7.4).

Basic amenities such as electricity constituted standard equipment in housing units throughout the towns. The towns have also been typically equipped with potable water. However, while public standpipes provided water for low-income quarters, housing units in the intermediate and senior staff quarters have been equipped with indoor plumbing facilities. Other fringe benefits for residents of CDC company towns – especially at the twilight, and immediately subsequent to the demise, of the colonial era – included "free" healthcare at CDC dispensaries, clinics and hospitals, low-cost supplies at CDC company stores, and subsidized funerals/burials upon the death of an employee.

Gridiron physical layout. One peculiarity of CDC company towns or workers' camps remains their physical layout, which is in conformity with the gridiron pattern. The streets orderly intersect at right angles and are flanked by housing units. However, except in the junior clerical staff quarters, there is a noticeable absence of physical planning and woefully inadequate sanitation facilities. In this latter regard, CDC camps are notorious for having only a few toilets to be shared by several families.

---

[22] Porteous, "The Nature of the Company Town."

Figure 7.1: A new CDC camp under construction: laborer camps. Notice the well-aligned buildings.
Source: Ambe Njoh.

Figure 7.2: Typical housing unit for a ranking low-income employee, Moliwe.
Source: Tabrey Construction, Buea, Cameroon and Ambe Njoh.

Figure 7.3: Intermediate Staff Quarters, Moliwe.
Source: Tabrey Construction, Buea, Cameroon and Ambe Njoh.

Figure 7.4: Typical house for a senior level employee at CDC.
Source: Tabrey Construction, Buea, Cameroon and Ambe Njoh.

An example of these toilets, which are typically of the bucket variety, is shown in Fig. 7.5. In contrast, housing units in the intermediate staff quarters, and especially those in the senior staff quarters, are served by well-aligned streets and furnished with enough space for gardening. However, it is worth noting that the streets and buildings in these once exquisite quarters are currently suffering from severe physical and functional obsolescence. The manager's building in Fig. 7.6.

Figure 7.5: Communal bucket toilet, CDC Camp, Moliwe (notice the bucket-holding compartments at the base of the building).
Source: Tabrey Construction, Buea, Cameroon and Ambe Njoh.

exemplifies this phenomenon. As a feature, the gridiron layout is a shared feature of all the living quarters.

The feature is rendered more conspicuous in the low-income districts by their congested spatial pattern. It is, however, less noticeable in the senior staff quarters where the housing units are sparsely distributed. Thus, when Njoh likens the structure of CDC camps to that of military barracks, he is talking of the low-income districts.[23] As shown on Fig. 7.1, the barrack-like structure of such districts in CDC company towns is obvious.

Uniformity of Style. This feature, as Porteous observed,[24] is characteristic of English company towns built before World War II. It is therefore no wonder that when the CDC, which emerged under the auspices of British colonial authorities in Southern Cameroons, embarked on a course to develop housing for their workers, they incorporated this feature. However, the reasons for this uniformity in Cameroon and in England differ. For the latter, one reason for the uniformity is that the building materials were "invariably those available locally."[25] Paradoxically, imported materials from Europe are among the features that

---

23 Njoh, "Urban Planning."
24 Porteous, "The Nature of the Company Town."
25 Porteous, "The Nature of the Company Town," 135.

Figure 7.6: CDC Manager's House atop a hill, Moliwe.
Source: Tabrey Construction, Buea, Cameroon and Ambe Njoh.

embellished the uniformity of buildings in CDC camps. Njoh draws attention to this point:

> In contrast to the assorted housing units in the surrounding environment, housing units in plantation camps were not only of identical design, but were also constructed of modern materials such as cement blocks (for the walls), steel (for the door and window shutters and frames) and aluminum sheets (for the roofs).[26]

Arguably the most important aspect of uniformity in the camps is the architectural style. As Fig. 7.1 shows, all the buildings are constructed based on a common blueprint. The last aspect of the uniformity worth noting is the finishing, particularly the painting, as the buildings in any given living quarter are usually painted the same color.

Spatial isolation. The CDC camps, like all company towns in general, are single-purpose entities designed to provide housing for workers. Thus, by design, company towns are usually located in places where the companies do business. In the case of CDC camps, they have historically been located in agro-plantation milieus such as large-scale farms for banana (e.g. Ekona Yard at its inception), rubber (e.g. Upper and Middle Costains, Tiko), oil palm (e.g. Bota and Middle Farms, Limbe), and tea (e.g. Tole, Buea) (Fig. 7.7).

---

[26] Njoh, "Urban Planning," 199.

Figure 7.7: Moliwe Camp exemplifies spatial isolation.
Source: Ambe Njoh.

These camps, and especially those of a smaller variety such as Saxon Horf (near Sasse, Buea), Mondoni (near Muyuka), and Idenau (near Limbe), have always been in remote locales. It is only in recent times, and thanks to urbanization, that socio-economically heterogeneous populations have been encroaching upon them.

Physical expression of economic enterprise. No account of CDC company towns or camps can be deemed complete without a word about the omnipresence of some agro-plantation-related activity. During the colonial and immediate postcolonial era, residents of these towns were acquainted with the bustling sounds and noxious odors of factories (e.g. the rubber factories of Middle Costains, Tiko), or palm oil mills (e.g. Bota and Mondoni). These residents were also familiar with noises from busy docks, wharves, and railway termini (e.g. Likomba, Tiko and Bota, Limbe).

CDC Company Towns as a Tool of Power and Social Control

To understand CDC company towns as a tool of power and social control, one needs to recall their origins. All corporations that operated in Africa during the colonial era were expected to contribute to the attainment of colonial development goals.[27] One of these goals, although hardly ever avowed, was the reinforcement of colonial power in colonized territories. The development of company towns constitutes one way in which the CDC has bolstered the colonial and postcolonial governments' power in built space in Cameroon. A more immediate goal of the company towns has been to instill in the workers the Western work ethic, minimize absenteeism, and, above all, facilitate employee retention. Applying Dovey's instruments to articulate power in built space,[28] the remainder of this paper is preoccupied with elaborating these points.

Force as an instrument of power. Physical features such as concrete walls, barbed-wire fences, and armed guards constitute visible and generously applied elements of force in built space. Recently, 20 CDC guards completed military training at Cameroon's Military Training Center in Koutaba. The corporation, however, did more than fence or install armed guards.

In many cases, these facilities are situated in isolated and secluded locales. Thus, elements of active force, in the form of armed guards, or elements of passive force, in the form of physical barriers or geographic distance, serve to guarantee the security of the camps or company towns. As in the case of Foucault's "Great Confinement", the strategic use of space and physical barriers nullifies the need for brute or military force as a means of assuaging real or potential threats to the camps and/or company towns. To be sure, the use of barriers and guards is intended to accomplish other objectives such as discouraging loitering and absenteeism by workers.

Coercion as an instrument of power. The expression of coercion in built space is similar to the use of force. However, coercion typically involves the use of artefacts or symbols that threaten, but do not actually use, force. As Marcuse stated, "coercion has physical force only implicitly behind it."[29] As an instrument of power, coercion finds expression in CDC camps/company towns through restrictions on the use of space. For instance, residents of low-income quarters have been forbidden from using recreational and other facilities in the senior staff quarters. This was especially true during the colonial era when residents of the senior staff quarters were exclusively of European extraction. At the time, racial residential segregation was also employed as an instrument of coercion. With the demise of colonialism and the concomitant departure of European residents, segregation as an instrument of coercion has been institutionalized along socioeconomic lines. Physical barriers separating the low- from the high-income quarters

---

27 Njoh, "Urban Planning."
28 Dovey, *Framing Places.*
29 Peter Marcuse, *The Forms of Power and the Forms of Cities: Building on Charles Tilly* (Springer Science: Building Media, 2010), 342.

are not the only social markers of exclusion in CDC company towns. Rather, the paved streets, manicured lawns, spacious yards and gigantic buildings that are unique to the senior staff quarters also serve as symbols of domination. The sheer size of these buildings is meant to advertise the resourcefulness of their owners;[30] it is also intended to subdue those over whom their occupants have supervisory authority without the need to resort to force.

Another variant of coercion that has been given physical expression in CDC company towns is internal surveillance. Here, the choice of elevated sites for the managers' residential facilities has two power-related objectives. The first is to symbolize and dignify the dominance of managerial power. The other is to facilitate internal surveillance and security. In this regard, and especially during the colonial era, the sites of these facilities were carefully selected to overlook the low-lying quarters of the low-income workers. Here, coercion is invariably manifested to the extent that those in the low-lying districts, the managed, are under the constant gaze of those at the elevated sites, the managers.[31]

Seduction as an instrument of power. Seduction entails the use of tactics designed to coax people into adopting a certain way of life and its attendant artefacts. This form of power is typically articulated in built space through the use of imported building materials, not because of their scientifically-proven superior quality but as a means of promoting a preferred culture. In the case of CDC company towns, it is no accident that building materials imported from Europe have been used in the construction process since the colonial era. Another Eurocentric feature of CDC company towns with far-reaching implications for acculturation is building design. For instance, the housing units for intermediate and senior level staff are of the self-contained variety, complete with kitchens. This effectively renders impossible the use of firewood, a well-known traditional African cooking fuel. Instead, occupants of the units are compelled to use natural gas, an imported cooking fuel. In addition, the CDC has effectively employed complex propaganda campaigns to promote Eurocentric culture in Cameroon. A common strategy in this regard is through screening of movie shows. Such shows constituted a staple of the entertainment diet that the CDC fed its employees in the colonial and immediate postcolonial period. Thus, as Njoh argued, "seduction is a potent and complex form of 'power over'."[32] In addition, during the mentioned period, the corporation operated its own primary schools whose curricula were replicas of

---

30 Cooper, "Urban Planning." Çelik, *Urban Forms.*
31 c.f. Anthony D. King, *Colonial Urban Development: Culture, Social Power and Environment* (Milton Park, Abington, UK: Routledge, 1976).
32 Njoh, "Urban Planning," 303.

British elementary schools. Furthermore, they instituted home economics classes designed to train workers' daughters and wives with European housekeeping skills.

Another element of Eurocentric culture in the spatial structure of CDC camps is the gridiron pattern. This was designed to promote a Eurocentric sense of order and economic efficiency. The small rooms that are standard for laborer or low-income housing, the dominant unit in CDC camps, are meant to encourage nuclear family sizes, a conspicuous aspect of Western families. It is clear that the one-room tiny housing units in the low-income quarters cannot conveniently accommodate a typical African family. This was especially true during the colonial era when African families were mostly polygamous. The history of colonialism in Africa is replete with accounts of Europeans working indefatigably to discourage polygamy and large families. In this regard, Bigon and Njoh noted that the Germans, Cameroon's first colonial masters, levied an extra head tax on men for each additional wife beyond the first.[33] Another feature of the camps suggesting that their founders were bent on promoting Eurocentric culture relates to toponymic inscription.[34] Here, there was a conscious effort to christen camps after European places or persons. Camp names such as Upper Costains and Middle Costains (in Tiko) and Saxon Hoff (near Sasse, Buea) illustrate this tendency. The Costains were named after the British construction company that built them.

Manipulation as an instrument of power. Manipulation includes efforts on the part of the state or agents acting on its behalf to bamboozle, and deceive, the citizenry. Most cases of manipulation involve the state or its agents distorting scientific knowledge to facilitate attainment of some desired cultural, social, political or economic objective. Instances of such manipulation with implications for spatial planning include the use of race or culture as a basis for access to socioeconomic goods and services. As already noted, CDC company towns were segregated by race during the colonial era. Manipulation in CDC company towns typically involves the supplanting of indigenous practices with Western equivalents. It also includes the use or misuse of (pseudo-)scientific knowledge to mislead the citizenry into using built space in a manner designed to achieve some goals of the governing authorities. Therefore, manipulation as a form of power thrives on the ignorance of the target population. The implied relationship between knowledge and power here validates Francis Bacon's familiar maxim that "knowledge is power." It is worth noting that CDC spatial planners dating back to the colonial era have always been uniquely knowledgeable in the version of planning – modernist

---

[33] Bigon and Njoh, "The Toponymic Inscription Problematic."
[34] Ambe J. Njoh, "Toponymic Inscription as an Instrument of Power in Africa: The Case of Colonial and Post-colonial Dakar and Nairobi," *Journal of Asian and African Studies* 52 (2016). Njoh and Bigon, "The Toponymic Inscription Problematic."

planning – that was one of the leading European export commodities of the mid-eighteenth to nineteenth century. Accordingly, knowledge of modernist urban planning rose to become an important source of power. Foucault sheds light on this phenomenon in one of his oft-cited works, *Power/Knowledge*.[35] For Foucault, there can be no power relationship without the correlative establishment of a field of knowledge. Similarly, there is never a body of knowledge without some form of power relation.

Segregation and power. The segregation question attained its zenith and assumed its most consequential form in Cameroon during the colonial era. In the context of CDC camps of the colonial era, the power of the colonial state was employed to bolster and legitimize the perceived superiority of Europeans over "racial others". By racially segregating CDC company towns, authorities were able to effectively control the movement of workers, especially the laborers. Racial segregation also enhanced the power of the European managers over their African employees by facilitating the former's surveillance of the latter. In contemporary terms, confining workers within a geographically or physically delineated space, and focalizing surveillance equipment on this space, has often been enough as a control measure. But the potency of spatial segregation in bolstering the power of "managers" can be appreciated at yet another level: low-income-only districts occasioned by segregation facilitate efforts to quell workers' riots, and the use of basic service provisioning to low-income districts for social control purposes – thus, supplying basic services as a reward for compliance and withholding them as punishment for recalcitrance or non-compliance.

Summary and Conclusion

The Cameroon Development Corporation (CDC) was created by the British colonial government in 1946. Rather early in its evolution, the corporation was preoccupied with the development of company towns, and especially workers' camps. This paper contends that these towns and camps did more than serve to accommodate CDC workers. They were designed, constructed, maintained, and managed as part of the broader colonial project. In this regard, the physical and spatial planners' expertise was summoned by the colonial state to maintain social order and articulate power in built space. The demise of colonialism did not witness a waning of the role of CDC company towns and camps in the geopolitical context of Cameroon. Rather, these facilities continue to serve as tools to enhance attainment

---

[35] Foucault, "The Politics of Health."

of laudable goals such as accommodating workers. During the colonial era, the paper contends, the facilities were especially considered viable tools for attaining rather covert goals of the colonial project, such as maintaining racial residential segregation, controlling workers' movement, disciplining workers, and facilitating exploitation of the labor power of workers. With the demise of colonialism, the indigenous leadership of the corporation has continued to incorporate company towns in their efforts to articulate power and maintain social order in built space. The specific instruments of power and social control often summoned for this purpose include force, coercion, seduction, manipulation, and segregation. This use of the opportunity to alter spatial structures to accomplish covert goals of the state is not unique to the CDC. Rather, it has always been part of modernist planning since its emergence in Europe in the 1800s. This suggests that in order to understand the purpose of planning projects it requires looking beyond official pronouncements avowing their *raison d'être*.

References

Abu-Lughod, Janet L. *Rabat: Urban Apartheid in Morocco*. Princeton, NJ: Princeton University Press, 1980.
Allen, James B. *The Company Town in the American West*. Norman, Oklahoma: Oklahoma University Press, 1966.
Bigon, Liora, and Ambe J. Njoh. "The Toponymic Inscription Problematic in Urban Sub-Saharan Africa: From Colonial to Postcolonial Times." *Journal of Asian and African Studies* 50 (2013): 184.
Bigon, Liora. "Bubonic Plague, Colonial Ideologies, and Urban Planning Policies: Dakar, Lagos, and Kumasi." Planning Perspectives 31 (2016): 205–225.
CDC. "Security Guards Complete Military Training in Koutaba." Accessed September 4, 2017. http://cdc-cameroon.net/new2014/security-guards-complete-military-training-in-koutaba/.
Çelik, Zeynep. *Urban Forms and Colonial Confrontations: Algiers under French Rule*. Berkeley and London: University of California Press, 1997.
Cooper, Nicola. "Urban Planning and Architecture in Colonial Indochina." *French Cultural Studies* 11 (2000): 75–99.
Dovey, Kim. *Framing Places Mediating Power in Built Form*. New York and London: Routledge, 1999.
Foucault, Michel. "The Politics of Health in the Eighteenth Century." In *Michel Foucault, Power Knowledge: Selected Interviews and other Writings, 1972–1977*, edited by Colin Gordon, 166–182. Brighton: Harvester Press, 1980.
King, Anthony D. "Exporting Planning: The Colonial and Neo-colonial Experience." In *Shaping an Urban World*, edited by Gordon E. Cherry, 203–226. New York: St. Martin's Press, 1980.
King, Anthony D. *Colonial Urban Development: Culture, Social Power and Environment*. Milton Park, Abington, UK: Routledge, 1976.

Marcuse, Peter. *The Forms of Power and the Forms of Cities: Building on Charles Tilly.* Springer Science: Building Media, 2010.

Meek, Charley K. *Land Tenure and Land Administration in Nigeria and the Cameroons.* London: H.M.S.O. Colonial Office, 1957.

Njoh, Ambe J. "Toponymic Inscription as an Instrument of Power in Africa: The Case of Colonial and Post-colonial Dakar and Nairobi." *Journal of Asian and African Studies* 52 (2016): 1174–1192.

Njoh, Ambe J. "Urban Planning as a Tool of Power in Africa." *Planning Perspectives* 24 (2009): 301–307.

Njoh, Ambe J. *Planning Power: Town Planning and Social Control in Colonial Africa.* London and New York: University College London Press, 2007.

Njoh, Ambe J. "Development Implications of Colonial Land and Human Settlement Schemes in Cameroon." *Habitat International* 26 (2002): 399–415.

Porteous, John D. "The Nature of the Company Town." *Transactions of the Institute of British Geographers* 51 (1970): 127–142.

Wright, Gwendolyn. *The Politics of Design in French Colonialism Urbanism.* Chicago, IL: University of Chicago Press, 1992.

Nicholas Sungura and Marlene Wagner
in discussion with Martina Barker-Ciganikova and Kirsten Rüther
8 Concrete Does not Cry: Interdisciplinary Reflections on and Beyond Housing

Here they are, ready to talk to us: two young professionals, an architect and a civil engineer, who go well beyond established boundaries of their disciplinary backgrounds. They reach out, experiment, and innovate. The focus of their work: end users, beneficiaries, dwellers, inhabitants, simply people. Both include the human element into professional fields primarily dominated by technical details, figures, and formulas. Although the importance and contribution of social disciplines to their fields are yet to be recognized, they concentrate on the importance of human interaction, communication, and community. Out of personal interest and professional curiosity, they apply interdisciplinary research methods. They go against the flow, visit archives to learn more about the history of the construction environment in their own countries. Or they include elements of self-reflection into architecture classes after a field trip to South Africa with students.

The idea behind this contribution arose out of a perceived need to balance the academic chapters in this book with a more practice-based, practical approach. We wanted to integrate the richness of observation of those who spend most of their time on construction sites rather than in archives or libraries. Nevertheless, academia is not at all foreign to our interviewees. Both authors professionally ended up where they are now by mere coincidence. Nicholas Sungura is a Kenyan civil engineer, with professional experience gained while working for a public institution mandated with infrastructure development in his country. Dreaming once of a career as a medical doctor, engineering turned out to be only his second choice. He concluded his doctoral research on risk management in public infrastructure projects at the Leibniz University of Hannover and currently works in Germany as a risk manager for a leading railway service provider. Marlene Wagner is an Austrian architect who has spent a great deal of her professional career implementing design-build projects in South Africa, also more or less by coincidence. She is a co-founder of a successful NGO called *buildCollective* and works as a part-time lecturer at a number of universities. Both left their known/familiar surroundings to develop their professional potential and skills abroad.

MARLENE WAGNER
- Born: 1981 in Klagenfurt, Austria
- Education: MA Architecture, Vienna University of Technology, 2010
- Special interest in: social architecture, design-build, non-formal spatial practices, alternative urban and architectural production
- Currently: founding member of NGO buildCollective for architecture and development; project assistant and PhD student at Vienna University of Technology, external lecturer at the University of Applied Sciences, FH Campus Wien, Kunstuniversität Linz
- Previously: external lecturer, Carinthia University of Applied Sciences, University of the Witwatersrand, Vienna University of Technology

NICHOLAS SUNGURA
- Born: 1978 in Nairobi, Kenya
- Education: Dr. Eng. Civil Engineering, Leibniz University of Hannover, 2016
- Special interest in: human element, risk management, public infrastructure, historical perspectives
- Currently: risk manager of rail infrastructure projects of a leading railway service provider in Germany
- Previously: civil engineer in a public institution mandated with infrastructure development in Kenya

For this publication, they shared their visions and views with us. We spoke about professional experiences, interdisciplinary approaches, and the contribution of architects and civil engineers to the study of housing. We thereby touched upon the complexity of construction projects, as well as recurring challenges and failures. Some of the questions asked were identical, while others were specifically tailored to their experiences. Although the two interviewees do not know each other, and the interviews took place at separate locations at different times,[1] their answers contain many commonalities. The following pages offer an insight into their professional worlds.

While analyzing the interview transcripts, we decided to bring the two voices together to show the commonalities and differences more clearly and to facilitate a reading across the variety of viewpoints. We were fascinated by how

---

[1] The interview with Nicholas Sungura was conducted by Kirsten Rüther in Hannover, Germany in July 2018; Marlene Wagner was interviewed by Martina Barker-Ciganikova and Kirsten Rüther in Vienna in August 2018.

centrally the importance of the human element featured for both Nicholas and Marlene in an otherwise technically dominated discipline.

The importance of the human element in the technical world: concrete does not cry!

Nicholas

Until, let's say, ten years ago, in the civil engineering course at the university, risk management was just a topic at the end of the chapter, somewhere, summarized by formulas: if this risk eventuates, the cost of the construction project will increase by so much money and the delay in completing the construction will be so many years. Those were just formulas. We were missing something. That's what I felt. We were missing the real people who are supposed to manage these risks. Who are they? Who are these people? Do they know what a risk is? Are they able to identify it? Does our risk awareness have something to do with culture? Does it have something to do with the training we received at the university? So, I said, "let's first of all define what a construction project is." Until then the engineering course focused on the technical aspects of a construction project. But then, during my research, I submitted the argument that a construction project is first and foremost a social project because we are building, say a dam, for the people. We are laying a railway line for the people. We are not just executing a project for construction's sake, the construction is meant for the people. And so, we have to find out what these people we are constructing for need. We need to engage them. And it is exactly here that a barrier arises. First of all, it would require of us engineers to leave our formulas behind and to receive the views and emotions of the public regarding the construction project under consideration.

You know, a construction project is like an animal in its milieu, like a lion that has to go and hunt, that depends on the environment for its resources. Similarly, I look at the country in which we are realizing a given construction project as its milieu. The required money, maybe from infrastructure development partners or investors, comes in to feed this project. So, let us imagine a construction site as a living thing, made of technical aspects and social aspects so that we have something like a techno-social organism in the construction milieu. Let's start looking at the emotions of construction practitioners because concrete does not cry; but human beings do. And when I attend the site meetings of a construction project, I become increasingly aware of the emotions of those in attendance. On the first day everything is good, things are perfect. Six months later, people start noticing that some payments were delayed. Or when it rained it didn't increase my money – money that I would have claimed as compensation for bad weather, and that is already a clash of interests! And those were some of the real risk factors. We are the people who execute a construction project yet we are the same ones posing risks to the realization of the project. It's not even the formula. The formulas we learnt in the classroom did not capture the scenario that the engineer could also be a risk factor affecting the execution of a project. As I see it, we engineers need to carry out self-reflection, go into ourselves and say, formulas are all good but we also need to remember human beings have emotions, they have aspirations, and above all, a construction project is first and foremost a social project. It is something we're building for the people.

Choosing the path of introspection in our work will create room for an array of insightful questions: Who are the people involved in the project? What is their level of awareness regarding the project? What is their cultural setting? What are they hoping for their lives with regard to the project? We need to look at every construction project as a living being, a techno-social organism. Developing awareness of the project as a living entity, having a lifespan like any other organism, would lead us to care for its wellbeing. We would ask ourselves: What are the things that can make the project sick? Like, if people demonstrate against it, if it's too expensive and then people say, "we don't want to construct it anymore, it doesn't make any sense for us." In my opinion, the aspect of complexity of the construction project has not been adequately addressed by the engineering fraternity in the past. Thankfully, this is now changing for the better.

Marlene
For me, architecture is always social. A house, a university, a school, but also your private home, there are people living in it so each building has a social component. The question I wonder about is why the kindergarten that we build in South Africa is called social architecture and why a kindergarten in Austria is not. It is interesting for me to apply what I have learned in South Africa in the Austrian context. There is more need for a more inclusive design and build process. To really focus on the process, the whole set-up, the stakeholders, the decision-making process, rather than the product, the fancy finished product. How did we get there and what is the potential of this building for people in its life as well as its afterlife? I have always been doing architecture in a very non-formal way.

Interdisciplinary entanglements: History? – Phew no!

How is the interest in an interdisciplinary encounter born? What led these two young professionals to step out of their traditional disciplines and to search for more elsewhere? What benefits were they able to identify when "borrowing" from other fields, both theoretical and practical? Being an interdisciplinary research group ourselves, we wanted to know more about this. We were particularly curious about the possible importance and contribution of social sciences and history to architects' and engineers' work. Although both colleagues apply an interdisciplinary approach, with respect to history, their answers differed significantly. While Nicholas puts historical (institutional) context at the center of his research focus, Marlene made a clear statement to our question of whether history was a discipline you work with: "Phew no!"

Nicholas
While doing my doctoral research in Kenya, I wanted to find out more about the history of infrastructure development in Kenya and the events that shaped the construction culture that is practiced in Kenya. I wanted to establish when the Ministry of Infrastructure was founded. When did it actually start executing its mandate? How did it evolve over the years? Who were the personnel in charge of it? When was the first time a Kenyan engineer was appointed to become the ministry's top administrator? So, I went to the Kenyan National Archives to find out more about the country's colonial history with special emphasis on Africanization of its civil service after Independence in 1963.

That was an approach we had not expected when in the research project we had speculated about the ways in which engineers would design research paths. We had assumed Nicholas would go to the laboratory, or a library, and just look at engineering books. But Nicholas had something in mind for which he needed to do extra research rather than tread the beaten path.

Because the role of the human element was at the core of my research, I needed to know, for example, how were Kenyans involved in the dams that were being constructed, say, in the 1950s? There was a water problem: to supply water to the population. How was water being provided? Who was designing these dams? Who was constructing them? How were construction projects set up? Who was financing them? Were there financial agreements in place? At the archives, I read memos signed by British personnel outlining the construction projects in Kenya. These documents served as my main source of information. They indicated the financing, the planned completion dates, the roles of construction practitioners, and the intended beneficiaries of the projects. Besides the Kenyan National Archives, the History Department at the University of Hannover has a very good library with material I used for my research. Notwithstanding these sources, I did not find information on Kenyan engineers in professional practice during the time-frame that my research focused on. I would read an entire book and it would only vaguely touch on construction activities in Kenya in general, only scratch the surface, highlighting the acute shortage of housing for Kenyans in urban areas. And that would be as closest to construction in Kenya as the sources went. This is what characterized my research venture: collecting knowledge from wide sources, looking for clues everywhere, and trying to interconnect them.

The archival work was very important for me. In my view, history has an important role to play in the life of construction projects. Supposing I just arrive at a stalled project where I have been appointed as an engineer tasked with resuming the building work, well, people will see walls coming up... the stalled project restarting. However, I would surely build better if I delved into the history of the project. For instance, can I establish why the project stalled in the first place? The construction work commenced, say, ten years ago, and then six years ago it was abandoned. To understand the reason why it was abandoned is beneficial for the future of the project. Because we could restart it now and if we didn't learn from the past, we could abandon it again. Sometimes the financing changes. We have development partners who come in and say, "we have this set of conditions. This is what you must fulfill in order to secure funding for realizing this project." Then after some time they pull out of the project due to one reason or another. We would then need to get new financiers. The new financiers would want to know what happened: "Why did you stop the project at the time?" So, somebody with a project memory who knows: "Aha! We started on the wrong footing, we didn't estimate the quantities of building materials well, we underestimated the role of the community, we didn't know that fifty kilometers away a railway would be constructed and that would make this project irrelevant. We did not connect with planners to find out what, say, the five-year plan is." Once I enter into the historical context, of a project, I come to the realization that I need to leave my formulas behind. The formulas are still important, though I now need to actively engage with the people, with the social dimension of the project.

From my experience, the entangling of disciplines is rather new to my engineering discipline, I struggled to find supervisors who were willing to oversee my research work from an interdisciplinary perspective. It was an uphill task! I had to argue my case to prospective supervisors aiming to convince them that it is the people involved in construction who determine the life of a project, and that the mind-set and emotions of these people have a direct influence on the outcome of the project.[2] For instance, when the operator of a machine on the construction site falls sick, and we are

---

[2] Nicholas Sungura, "Der Faktor Mensch bei der Risikosteuerung öffentlicher Bauvorhaben in Kenia", translated "The Human Element in the Risk Management of Public Infrastructure Projects in Kenya" (unpublished Dr. Eng. diss., University of Hannover, 2016).

unable to find a suitable person to replace him or her such that the construction stalls, what do we then do? We would need to talk to one another, we need to enter into negotiations about what to do next. These negotiations are not there in the textbooks. In our search for workable solutions, given such a scenario, we need alternative approaches, perhaps, from other disciplines. I borrowed concepts from biology and mathematics in my research. Using the concept of cybernetics in biology, I imagined the construction project as an organism capable of balancing the tensions it experiences during project realization. The capacity of balancing its tensions aims at preserving its life. This capacity depends on the persons involved in the project. Using game theory in mathematics, I imagined the construction undertaking as a game. In the construction game, I considered the two main players to be the project owner and the community intended to benefit from the project. I assigned the role of referee to the engineer. Several fascinating scenarios between the players of the construction game emerged. The complex interactions between the players could not be modeled solely by use of engineering techniques. Thankfully, I found two supervisors who were willing to embrace this approach; their openness signaled a trend that is changing. A trend in favor of interdisciplinary approaches in engineering.

Marlene was also looking for new ways to turn "ordinary" architectural knowledge into meaningful design projects which are pushing forward not only ideas but society more generally.

Marlene
My focus on design-build architecture over the last years has been more of a coincidence. I attended a design-build course at the Vienna Technical University to realize a kindergarten in Orange Farm, South Africa in 2005. I did not have much knowledge on South Africa or construction at that time. But I was motivated to realize and implement a project, which ordinarily in architecture you start doing at a much later stage, at the age of 40. For me, working in this new environment showed me that architecture could also be (change word order) something else. It made me believe that architecture might have a power to do something more than just giving the space, perhaps even a positive impact on the global scale?

Doing design-build architecture is doing a different kind of architecture production. It is not equally accepted as it is not the formal established and over-regulated way of architecture. For me personally, the potential of design-build is about a collective approach and about trying to focus on the process rather than the product at the end. I hope its ok to place this further down. I believe it is more understandable to explain design-build and then my approach of Social Architecture.

The biggest difference probably to formal architecture is that in design-build, the layperson and the designer also become the implementers. Design-build can be done with an educational approach at architecture faculties or also as an architectural practice - as we approached it with buildCollective. So, for example, Austrian, or let's say European, students design a classroom during the university course for clients that would not have the means for this service, and then, for the implementation and construction phase, they go on site, for example in South Africa insert comma here and work together with local client and construction team on the implementation. In ordinary architecture, the role of the architect is comparatively small. The creative design is some 10 percent of the work of the architect. The architect hands in the plans and then the construction company takes over and makes the rest. With design-build, you can have control over the entire process. You have influence on construction and you can design on the site. You work together with students, volunteers, suppliers, users and the broader community. So, you have to make a lot of decisions on the go, you need to have control and customize the process, you manage the construction site and sometimes even organize maintenance and actively influence the use of the space.

This kind of architecture – design-build between the global North and South, working in different environments and, as I like to frame it even further, "Social Architecture" – is trans-disciplinary. Social Architecture combines both theory and practice and spans a huge field of activities. It is a journey of development together with whoever is on the team, European and African universities, governmental institutions, local communities and users. The main idea behind this is to remove hierarchical boundaries and to create more of a family design and construction business. Let everybody have a say and balance the different needsand interests to create something meaningfull and to learn from each other. Ethnographic and sociological skills are needed. Qualitative research methods and skills on how to conduct interviews are required. As an architect, I am always pushed towards seeing something others don't, trying to convince user and client about the future reality. Architects are envisioning something that is not even there; that's the design process. If we design a house, I have to see it already there; I have to faciliate and guide people into an envisioned reality.

For a considerable time now, Marlene's particular role has been to translate and transfer design-build processes between continents and different professional and social settings.

Before and after a design-build project with students, I try to incorporate elements of self-reflection into the university architecture classes. I try to sensitize students and apply reflective methods: in what way did the experience change them? What impact did the project have on them? This is often not really supported by the architecture school, so it happens that the main professor leaves the class when I start talking about "these social things" in a technically dominated field. So, the set-up is difficult. Many of the qualitative research methods and approaches I apply in my work, I just made up for myself on the go, on the construction site, through books. It is just from my personal interest, nobody ever gave that to me. It is my personal drive to look into books, to have discussions. As a matter of fact, young Austrian architecture students do not know much about Mandela, apartheid or townships, so I need to give them some background. Another source of information for me is the local knowledge, the individual stories and histories of the people you work with. Everything we did was always in the process of making. All these facets combined make up my idea and notion of the space I work in. I am grateful I had a lot of freedom in these past years to develop myself and just to try out. Now that I am back in the Austrian context, the word seems to be "real-world laboratory or living-lab" and describes what we have actually been doing, practicing without even knowing this word.

The role of architects and civil engineers with regard to housing

As we ourselves have been committed to the study of housing in our research project, we naturally asked a number of questions with regard to that particular field. What is the biggest contribution and potential of architecture and civil engineering toward the study and planning of housing? At which stage of the construction process do the architects and engineers have the power to effect the most change? Where do they leave their imprint? Both Nicholas and Marlene are, of course, committed to infrastructural projects other than housing. Yet we were curious about the kind of input they would bring to the field of housing where a lot of cooperation and interchange happens between the respective disciplines they and we represent. Do professionals like Marlene and Nicholas have the potential to create more than a mere living space, to design more than just a physical structure and lay the basis for making a house a home?

Nicholas
The magnitude of a housing project in comparison, let's say, to a dam project may be smaller depending on the variables under consideration. But we talk about housing units, we talk about the state, pledging: we are going to provide 1.5 million houses, or housing units, in the next five years. Then areas have to be set aside to construct those houses. First, there is what we call the physical plan, that is to say, the area has to be zoned, this is done by physical planners in a given zone. Then maybe they say there'll be housing estates, maybe one estate having about three

hundred houses, for example. And there is a standard house, like it's one house repeated three hundred times. The architect will design that one house and say, all right, that is what a model house will look like, and we are going to have them all around in this way. The engineer will then come and say, "all right, if the houses are to be spaced in this manner, then this is where the main roads and access roads need to be. We need water, so this is where the water points are going to be, to connect them to the dams." We also investigate the soil. We say, "ah, if this is the kind of soil, these are the kinds of foundations we need, and this is exactly the kind of reinforcement we need for the columns and house walls." The engineer is integral to housing, in fact he's the one who realizes the dream of the architect. The architect will give her idea, her housing design to the engineer, and the engineer will then execute it.

We wanted to know more about the actual living and dwelling conditions. Beside roads and sanitation, there are the real houses, the spaces occupied by people. Does an engineer have an impact on their quality of living? How can she or he help to improve the living conditions?

Nicholas
From an engineering point of view, I say, "okay, if this is the house design, what's important for me, if I were to be the one to occupy the house: is there enough daylight?" I need to figure out: where does the sun rise in the morning and where does it set? Because that tells me where the windows need to be. There is no need for people to live in a house that is dark most of the time. How far apart should the housing blocks be? Because I need to consider the shadow cast by adjacent houses. During the day, if there is a shadow that follows the house, I need to space the houses apart. I would also need to consider how far away the water point is, because sometimes there is the situation of people having to go and maybe fetch water, in case there is a problem with the piping of the water. How far would they have to walk to access the water point? I also try to imagine the needs of the people who choose to live at the location in future and would be having cars. Where could I locate a car park? Is there a market nearby? Are there schools nearby? There is no need of constructing housing units deep inside the bush if there is no school in the vicinity. I would need to consider families and their needs. How does a model family look like? Is it a family of two or three children? All these aspects come together and provide vital information to enable me carry out the engineering design of the housing units.

And what if, notwithstanding all the meticulous planning and calculations, the implementation phase takes its own path? The Western model of nuclear family is challenged in African societies and living arrangements might encompass a range of blood and non-blood relatives one conceives of as family. Do engineers have a solution for assembled family set-ups? How does one actually plan knowing that the houses will be used in different ways from the original design anyway?

Nicholas
We have a term for it. We call it the design capacity of a house. So that means, when I design the house, I can say this house is for five persons. That is its design capacity. But it does not mean that only five people will live there. Because we have experience of houses with double the number of occupants. But for purposes of design, we need to quantify the building materials and say it's going to require so much cement and sand. We need a design basis to be able to calculate for sanitation of the solid waste or liquid waste; we need to know how many people are living at a given location for us to determine the sizing of, say, the potable water or wastewater treatment tanks. So that is the one point. But once these houses have been rented out, there is no chance whatsoever of making sure that only five people are living in a given house. In order to cater for a possible overload of the system we have designed, what we can do as engineers, when we have a design capacity of, say, five persons, we use a numerical factor. In the formula we say, "let us factor the load in our design by 25 percent more, so that in case instead of five there are seven or eight persons, they can still safely live there." We do it using the multiplication factor in the formula. But in real terms it doesn't mean that only eight people will live there; they could be ten or more; and when such scenarios happen, the designed system begins to fail because its capacity has been exceeded. Then we realize the piped water is not enough the population at a given location, or it takes a longer time than planned for the sewage from the housing units to be safely disposed.

Marlene was very passionate about the role architects may play to ensure housing projects amount to more than just technological and pricey designs.

Marlene
The potential of architecture is to create alternatives, maybe different typologies, different materials, and different processes that can turn it into more: that can make it a home; that can make it an income. That is definitely architecture's role. The problem is there is no architect involved most of the time. There is the construction company – a general contractor, especially if it's a governmental project. The plan is already there, and any construction company can make an offer: "We build so many houses for this price, even offer mass prices." The bigger the company, the better, so there is no interest that there is an architect involved. The architect can make a spatial benefit; create a better space, maybe also a space more flexible and adaptable for people.

The architect, most of the time, had better or more ideas than what you see in the outcome – what is left of the design after fighting for budget, fighting with the client for what is actually needed, fighting with the construction company, fighting or rather hacking the regulations and norms of the government and engineers. I think being an architect is really this umbrella position, that is natural to architecture, between theory and practice, between drawing board and construction company. At least that is what I also hope to see and, to work in this complex interdisciplinary field, it's kind of what we have to do in architecture.

Architecture is the social glue in the making of space between disciplines, or the creative glue. It pushes the limits. The engineers, for example, often stick much more to the rules and the books, also because of the responsibility they have. But it is definitely the architect who has a totally creative job to balance all the needs. The material can do that, the user needs that, the construction company wants that, the client wants that, now make one thing out of all of that. That is also why in my opinion interdisciplinary work is totally natural to architecture. I believe that architecture can envision things.

On the construction site the reality-check happens and, one needs to move forward; every day on site costs money. It is not possible to sit on site and discuss for too long neither design issues nor social issues because the project cannot afford the digger one more day. So, you just have to take decision after decision, in the design and especially in the construction process. To always think ahead, to visualize something ready that other stakeholders cannot imagine yet. On the other hand, there is also the problem of architects: that we tend to fall in love with our own ideas and do not listen enough to others. Then it is not a participatory process anymore and you will lose partners in the kind of architecture we do. Architects need to envision but not impose their own vision over all the others. They need to listen.

Involving the community, involving the professionals

Both Marlene and Nicholas emphasize engagement with the local community as the alpha and omega of their work. They both believe the success of a project depends on the degree of involvement of the local community. Is the local community consulted? Do people have a say? Are their wishes heard or, even more importantly, respected? If so, there is a high chance of accomplishment. If decisions are imposed, there is a higher likelihood that something will go wrong along the way and the project will stall or fail. But who is the local community? Who is allowed to represent it and have a say? And who engages with whom in the end? The community with the professionals, or vice versa? Unsurprisingly, the interviewees did not manage to answer all our questions.

Nicholas
When the engineer decides to engage more with the people, he then has to leave the office where he is drawing and designing and do more work with the community, and sit with the people, maybe organize forums. We need to have, say, a community day, we are collecting ideas, say, at the community market place. We intend to, let's say, rehabilitate this village road, or put a new surface on an existing all-weather road: "What do you think? Do you want it? Do you need it? Or would you like this road to be wider, or would you like it to also go into two more villages?" So, this work that I have come to realize is necessary, to engage with the community, unfortunately was not incorporated in the university training. Because when I go to my civil engineering course, I go to mathematics, I go to physics, I memorize and apply countless formulas and I come out of college in the end and I have my degree. But there is not much emphasis on people, community. Already, the way the course is tailored, it is so technically inclined, something which I can partially understand. But it neglects the social aspects: for whom are we actually going to work? And maybe it is now more often the case that the projects are becoming more complex to execute. It is a wake-up call that the new engineers who are being trained should be receiving maybe 10 percent more social skills than has been the case before. Because when I go to the village, the people I interact with don't care about my formulas. They don't even need to know that my formulas exist. Maybe they know I will draw something. Then they call it, as is the case in my village, a map. They say, "oh, he will come with a map, and this map is what he's using to build the road." That's all. But of course, it's not called a map, it is a design plan, and it has technical validity, but they don't need that. They just know I will come with a map. But they need me to know that the planned road is important or not important for them. They need me to provide them with information addressing their concerns: when this road is being constructed, will they get jobs, will they be allowed to work on that road, or will I bring my own workers? Because depending on what the contract model is, they may even choose to protest and say, "okay, if our children are not going to get jobs here, don't construct the road. We want a road that will generate jobs in the village." So, these are many things that we have to learn these days. And even for the engineers who have been, say, long enough in the profession, it may seem as if the train has already passed them by yet I believe we all have room to learn because the community is very, very important.

Under Marlene's tutelage, the self-built suspension pedestrian bridge over the Mzamba River in Eastern Cape, South Africa was built between 2014 and 2016. It involved the local community, the NGO *buildCollective*, the architecture faculty at Carinthia University of Applied Sciences and many other contributing individuals, including students, volunteers, consultants, and supporters. The project won several awards; a documentary and a book were released after its realization.[3]

Marlene
As for the bridge, that was not our idea. The community approached us, that there are people dying because of the river. Sometimes it floods, and the connection to get food, education, and healthcare does not exist. There we had to undergo even environmental impact assessment because it's on public land and in an environmental protection area. Of course, each project differs. It is much more important to have a participatory approach and community involvement in the public infrastructure because there is nobody to hand it over to. It is always a big challenge how to balance things because sometimes the user is not even interested. Just give me a building, they seem to say. I do not want to be included in the whole design, they say. But you need the community to be involved, so that they can take care of it. Government trusted us to take care of it. We got the South African Sustainable Architecture Prize and I was asked: "There is a similar bridge in the neighboring province that got destroyed by the community. How can you make sure it is not happening to your bridge?" "Well, it is not our bridge, the request came from the community and there was a steering committee and the whole decision-making process, from the set-up how high the bridge needed to be, from the whole talking with government, getting the environmental impact assessment and so on." The community steering committee was made up of political representatives, traditional leader, and just community members from both sides of the river, women and men; it was really nice. In my experience, working in the countryside is very different compared to the city, the unity and self-organization, the whole traditional system is still in place; that is why it was much easier to work with this alternative set-up. On the construction team, there were never more than five to eight Europeans as compared to ten or twenty South Africans on the site. The team on the construction site did not have any special technical knowledge; some used to work with us before at the construction of the schools. And then also it is a very rural community, so everybody is kind of handy. The bridge design was simplified, every single part of the bridge had to be light enough to be carried because there was no road. So that again influences the design, and then you just screw. And screw. The material was steel, it is 140 m long bridge, and the pylon is 15 m high. We spent three years on this project. I believe

---

3 http://buildcollective.net/onsite/bridgingmzamba/. Besides the bridge – the NGO's most famous project – the co-founders Marlene Wagner and Elias Rubin also realized other projects including education facilities, classrooms, schools, workshops, and water points.

that architecture, because it spans a big field between design and construction, really has the power to be an enabler, for people to learn more about construction, and to have a say. It is just that in participatory design-build architecture, projects need to be designed in a way that laypeople can be involved in the different phases. They are a kind of educational project for everybody involved. This requires more management at the beginning, but generally I believe that, especially considering the South African housing shortage, it should be made possible with funds available from the government so that people can build their own homes as skills are there.

What are real houses?

Where there is housing, people often need space to produce goods, to offer services and to subsidize family incomes. This aspect is often neglected both in theory and practice when housing is conceived of as a mere physical structure. The state and construction companies promote a low-cost philosophy, be it in social housing, home-ownership or site-and-services schemes. The target is to save costs wherever possible. Those who offer the lowest price win the tender. This philosophy is in stark contrast with issues of maintenance, longevity, high sensitivity, and the complexity of housing projects more generally. Cheap material, repair, and overcrowding quickly become a problem. As a result, intentions to regulate people's lives often clash with people's understandings of housing as a place of work and belonging, community cohesion and identity or as a space that provides social benefits – be it valuable support networks, neighbors, friends or sharing childcare duties: "The sign of a material house is an illusion when no system of institutionalized expectations is in place to connect the physical structure (house) and the range of functions it is assumed to provide to the resident: safety, security and health benefit."[4] It looks like it is a house, but it is not one. It is a "non-house".

Nicholas
First of all, I would challenge the planners who tell us about low-cost housing. They should tell us which costs they are talking about. Are they talking about construction costs? Are they talking about maintenance costs? They have to tell us which cost is being referred to. Or are they talking about the rent that the tenant will pay? For example, maybe I'm saying it is low-cost, and this means when the person is going to rent it, he will pay eighty Euros for one room. But if I just say it is low-cost because it cost me a hundred million Euros to construct, I will also have to say what the lifespan

---

[4] Tess Lea and Paul Pholeros, "This is Not a Pipe: The Treacheries of Indigenous Housing," *Public Culture* 22 (2010): 191. See also for a more detailed discussion on the non-house syndrome.

of those houses is, before, say, a renovation is done. Is it five years before we come back and paint again? Is it ten years before we change the piping again? So, is it low-cost now because we are using cheap building materials that can get damaged after three years, or even after six months, and then we have to replace it? This is what is seldom talked about in the open. It could be a strategy to sell the project, to attract financing, it could also be a strategy to attract the support of the public. Because when the public hears, "oh, housing at low cost," many people are led to think that they can afford to rent or purchase such houses. But they are not told about the maintenance of those houses. Does it mean that if the state builds the house, it is now the cost of the tenant to maintain it? That is often not explicitly communicated. Even if it were clarified that, "okay, we're building the house but it is your cost to maintain it," then people may realize that actually it's not low-cost at the end of the day. The question remains: can the calculations of the housing developers tell us how much it is going to cost to maintain that house ten years from now? To change a broken sink, to change the wiring if there is a wiring problem, those are the silent aspects that become clearer the moment there is damage to be fixed.

Marlene
The problem in South Africa is not the building itself. The buildings, especially in this climate, do not need air conditioning or high-tech materials to create a good room climate. You can design the house quite cheaply, low-maintenance, self-sufficient, especially within the standards of the RDP housing program [Reconstruction and Development Program]. I believe that a big problem is for the government to allow alternative design strategies and construction material to be tried out, but I don't know what happened in the last two years. Of course, you have good architects in South Africa and they all put proposals for alternative housing models. There are some interesting ideas with different typologies so the owner can, for example, easily rent out a part of the house to generate income. As non-South-Africans do not qualify for the RDP housing program – the post-Apartheid promise of free houses for all South Africans – there is the problem of the so-called "backyard shack," meaning that people informally rent out an inadequate self-built space in their backyard. In order to tackle this problem, South African architects started designing houses with two entrances and which can be easily extended. The South African beneficiary of the RDP house can formally rent out a room which generates income while the non-South African resident is not living in a backyard shack but in a real house with an address.

The other side of it is that this rental system is not controlled. So, for example, the south African RDP house owner can make the Zimbabwean tenant suffer by obliging him or her to pay I don't know how much rent for a small space. That is another issue. The space and construction are not a problem. It's the political will *and the money flow. I am talking about ordinary housing now, not even ecological construction. Just better planned typologies of housing to meet existing needs and processes that take into consideration the reality of the users.*

In South Africa, social housing is basically for rent. An RDP house you would not call social housing. That was something new for me to see, there is a whole different understanding and system of housing programs as compared, for example, to Austria or to Kenya, where it is more common to rent, not to own their house, they are fine with a flat. In South Africa, this promise of a "free house" of the post-Apartheid government is so strong that people want a "free house" as promised. The end-users already have a certain idea, expectations of how their house should look like. Now you as an architect come, trying to convince the government and the end-user that a different design might be better, but it is really not supported to try out case studies of different typologies or different set-ups. People do not want just any kind of house. It is the promise they got with democracy and the RDP program and that is how the house should be. It is also a marketing strategy for the government to advertise itself. We give you a house. This year we deliver so and so many houses. That sounds better than to say that we will build a block of flats. But the problem is, after a while, especially in the outskirt areas, the problem is not only with the house or the architecture of the house, but mainly with the zoning. Because what is allowed to be on the land, it is just residential zoning, which kills the whole income generation possibilities of people. To do business on the land is not allowed and also the government keeps the land. You never get the land; you just get the top structure, the house construction. You are not allowed to sell the house, so it is not a real asset, and you are not allowed to have your shop, which was your income in your former place. Now, when you are transferred from an informal settlement into a new housing development in the periphery, you have your house but not in the same place, and you are without your social network. This house, if it's nowhere, you have your flushing toilet, but you cannot pay your electricity anymore. It's not a shack, it's not corrugated iron, it's a brick house, but that's also it. You have a safe structure, nothing more. The construction company consumes so much money; it could besides being a real home within a social network, the building process could also support economic and educational features. But for that you need proper management and policies and capable construction companies to implement it. It is very difficult to try to convince the government or a construction company to do something differently, no matter if in Austria or South Africa. If you want something different, there is always a big discussion. Construction companies just try to get as much money as possible. Funding is coming from the government, and the cheaper they can build the houses, the more money is left for the company. This is not a system that supports a different, alternative way of doing things.

Reflections on institutions, complexity, and communication

The network of actors involved in a housing or construction project involves many more participants than engineers, architects, and the local community. It is like a web linking different corners and (hi)stories. Besides the people who receive the construction – the end beneficiaries – there are economic players, including banks or international donors, physical planners, construction companies, and research institutions. They are engulfed by the omnipresent state. An increased number of actors often means more complexity and an increased need for communication to avoid misunderstandings. This again puts pressure on the budget and timeline of each construction site. In our research project, we conceive of housing as not only a "physical frame"[5] of everyday urban life, but as a social, cultural, and legal network of relationships between various players, each of whom cultivate their respective interests. These diverging interests need to be accommodated. Are there particular ways of engaging with the institutions in order to push through a certain dimension of the project, or to create awareness? While for Nicholas, who has work experience in public service in Kenya, the state is the most important actor to engage with, Marlene, a co-founder of an NGO, also cooperates closely with (European) private companies while searching for funding.

Nicholas

Yes. We are very aware in my country that the state is alpha and omega. Because the state provides the framework allowing us to practice our profession. The state licenses the engineers who can practice the profession. The state is the one that approves the construction project to be realized. That is why I can't just wake up and say, "now I like this place, I want to build a bridge." I am required to seek approval from the state to implement the planned project, and the state has the last word. The state provides the framework within which infrastructure can be executed.

We say the state has no face; it is faceless. But we feel its institutions. For example, if there is a conflict on the construction site, the aggrieved parties go to court. So, the court is an arm of the state. I have two options to practice as an engineer in Kenya: I could work in the Ministry of Infrastructure, inside the government system, so to say, or I could work in the free-market economy, as a private engineer having his own engineering office. If I'm in the Ministry, I apply my skills to execute the state's plan. And the state has, say, a five-year plan, a medium-term plan, maybe it says in the next five years our focus is on schools. So, the efforts of

---

5 Alison Hay and Richard Harris, "'Shauri Ya Sera Kali': The Colonial Regime of Urban Housing in Kenya," *Urban History* 34 (2007): 504.

its technical personnel are geared towards realizing that objective. And as an engineer I can't change that plan. I cannot because this is how the state is even marketing itself. And an engineer in the Ministry executes the state's infrastructural agenda. He goes to supervise the work on the construction site to make sure that that school is being constructed according to the budget that was set aside. Whether that budget is enough is another question altogether. It is also worth noting that, there is a government of the day and each government has its own development agenda. For instance, one government can say, "our plan is infrastructure, we want railways, we want roads." As a result, that is where the its resources will be channeled to. It comes as a policy.

Nicholas has some particular comments on the complexity of construction settings:

The complexity of a construction project enhances the need for increased use of interdisciplinary approaches. The required initiative needs to come from the engineers themselves because, yes, we have the drawing pen and we have the drawing board. And we have the technical knowledge, but that is not enough; we need to work with other non-technical disciplines. I acknowledge that if we work with other disciplines, it does make the construction project more complex, that's for sure. I mean, it's easier when somebody says, I'm just doing it alone, for then I can make decisions quicker. The more the number of interested parties sit on the table, the more players there are to satisfy, and such a setting calls for more compromises to be made. In our time, we need technicians who are also willing to say, "okay, I admit it is more complex and time-consuming to design a project in this manner, as I now consider your interests. I am now able to expand my thinking and increase my awareness of the significance of the project with your concerns in mind." And then the project financiers also need to be able to agree, "yes, we are willing to continue being part of the project, although it will cost us two hundred million shillings more. We think we are better off implementing the inclusive design solution that costs more than spend two hundred million less, only for the project to not be used as projected. Because we are also looking at the rate of return of our investment." The cost of an infrastructure project is justified by the accrued benefits from its intended use. The more people are likely to use the railway, to use the dam, to use the schools, the more sense it makes to implement the project, and which eventually yields the benefits for which it was constructed. And I think, if we as technicians can open our minds and appreciate other professions and accept that an infrastructure project is not only a technical project, but also a social project, then I think that would be a good start. This approach will not eliminate risks from the construction site, because life is full of risks, anyway. I see the interdisciplinary approach as more conducive for risk management. We don't talk about eliminating risks in infrastructure projects, we talk about managing them, because some risks will eventuate anyway. Could we join our efforts so as to mitigate the impact of eventuating risks?

Marlene
Most of the funds and money for our projects are coming from private people in Austria. We do projects with local grass roots organizations, with clients that don't have money so it needs a different set-up, and we collect money on our own. We also received money from companies or development funds of the Austrian municipalities, but the biggest contributions are from private people. These were the biggest amounts, they trusted us, they know our work; they often have some kind of relationship with South Africa. As an architect working between cultures and income classes, I can be the translator between needs, between users and clients, because I am on site.

For me, these design-build projects with universities also have their limits. To design and build a house with 20 students and 20 community members in just seven weeks is quite... there are a lot of risks, you push all participants already quite to the limit, if you just want to do the design and build the house. If you also want to take into consideration cultural issues, learn about history, then you will never end up building in the framework of one term given by the university structure. That is why I also tried to convince partner universities to do the course for at least a full year, not just one term, because then it's much easier to have a longer design and transdisciplinary learning process. But with the regulations of the university in Europe, it did not work. Then I tried to set up collaboration between Wits University and the FH Kärnten [Carinthia University of Applied Sciences], but the terms are completely the other way around so it really did not work out, both sides being very opposed. The Austrians saying, "we cannot change anything, the Africans have to do so", and South Africans saying, "no, why again should we change our schedule for Europeans?" I took some of my South African students on site, but not as part of the regular course, rather in a way as a volunteer workshop to team up with the local construction team, which went really great. For me it was frustrating that despite the many years of working with the European universities, we are still in the same set-up as when I was a student. This design-build practice in the Global South did not develop in the way I believe it would be necessary.

Of straw and clay and stamps

Discussions on the use of building material have always played a pivotal role in the housing and construction industry. Our archival research in The National Archives in Kew, UK revealed that few other topics were examined so prominently and in such detail among British colonial officers as building material.

The debates were highly technical: which material to use for whom and, most decisively, how much would it cost the taxpayers? Corrugated iron or mud and wattle? Stone or cement? Imported or local? All had their pros and cons and only seldom was there a univocal reply to any of these questions. The search for answers has not ceased with the demise of the colonial period. Against the backdrop of the scarcity of resources today, the discussion on more sustainable and ecological solutions gains even more prominence. One of the most important questions to answer remains: what type of building material do dwellers desire?

Marlene
In our work, we did experiments with alternative materials. We did projects with, for example, straw-clay for better insulation. Especially in the Johannesburg climate this material supports a good room climate. But you need a load-bearing structure, for example, out of concrete pillars and steel trusses. We try to produce as much as possible on site, the trusses and pillars included. As a way of building up the local construction team: that you go through the same process over and over again, so that it can be pre-produced at some stage even without us; and that it creates income-generation for the local team while there is no big project going on, but they can pre-produce pillars and trusses that are then later bought by the universities. There is a lot of learning, and long-time guidance and collaboration there. We developed the system for classrooms, with self-built pillars and self-built trusses and the light-clay infill. We went to the Housing Department in Ekurhuleni Province because there is an existing housing program which allows South African citizens to apply not only for a house from the South African government but also for money to build their own house, provided that they match the application criteria. But I have never really seen it actually work. We had a lot of meetings, and we showed how it's designed and how it's cheaper, and more comfortable than the ordinary RDP house design, but it never worked out.

But I think the problem was that we were not South Africans. It is very tough to get into the business: Like everywhere, the construction industry is corrupt, so as an Austrian, how to get a contract with the government; as young architects, how to get into the system; with the township crew, how to get in the system; with alternative material... all at once, to get into this funded housing schemes is very difficult. We would have liked to build some show houses. In our projects on private land, we could experiment a lot, but it's different on land for a publicly funded housing scheme. So, we had a lot of meetings with the government, trying to convince them that they trust us to make a show house, to show them that the material is fine, that the community can do it on their own, but it never really worked out.

For me the main motivation for using straw and clay is because one can build ecologically. First and foremost: to reduce concrete. The idea was also to try something new, something that is easy to work with. To have better indoor quality. Straw-clay is a natural insulation; it has better insulation quality than a concrete brick. Also, this alternative wall infill is something that is workable for everybody. You do not need special skills. For the main load-bearing structure, of course, you need a professional team, but as regards the straw-clay infill, anybody can do it. I can show you in half an hour more or less, and then after one day of guidance you can do it yourselves.

But then people, they do not want straw and clay houses, they want concrete, steel, and glass architecture. At first, there was a lot of skepticism because it's earth, community team members would see earth houses as outdated. Plus, the government has the program to "eradicate all mud schools," it is really "anti-earth" and anti-natural building materials. It all depends on the milieu; the rich people want green, ecologically built houses. It is the same in Austria, working-class people don't want or care about a clay house; it is something you want if you have extra money and you can afford an environmental consciousness or the time to care about ecological issues. But because community members in South Africa have been working with us for such a long time and experienced that it's really a better room climate inside a straw-clay insulated house, it keeps the inside warm while it's cool outside. We could show participants, for example, how much money you need for a square meter of concrete bricks and how much for straw and clay. The straw and clay infill depending on availability and context in mass production would of course be cheaper.

To officially build with alternative material, you need a formal approval that this material certifies as construction material. This costs a lot of money. You have to go through a special process, not if it is your private house, but for public construction. We tried to do some testing via cooperation with the South African Bureau of Standards and also with engineers of the University of the Witwatersrand and the Carinthia University of Applied Sciences but then another project came in and we just could not afford it.

The bridge project is a completely different project because it's public infrastructure and one needs to comply with a lot of different regulations. You need engineers to calculate forces. With a house, you have a span width and forces you can calculate as an architect. For the 140-meter-long suspension bridge, we had to work with engineers. A Swiss engineering company donated their time to calculate – which is not an architect's job, but an engineer's – to get the stamp for the structural issues. The Swiss engineers calculated everything, but to get all the approval and submit the application with government for the structure of the bridge, we had local engineers. The main issue is the responsibility: the engineer with his stamp that proves that this structure is sound. That is in a way also a kind of donation, because we built it, so they need to trust us, it is not how architecture and construction work ordinarily.

Dignity, language usage and living in lack

Besides agency and governance, language usage is one of the three analytical layers through which we look at housing in our research project. The use of terminology in the field of housing and the way language in its broadest sense is used to (de)stabilize or establish power relations between the players is of great interest to us. Why and when are certain expressions being used? What is a "slum" and where does it originate? At certain periods specific words become *en mode*. When they are no longer required, attempts are made to erase them from public discourse. The Eurocentric framework for analysis has also been one of the reasons why, in colonial as well as postcolonial settings, it is deemed necessary to focus on the slum, the most prevalent "other" as opposed to European forms and norms of housing. Do engineers and architects reflect on language usage? Does it make any difference to them which term is being used? And do they come up with alternatives to express their dissatisfaction with the vocabulary at hand? We animatedly talked through these issues together.

Nicholas
I can't make much of the term slum. I use the word shelter in my work. I see shelter as an umbrella terminology that allows many possibilities under it. I use housing to mean a planned, structured kind of dwelling, you know, where there is a plan, like, this is where there are shops, and these are houses for families with three children, these are houses for families with seven children, that is now housing to me. But when I use shelter, I use it to also accommodate people who simply have something over their heads. It could be cardboards, paper carton boxes, they're just using it to protect themselves from the elements, and they keep staying there. Such shelter forms are thus less secure, they can be demolished more easily; houses are more permanent. I realize that if I just choose the word housing, then there would be many people who are not accounted for. Yet they are having shelter, they're having something over their heads protecting them from the elements. Many of them don't even have an address. It's not a registered address because they can move with their shelter. For instance, they could be staying at a given location today and tomorrow when there are demolitions, they can take their structures somewhere else and stay at another location. But still at the end of the day when they come home from their daily endeavors, that's where

they come back to: to their form of shelter. And at the end of the day, we always need to remember; it is a human being coming back home, irrespective of the form of shelter.

From an engineering perspective, we also look at sanitation, where do the people in such shelter forms shower? Where does their liquid waste go to? Because we have to account for it, we have to drain it. There are very many aspects that need to be taken into account. Let's take an example: accessibility, how do they get to their shelter, how do they access their shelter? So, we need to plan for it and we would have to, first of all, acknowledge they are living where they are. And then to say, okay, if you are staying around this area, let's now think of communal toilets or communal bathrooms. If you need to shower, these are the common areas for showering. On such a basis, it becomes easier to plan for the necessary sanitation, because we are also responsible for public health. We need to design sanitation in order to prevent the outbreak of diseases such as cholera. I prefer to use the term shelter experience to slum. I cannot make much of the term slum.

Shelter experience, for me, may mean that dwellers lack a personalized bathroom, for instance. Their personalized experiences are: they lack. So, they are more inclined to use communal facilities, if these are available. For them, for the dwellers in that shelter experience, community means a lot. So that means we need to appreciate and acknowledge these shelter dwellers. We need to plan for them, which now brings me to housing, because housing, as I now use it, implies there is a plan. The engineer comes in and says, all right, I know you are staying here. We are all accountable for safeguarding public health. The solid waste management trucks cannot pick your solid waste directly from your form of shelter for lack of access roads. So, let us have a common area for solid waste disposal. Then it becomes easier to pick waste from there. As you can see, engineering is part and parcel of this. Wherever there are human beings, solid waste is being generated. I see the engineer as having a clear role to play in this shelter setting, and he cannot just distance himself and say, I'm only constructing housing schemes. We are inside this shelter theme, part and parcel. I'm not going to the person living in that shelter experience to get money from him and say, we want to build you something, it is the state that is responsible for building the required sanitary facilities and providing the needed sanitary services.

Marlene

When it comes to vocabulary, you need to use some words. I have not found the right answer in architecture on how to talk, what words to use: slum, shelter, shack. So, I was quite surprised, when I looked up academic work of development studies hoping to find an answer. But no, there is also no certainty about the wording, so maybe we as practitioners do not have to worry too much. But I think it's very interesting, also for me, more between North and South, not so much between disciplines. For example, in the collaboration with European architecture universities. The students wanted to call the project "We build a school for Africa." Most were fine with that slogan but I was not because we built one classroom for one village in South Africa and, of course, one cannot claim to build a school for Africa, the whole continent.

In the South African university context, when I went to doctoral seminars at Witwatersrand University people were also discussing, "how can we call a township?" because this is also not the best term. Okay, I thought, so the local academic experts also don't know. Next day, I was on the construction site, and it was really nice to take the university discussion onto the construction site, over lunchtime, discussing how to call a township. The community construction team did not like the term township; they liked location much more, which from my perspective would be much worse. So, the terminology I use is something I try to do very hands-on again. I feel that in discourse in architecture "slum" is okay to use. For me, in my thesis, I created for myself the category "non-formal" because informal is normal and is everywhere, it's just not formally accepted but it's not something extra, it's interwoven into everything. I don't like the word informal. I was actually getting on everybody's nerves for being the 'word police' on the construction site. But in practice, on a construction site, you can hardly discuss these things. So, either you make something up, or everybody lives with it, or you use something that everybody understands. But that is also the nice thing on the construction-site again. To do something interdisciplinary, cross-culturally with your hands, you learn a different way of communication. Then the word is really not important anymore, it is a code of profession, not of culture anymore.

Frustrations and breaking points

Notwithstanding meticulous planning, best intentions, careful and lengthy preparations, involvement of communities, and protracted discussions with stakeholders, something always goes wrong on the construction site, in the implementation phase of the project. The discrepancies between theory and practice, between provision and planning on the one side and implementation and building on the other, have been frequently discussed in academic literature on housing. When, where, how, and why do disruptions and wrongs happen according to the practitioners? Are these more likely to happen during one particular stage of the process than the other? And can someone be held accountable?

Nicholas
I can hardly imagine that there could be one single answer to this, but there are many contributing factors. For me, first of all, it is the conception of a project. Who decides that this project is important? Is it the technicians? Is it engineers sitting in the office and saying, "oh, it is important that we build a dam?" Or is it a voice from the people, from the grassroots, that people say, "we need a bridge, we need to cross from this river bank to the other?" Because where the project initiative is coming from is actually a decisive factor in making the project a success. That is one point. The second point is the political will. You know, projects will not just happen unless politicians say yes. Because elected politicians are the ones who actually approve the funds to be disbursed to realize infrastructure projects. So, the politicians also need to have an awareness of the importance of the infrastructure being constructed. They need to be integrated in these projects. And the politicians have their own interests, too. For example, if he notices that a planned road will not pass where his voters are living, he may not support its construction. Thirdly, there is the aspect of us technicians ourselves: not accepting that a technician's or an engineer's knowledge is not enough to realize a project in its entirety. I may need to work with sociologists, professionals who have knowledge of demographics, who can inform us, say, about demographic trends for the next five, ten years. They could be telling us: we think people are going to live more in one area than another. In my limitation, I may just sit down at my drawing board as an engineer and say, "from the engineering point of view, this or that is the best route," but maybe the people with knowledge on demographics can tell me, "actually in the next fifteen years that area is less likely to be preferred for habitation, most people are going to move to a different area. So, find a solution to design the planned road with that information in mind." This is my message to, engineers: let's open up, let's work more with other disciplines.

Another aspect is that in the construction undertaking most actors tend to maximize their gain. For instance, if somebody knows that his property has a certain measurement he is inclined to use all that space, to build as many housing units as possible. For the sake of maximizing his profit. And in that regard other aspects that are important to tenants, such as "where do we hang our clothes to dry" may not receive adequate consideration by the property developers. Or, say, what about lighting during the day? There are actually some places, some rooms, that are always dark. People using those rooms must always switch on artificial light during the day to be able to access such rooms. Perhaps this is the face of greed: the drive to maximize personal profit at the expense of creating a humane shelter experience. I have regrettably observed that, sometimes, when property developers realize they could make an extra Euro at the expense of guaranteeing, for example, ample daylight for the houses under construction, they are willing to choose the option that ensures their personal gain. The option seems attractive to them as long as they are not the ones to occupy the houses. . ..

Marlene
Where do things go wrong? In communication! That happens at every step. I would definitely say in communication and in the transfer of information, even within the same discipline. It is really not just the theory and practice, but it happens at every step. It's the change of media, every time you change media, which is the communication, if from the first idea... followed by sketch, then you start to draw something, then you draw an actual plan, which changes again everything, then you build a model, so every time you change the media, you translate the meaning and the idea. Then you have to prepare a detailed plan and it changes again and to translate this drawing into a real thing, it changes again... Even if it is just one person who builds his entire house by himself, the construction – the implementation of an idea into reality – keeps changing in translation.

Nicholas
Unfortunately, I have observed several cases of dishonesty in construction. The level of trust between the main decision-makers is at times very low, and fairness in the face of unexpected outcomes is not really practiced. How I wish I could hear something like, "okay, that risk happened, it cost you a lot of money, let me compensate you." The reaction I encounter more often could be verbalized, "let me save myself," so self-interest becomes the order of the day, and when everybody has self-interests to protect, then we always have a conflict potential. And the risk we all feared most, that the cost of the project will exceed our budget, ultimately eventuates, because we now have to engage lawyers. And lawyers cost a fee. We end up going to court, where the judge says, "first of all you must stop the construction work." The construction site becomes an exhibit for the judicial proceedings. While the construction has been halted, the money lent by credit institutions to finance the project is still accruing interest. So, we are not building at the moment, because we are stuck in court, fighting each other. And when we go to the construction records, we find that we have court cases that have taken ten, fifteen years, even twenty to be settled. And it's often taxpayers' money that foots the bill arising from such legal proceedings.

Marlene
Housing construction in South Africa (as in postwar Austria) is an economic machine; it supports the economy by implementing people's dream and life goal of

owning a house. I did my thesis on Cosmo City, a satellite city of Johannesburg.[6] In construction, the more mass production, the cheaper it gets. It's money; the construction business is a corrupt system everywhere... the problem is always the money, and we now even see it in Vienna. I left Vienna where there was nothing going on; now we have a large need for housing people again, we would actually need to build 20,000 flats every six months to house all the people in Vienna. So, there is now a completely new dynamic in the housing market or housing construction in Vienna. You could also say what a great chance to change things, but, again, it has to happen so fast and as cheap as possible that, of course, the quality gets corrupted. It is easier to go for the known system instead of alternatives of material, construction process or ownership. It is very clear for the government where the money goes, it is very clear for the construction company as well.

When working together with Austrian and South African universities on the design-build projects I really try to include self-reflection into my courses after a field trip. With students we did little exercises, to find out where decisions were made, to reflect on the whole exercise after the process had been finished. They had to summarize their experience with the design-build course, what they had done for more than a term, now that they were back from the South African construction site. And I wanted to know whether they could describe it in one word. So, one of the students said, "AFRICA". That was so disappointing for me, that was actually one of the reasons why I said I do not want to do it in this way any more. I don't want to get hundreds of Europeans to South Africa; firstly, I always have to explain and to start afresh, kind of, explain that we do not use certain words or names for people, and so on, it really started there. For me, the idea was always to show European students something different, a different way to look at the world, a different look at the North and South, different cultures, but I am afraid for many it made "Africa" even more exotic. The collaboration and exchange between Austrian and South African architecture students were much better then, because they talk the same architecture language, but if it is just the local community in a rural or poor area, the perspective of the Austrian guest does not change much – the perception of the South. It is still common belief that you go somewhere, bring your design, bring your house, your technical solution and impose, instead of listening and really collaborating.

---

6 Marlene Wagner, "A Place under the Sun for Everyone – Basis for Planning of Inclusive Urban Development and Adequate Architecture Based on the Analysis of Formal and Nonformal Spatial Practice in the Housing Development Cosmo City, Johannesburg" (Thesis, Vienna University of Technology, 2010).

I always believed these educational design-build projects need to offer a safe space to experiment. For some students it's just a nice opportunity to improve their CV, for others it is life changing (points to herself). The same is the case for local community members of the construction team. For many it's just a well-paid job, a very friendly environment to work in but nothing further, and for others, they stay in construction or they open up their own company where they apply their skills. So, there are very individual experiences. But for me, the South-North cooperation was not fulfilling anymore with the universities or architecture school, because they did not change their systems of delivering the building. The whole construction process is great, but it's always new European students while the local people already have a lot of knowledge which makes it really difficult to move forward.

Spaces in-between and perspectives from afar

Last but not least, we were eager to find out more about the personal experiences of our interview partners. They both travelled in-between spaces. They left their ordinary environments and searched for more knowledge and skills in different contexts. Nicholas, a Kenyan in Germany; Marlene, an Austrian in South Africa. From hindsight, how do they look back on South African and Kenyan construction sites from afar, incorporating their know-how from abroad? What lessons did they learn from people on the spot in their immediate surroundings? And, through their extensive experience and close contact with local communities, were they able to find out what people really want with regard to housing?

Marlene
That is difficult… the South African wants something different, and even the rural South African wants something different. It's so much more the local context again, that I would never ever, how could you say, make a global manual on how to build. Of course, you look at the general climate, but then you also have to look at the microclimate: it makes a difference if there is a lake, a city or woods. If it's good architecture, it takes a very close look at the context, on the user and on what people want. Of course, in the context as a European going with money to the South, it is very hard to hear what people want. I think that generally in South Africa, because of the traditional round hut and the climate, life happens a lot more outside. So, it is about the space between the buildings, something we should look at in more detail and take better care of, also in Europe – the shared public or semi-public space. Also because of our culture, and the temperature, we have cold winters, people spend much more time inside, but still it is the quality of the shared space that should receive much more attention. In South Africa, for me the number one is the

climate; it is easier to build. I think in Austria it will soon be harder to build. If you get these extreme summers and extreme winters, you have to build something that works fine in both conditions. Besides, the family structures change, we have only single people living in bachelor flats now, we do not have the big families anymore. I am sure that is also changing in African countries. And there is also always the representative porch and fence, that's a suburban issue. That is in Lower Austria the same as in Cosmo City in Johannesburg, that you have the representative aspect.

And the lessons learned?

Uuh, that is a tough one. In general, I think what I learned from the people on the spot, my work, and from having lived in South Africa... I do not know where it comes from, from the construction site or maybe from poverty, maybe it is poverty that makes you more flexible, and more adaptive and more willing to find a quick solution, improvisation and these things. That is definitely what I have learned, how I work and how I improvise now. There is anyway not the one right way of doing things... maybe that also comes from the very informal context as much as from the construction site, that there is not one procedure, there is ten different ones, so nobody will even tell you, do this. In Austria, maybe you have a plan B, but in general we have, this is the only way and bureaucracy, and as long as you do this and bring this, it will work out somehow finally. This is not the case in South Africa, there is no safety net, it can always change, you always have ten different plans, and you improvise you negotiate, and you balance. We will have to look at these skills much more here.

Nicholas
In Kenya, just like in Germany, engineers do place great emphasis on administering so-called watertight contracts that legally bind the parties involved in realizing the project. Such contracts work on a strict reward-and-sanction basis. It is my view that the parties to a contract need to agree about what is to be constructed, and have the agreement documented. This agreement should then serve them as a guide during project execution. However, overreliance on watertight contracts represents, for me, a tendency among engineers to place trust on fixed structures to regulate the construction undertaking. At times I have the impression that engineers assign the construction contract the role of autopilot for the infrastructure project. When this becomes the case a construction contract becomes a kind of formula, like the many I memorized in college, only that this version of formula contains many clauses and legal jargon. From my experience, conflicts on the construction

site are far from being banished by cleverly formulated contracts. I have been on sites where project participants successfully realized projects despite the construction work being administered by contracts with loopholes. In the same vein, I have been engaged in projects with watertight contracts, having minimal gray areas, if any, yet these same projects were often interrupted by court injunctions. In between these diametrically opposed outcomes on site, I am learning that project realization is dependent on the commitment of those involved to cultivate and practice a culture that preserves the life of the construction project. Whenever I image culture, I see people. The human element is at the core of every project. The success or failure of the project depends on the culture that the project participants involved choose to practice, regardless of the country in which they are executing the project. I imagine that this observation would apply for housing projects, too.

And the lessons learned?

A game changer for me has been nurturing an awareness of the construction project as a living entity. The project has life because of all the people who take part in it, actively or passively. All the persons who effect or are affected by the project breathe life into it. The project first lives in the human mind and is then birthed on the construction site. The state of a construction project reflects the prevailing relations among all persons involved, the project initiators and the intended beneficiaries. Engineers can erect the most robust houses possible, but only when the needs of the dwellers are addressed will the houses be transformed into homes that shelter. Formulas are all good and have their place in the engineer's life; however, we cannot talk with numbers. Numbers can only tell us so much. We as engineers need to develop an awareness for social competences to complement the technical ones that our training endowed us with. It is time to mindfully look around us and begin talking with other project participants who represent other disciplines. I imagine a better life for construction projects if we all work together.

We wish to express our deep gratitude to Marlene Wagner and Nicholas Sungura for their openness and willingness to share their professional experiences with us.

References

Hay, Allison, and Richard Harris. "'Shauri Ya Sera Kali': The Colonial Regime of Urban Housing in Kenya." *Urban History* 34 (2007): 504–530.

Lea, Tess, and Paul Pholeros. "This is Not a Pipe: The Treacheries of Indigenous Housing." *Public Culture* 22 (2010): 187–209.

Sungura, Nicholas. "Der Faktor Mensch bei der Risikosteuerung öffentlicher Bauvorhaben in Kenia." Translated: "The Human Element in the Risk Management of Public Infrastructure Projects in Kenya." Unpublished Dr. Eng. diss., University of Hannover, 2016.

Wagner, Marlene. "A Place under the Sun for Everyone – Basis for Planning of Integrative Urban Development and Appropriate Architecture through the Analysis of Formal and Non-formal spatial practice in the Housing Area Cosmo City, Johannesburg." Unpublished thesis, Vienna University of Technology, 2010.

List of Contributors

Martina Barker-Ciganikova is currently a post-doc researcher at the University of Vienna. She holds MAs in African Studies, Social and Cultural Anthropology and International Development. She conducted her PhD (2010) within the interdisciplinary research programme Vienna School of Governance. She has been teaching courses on democratisation, political and electoral systems, governance and development cooperation since 2007. She has extensive work experience in various international organisations, such as the OSCE, the EU, and the UN in the fields of democracy/electoral support and governance. Studying housing, Martina has discovered an additional research interest. She applies governance, both as a concept and as an analytical tool, to analyse housing in all its variety and multiplicity.

Liora Bigon is an urban (planning) historian. A Senior Staff Member in HIT – Holon Institute of Technology, she specializes in (post)colonial urban history and planning cultures in sub-Saharan Africa, with an emphasis on West Africa. She has published widely in these fields, including articles, books, and edited collections. Among the latter are: *Garden Cities and Colonial Planning in Africa and Palestine* (Manchester University Press, 2014); *French Colonial Dakar* (Manchester University Press, 2016); *Gridded Worlds: An Urban Anthology* (with R. Rose-Redwood, Springer, 2018); and *Grid Planning in the Urban Design Practices of Senegal* (with E. Ross, Springer, 2020).

Carl-Philipp Bodenstein studied African studies and social anthropology at the University of Vienna. Within the current project on "Employment-tied housing in (post)colonial Africa" he has been working as a research fellow (pre-doc) on the Zambian case study (Livingstone) and is currently writing his PhD thesis. His research focuses on spatial history and the historical geography of urban spaces.

Sofie Boonen graduated as an engineer-architect at Ghent University in 2009 with a dissertation on the urban form of the city of Lubumbashi, Democratic Republic of Congo. From 2009 to 2013 she worked as the main researcher on a 4-year research project, financed by the Flemish Research Fund, entitled "City, architecture and colonial space in Matadi and Lubumbashi, Congo. A historical analysis from a translocal perspective." In June 2015, she joined the Brussels-based architectural office DDS+ where she is in charge of the firm's external communication. In 2019, Sofie Boonen obtained a PhD-degree from Ghent University with a dissertation on Lubumbashi's colonial urban history. Together with Johan Lagae she has published several book chapters and articles in international academic journals on the architectural and urban history of Lubumbashi and presented papers at several international conferences. With Johan Lagae, she has also contributed to art exhibitions, mainly in collaboration with Congolese artists Sammy Baloji and Patrick Mudekereza.

Donatien Dibwe dia Mwembu is a historian with a doctoral degree from the Université Laval in Quebec, Canada. He is currently Professor of History in the Department of Historical Sciences at the University of Lubumbashi (DR Congo). Since 1990, he has been interested in social history, especially urban popular cultures. In collaboration with Bogumil Jewsiewicki, he leads the *Lubumbashi Memorial Project*, of which he is a chairperson of the local scientific committee. He is also director-coordinator of the *Observatory of Urban Change*, research center of the University of Lubumbashi and has an extensive publishing record.

Johan Lagae is Full Professor at Ghent University teaching 20th Architectural History with a particular focus on the non-European context. He received an MSc Degree in Engineering: Architecture from Ghent University in 1991 and obtained a PhD degree with a dissertation on 20th-century colonial architecture in the former Belgian Congo from the same institute in 2002. In autumn 2007, he resided as a *Chercheur invité de la Fondation de France* at the *Institut National de l'Histoire de l'Art* in Paris and from September 2019 till January 2020 he was a fellow at the *Institut des Études Avancées* in Paris. His current research interests are colonial and postcolonial architecture in (Central) Africa, African urban history, colonial photography and colonial built heritage. Between 2010 and 2014 he acted as co-chair of a European Community funded COST-action entitled 'European Architecture beyond Europe' (www.architecturebeyond.eu), and is co-founder and editorial board member and since June 2019 co-editor of *ABE journal* (http://journals.openedition.org/abe/). He has published widely in edited volumes and international journals such as *Third Text*, *Journal of Architecture*, *Cahiers africains*, *Photography & Culture* and co-authored several books and journal issues, among others for the architectural journal OASE. He is also active as a curator and has contributed to several acclaimed, Congo/Africa-related exhibitions, such as *The Memory of Congo. The Colonial Era* (Tervuren, 2005), *Congo belge en images* (2010) and, most recently, *À chacun sa maison. Housing in the Belgian Congo 1945–1960* (Brussels, 2018).

Martina Kopf is Senior Lecturer in African Literatures at the Department of African Studies, University of Vienna (Austria) and Elise Richter-Fellow with a project on "Concepts of development in postcolonial Kenyan literature." Her work focusses on African literature and (post-)development thought; postcolonial feminisms; memories of violence and the ethics of representation. She has published in peer-reviewed journals and books, including the *Routledge Handbook of African Literature*, the *Journal of Commonwealth Literature*, the *Journal of Literary Theory*, *Stichproben – Vienna Journal of African Studies* and *Matatu – Journal for African Culture and Society*.

Ambe Njoh is a Professor of Environmental Science and Policy in the School of Geosciences at the University of South Florida, Tampa, Florida, USA. His academic and professional background is in urban planning and international development. He has written extensively on these and related subjects. In this regard, he is the author of eleven books, more than a hundred peer-reviewed articles, book chapters, technical reports, and papers in scholarly and professional conference proceedings. His most recent book, *Nature in the Built Environment* is in-press at Springers Publishers and slated for release in March 2020. He is a 2019/2020 recipient of the United States Ambassador's Distinguished Scholars Program (ADSP) Fellowship, and on assignment at Mekelle University in Ethiopia.

Kirsten Rüther holds the professorship of African History and Societies at the University of Vienna's African Studies Department. After a longstanding interest in issues of Christianization and colonialism, and apart from an ongoing interest in studies of kinship, biography and family history, she has identified a further research interest in the study of African cities, more particularly housing. Her empirical research area is Southern Africa. Within the current housing research project she focuses on Lusaka and Livingstone, Zambia, and, as Principal Investigator, is responsible for the overall coherence between the three sub-projects. She supervises several doctoral theses (on other topics than housing) and is keen to link teaching in BA and MA curricula to this project's research focus.

Nicholas Sungura is a civil engineer with a doctoral degree from the Leibniz University of Hannover, Germany. He works in teams realizing public infrastructure projects in Kenya, and in Germany. He has a special interest in geotechnics and in the social dimension of infrastructure projects. He periodically contributes articles on geotechnics. He is currently researching on the nature of interpersonal bridges in Scrum Teams realizing railway projects in Germany.

Marlene Wagner graduated with distinction in architecture studies at Vienna University of Technology. She is a founding member of the not for profit organization buildCollective for Architecture and Development. In collaboration with international NGOs, universities, grassroots organizations and diverse public and private stakeholders, she realized a large number of educational buildings, social and technical infrastructure, art and public space projects as well as organizational and educational development frameworks. She spent seven years in South Africa where she worked on projects, taught and conducted research. She established collaborative partnerships with institutions and organizations in Germany, Italy, England, Switzerland, Slovenia, USA, Tanzania and Kenya. Besides her PhD studies and cultural projects, she is a project assistant in an Urban Mobility Lab at Vienna UT. Marlene works, teaches and does research on social architecture, formal and non-formal spatial practices, critical spatial production, transformative process, methods, mediation and participation of design between local and global scale. www.marlenewagner.online, www.buildcollective.net

Daniela Waldburger holds a PhD (2012) in African Studies from the University of Vienna. Earlier she studied Social Anthropology, African Linguistics and General Linguistics at the University of Zurich. Since 2004 she has been teaching Swahili and Linguistics (sociolinguistics, language and power, discourse analysis, visual grammar etc.) at the Department of African Studies. Beside her research interests in Swahili Studies she has a strong research interest in the intertwining fields of language (mis)use and power (ab)use.

Index

absenteeism 26, 179
acculturation 180
administration 2, 8, 23, 33–35, 37–38, 42, 44–45, 54–55, 59, 69, 72, 74, 79, 133, 150, 164, 170, 184
advisory boards and committees 7, 32
– Housing Area Boards 53, 63
– Township Management Board 35, 57–59,
– Urban Advisory Board 38
African Fruit Company 170
African Housing Ordinance 32, 34, 39
African quarters (African areas) 13, 35, 53, 69
African Urban Advisory Council 50
agricultural production 68
agriculture 18, 42, 169–170
amenities 31, 48, 56, 151, 173
apartheid 44, 89, 121, 128, 168, 183, 193, 200–201
appropriation 1, 16, 21–22, 24, 86, 93–94, 101, 120
architects 17, 69, 75, 85, 91–92, 94, 142, 186, 189, 192–193, 195–196, 200, 202, 205, 207
archival records 21
artisans 11, 47, 49
Asian 10, 36, 168, 181, 183–184
Atkinson, George 10, 34, 63
Austria 186, 188, 201, 204, 206, 211, 214, 218
autobiography 47–48, 51, 65

bachelor housing. *See* housing categories
backyard shack. *See* housing categories
Bakweri 170
barrack 17, 22, 26, 28, 176
bathroom 109–111, 115, 117, 156, 208
becoming urban dweller V, 22–23, 31–32, 36–37
bedroom VII, 83, 89, 172
Belgian VII, 4, 23, 25–26, 66–71, 75–76, 84, 89, 93, 95–96, 141–150, 152–155, 159, 162–166, 218

– belge 67–69, 72–73, 91, 96–97, 125–128, 133–134, 139–140, 142, 150, 153, 165–166, 218
Belgium 3, 67, 75, 85, 143, 145, 147, 163–164
Bentham, Jeremy 168
bidonvilles 66, 68
Bismarck 169
Bordeaux 92
Boudon, Philippe 24, 67, 92–93, 95
boycott 23, 36, 64, 115
boyerie. *See* housing categories
brick house. *See* housing categories
British South Africa Company (BSAC) 34
Brown Report 44, 54, 57
Brussels 19, 67–69, 72–73, 77, 79–80, 84–87, 94–97, 143–144, 150, 163–166, 217–218
buffer zone 72, 146
building materials 14, 20, 176, 180, 190, 195, 200, 206
– aluminium 177
– brick 51, 201, 206
– concrete/ cement VI, 108, 141–142, 161, 177, 179, 185, 187, 189, 191, 193, 195, 197, 199, 201, 203, 205–207, 209, 211, 213, 215
– corrugated iron 51, 201, 205
– steel 177, 198, 205–206,
– straw-clay 205–206,
– wattle (and daub) 9, 111, 205
– wood 161, 213
Building Research Station 19, 34
building standard 42
Bujumbura 66, 69
Bulawayo 37, 65
bungalow 172

Cameroon V, 4, 8, 22, 26, 167–172, 174–176, 179–184
Cameroon Development Corporation (CDC) V, VIII, 26, 167–168, 171–183

camp de travailleur. *See* housing categories
casual labor. *See* labor
central Africa 34, 40, 45, 63–64, 66, 68, 95, 143, 164
Central African Council 34
Central African Federation 37, 40, 44, 52, 54, 62
Centre extra-coutumier 72, 75, 96, 124, 129–130, 150, 165
cité frugès 24, 67, 92
cité indigène VII, 70, 73, 77, 124, 126, 130, 153
citizens 8, 26, 32, 41, 44–45, 57, 205
civil resistance 4, 53, 65, 110
civil servant 15, 37, 39, 43–44, 46–50, 57–58, 61
civil service 47, 57–58, 60, 63, 189
civil unrest 36
class 2–3, 8, 13–15, 19, 24, 26–28, 30, 33, 37, 41, 57, 65, 81, 103, 108, 117, 137, 148, 173, 181, 185, 192–193, 204, 206
– African class 27
– class distinction 103
– class position 37, 57
– middle class 8, 13, 26, 30, 41, 117
– political class 19
– working class 14–15, 27
cleanliness 25, 141
clinics 51, 173
– hospital 35, 47, 141, 146–147, 161, 172–173
club house 172–173
Colonial Development and Welfare Act 31, 172
Colonial Housing Research Group 34
Colonial Office 10, 34, 44–45, 55, 57, 63, 170, 184
colonial state V, 1–2, 7–8, 11, 16–17, 21, 23, 25–27, 31–32, 40–42, 52, 62, 141–146, 149–154, 162–163, 167, 182
color bar 37, 53
colored people 169
communal facilities 208
communication 16–17, 25, 39, 123, 142–144, 185, 202, 209, 211, 217
community 1–2, 17, 22, 25, 54, 68, 72, 76, 146, 185, 190–192, 196–199, 202, 204–206, 208–209, 212–213, 218

Compagnie de chemin de fer du Bas-Congo (BCK) 128, 130–131, 135
company town 26, 167–168, 172–173, 176–184
construction project 186–191, 202–203, 215
construction site 21–22, 103–105, 185, 187, 190, 192–193, 196, 198, 202–203, 209, 211–215
construction worker 103
control IV–V, 4, 6–9, 14, 16, 18, 22, 26, 29, 41, 43, 45, 54, 74, 76, 103–104, 109, 145, 147, 155, 161–162, 167–169, 171, 173, 175, 177–179, 181–184, 192
– colonial control 7, 171
– social control V, 18, 29, 167–169, 171, 173, 175, 177–179, 181–184,
– state control 6
cooking 12, 20, 85, 142, 158, 161, 180
Copperbelt 8, 31, 34, 40–41, 58, 63–65, 145
cordon sanitaire 70, 96, 127, 141, 146
Costains 177–178, 181
council 7, 10, 12–14, 21, 27, 34–35, 37, 43–44, 46–47, 50–51, 53–56, 59, 61, 63, 105–106, 110, 149, 161
Crown territory 170

De Meulder, Bruno 68–70, 80, 86, 89, 91, 95
De Schiervel, Xavier Lejeune 68–69, 79, 82–83, 96
democracy 201, 217
Democratic Republic of Congo 3–4, 6, 217
– République Démocratique du Congo 80, 94–96, 123
demolition 207
Department of Local Government and Social Welfare 45
design V, VII, 14, 16, 28, 36, 64, 66–67, 69–70, 79, 81–82, 84–85, 92–94, 142, 145, 163, 168, 177, 180, 184–186, 188–189, 191–201, 203–205, 208, 210, 212–213, 217, 219
design-build 185–186, 191–192, 199, 204, 212–213
development
– capitalist development 24, 99, 103, 107, 110
– colonial development 31, 172, 178

– development discourse 27
– development funds 204
– development industry 100–101, 112
– development studies 100
– economic development 7, 23, 66, 68, 150, 167
– housing development. *See* housing
– industrial development 18
– infrastructure development. *See* infrastructure
– urban development 5–6, 8, 12, 18–19, 24, 27, 35, 65, 99–102, 118, 145, 165, 180, 183, 212, 216
direct representation 52–53, 56
discipline 1, 4, 15, 25, 76, 156–157, 162, 168–169, 185, 187–191, 193, 196, 203, 209–211, 215
disease 99, 106, 208
– sickness 39
displaced persons 170
domestic servant 12–13, 155
domestiques 124–126
domination 22, 40, 180
dweller V, 4–6, 14–16, 20–23, 27, 31–33, 36–37, 42–44, 46, 50, 53, 69, 113, 141, 185, 205, 208, 215. *See also* inhabitant

economy 7, 10, 14, 36, 40, 45, 62, 64, 67, 98, 102, 107, 146, 166, 202, 211
– cash economy 7
– colonial economy 62
– low-wage economy 10, 14, 40, 45
education 19, 29, 46–47, 51, 53, 69, 144, 147, 149, 153, 172, 186, 198
election 32, 36, 53, 59
Elisabethville V, VII–VIII, 6, 22, 25, 68, 70, 72–75, 77, 80, 82, 86, 96, 121–129, 131, 133–137, 139–141, 144–147, 150, 155, 161, 164–165. *See also* Lubumbashi
emancipation 1, 7, 23, 85
employee VIII, 9–13, 15, 26, 34, 42, 51, 55, 59–60, 63, 65, 85, 91, 104, 110, 147, 151, 155, 163, 168, 172–175, 179–180, 182
employer V, 1–2, 9, 11–13, 15–17, 22–23, 25, 31–32, 34, 37–43, 45, 47, 55–57, 60–62, 64, 75, 147, 149, 155
Employment of Natives Ordinance 39, 60

encampment 170
engineer 18, 22, 33, 38–39, 45–46, 142, 152, 156, 185–191, 193–197, 202–203, 206–208, 210, 214–215, 217, 219
engineering V, 14, 18, 23, 25–26, 45–46, 67, 85, 91, 141–143, 145, 147, 149, 152, 158–159, 163, 165, 167, 185–191, 193–194, 197, 202, 206, 208, 210, 218
enterprise 2, 28, 39–40, 67–69, 85, 93, 173, 178
entitlement 16, 31, 42, 44, 47, 57
eurocentrism 5, 26, 167, 180–181, 207
Europeans 34–35, 40, 47, 50, 58–59, 68, 70, 145, 149, 158, 169, 181–182, 198, 204, 212
– European housing. *See* housing
– European staff 32
eviction 9, 20, 36, 107
exploitation 6, 128, 131, 134, 183

family
– family housing. *See* housing categories
– family income 107, 199
– family life 41, 85, 148
– family quarters 13
– family relations 7
– nuclear family 23, 85–86, 149, 181, 194
– worker's family 10
farmers 7, 34, 41
fee 35, 56–57, 60, 211
Fiction (novel) V, 6, 24, 98–120
finance 11, 17, 45, 58–59, 104, 106, 211
flat. *See* housing categories
Foucault, Michel 168, 179, 182–183
foyer social 76, 85, 96, 148, 165
France 6–8, 28, 94, 97, 121, 171, 218
franchise 42, 53–54, 61–62
funding 81, 190, 201–202
– funds 15, 34, 45, 55, 61, 199, 204, 210
furniture 49, 105, 156–158

garage 107–108, 172
garden 18, 26, 28, 79, 82, 89, 142, 148, 156, 172–173, 217
– orchard 172
gatekeeper state 16

Gécamines 128, 131, 135–139, 143, 147, 151, 156, 165
gender 2, 4, 7, 24, 27–29, 38, 49, 65, 88, 98–99, 103, 113–114, 117–120
German 169–171
Global South 98, 103, 204
golf course 173
governance 3, 19, 29, 37, 64, 68, 99, 207, 217
gridiron layout 176
– grid-pattern 73, 77

habitat V, 18, 29, 91, 100, 107, 112, 120–121, 123, 125, 127–129, 131, 133–135, 137–139, 170, 184. See also housing
hawker 13, 105, 113
head tax 181
health V, 1, 12, 14, 18, 25, 29, 39, 72, 106, 141–143, 145, 147, 149, 151–157, 159–163, 165, 168, 172, 182–183, 199, 208
– healthcare 8, 147, 173, 198
– santé 127, 154
health office 12
high-density 19, 21
hinterland 67, 171
Holforth Company 170
home-ownership 11, 15, 36, 46, 57, 61–62, 69, 75, 108, 199, 212
homelessness 118
hospital. See clinics
household 14, 22–24, 56, 67, 85, 103–107, 110, 112–113, 117–118, 142–143, 159
housewife 76, 84–85, 117, 158–159
housing
– European housing 47
– housing allowance 10, 40, 56–57,
– housing development 201, 212
– housing provision 1, 10, 13, 35
– housing shortage 10, 12, 17, 85, 199
– logement 68, 83–84, 96, 121, 132–133, 135–137, 158
– maison VII, 79–80, 82–85, 91, 125–126, 130, 132–133, 135–138, 143–144, 152, 154–156, 158, 165, 218
housing categories
– bachelor housing 11, 146, 214
– backyard shack 200

– boyerie 125
– brick house 201
– camp de travailleur 128, 130–132, 136, 138
– family housing 11, 41
– flat 104–105, 109–110, 116, 201, 212, 214
– free house 200–201,
– municipal housing 11–12, 40
– permanent housing / les camps permanents 11, 26, 31, 50, 133
– self-help housing 11, 51
– servants' quarter 172
– shelter 2, 23, 29, 85, 105–106, 152, 207–208, 210, 215
– single-family home 17, 28, 67, 85, 91
– two-story house VII, 82, 88
– unauthorized housing/ settlement 16, 42, 62–63,
– workers' camp V, 25–26, 69, 91, 146, 148, 167, 172–173, 182
– workers' housing 150, 156, 163, 172–173
Huxtable, Ada Louise 92, 96
hygiene V, 18–19, 25, 141–143, 145–147, 149, 151–157, 159–163, 165
hygiénique 133, 138

Idenau 178
income VIII, 2, 11, 14–15, 24, 29, 59–61, 99–101, 104, 106–107, 113–114, 117–118, 173–174, 176, 179–182, 195, 199–201, 204–205
independence 6, 8, 19–21, 24–25, 27, 32, 36–37, 44, 51–52, 58–59, 62, 65, 80, 86, 89, 91, 101, 103, 110, 189
Indian 13, 36, 43, 100, 108–109, 169
industrial worker. See worker
inequality 4, 19, 29, 33, 47–48, 98, 100, 103, 113, 120, 144, 166
informal structure 23, 67, 91
infrastructure VII, 1, 6–7, 18–19, 43, 46, 53, 55, 69, 78, 87, 89, 91, 93, 98, 132, 150, 160–161, 185–187, 189–190, 198, 202–204, 206, 210, 214, 216, 219
– basic infrastructure 93
– informal infrastructure VII, 87
– infrastructure development 185–187, 189
– infrastructure project 6, 150, 185–186, 190, 203–204, 210, 214, 216, 219

– material infrastructure 46
– physical infrastructure 6
– public infrastructure 69, 185–186, 190, 198, 206, 216, 219
– rail infrastructure 186
– road infrastructure VII, 78
inhabitant VII, 4, 21, 23–24, 67–70, 74–76, 78, 80, 82, 84–86, 88, 91–94, 150, 153–154, 185. *See also* dweller
interdisciplinary VI, 3, 22, 85, 185–191, 193, 195–197, 199, 201, 203, 205, 207, 209, 211, 213, 215, 217
International Labor Organization (ILO) 141

Jantzen und Thormalen 171
Johannesburg 5, 29, 118, 205, 212, 214, 216

Katanga V, 6, 8, 19, 25, 70, 72, 93, 96–97, 121, 123–126, 128, 130–136, 138–141, 144–147, 149–151, 153, 156–158, 160, 163–166
Keka/ Tiko 170, 177–178, 181
Kenya VII, 2–5, 7–13, 15, 22, 24, 27–29, 36, 70, 72–74, 93, 95, 101, 103, 108, 113–114, 123–124, 130, 186, 189–190, 201–202, 214–216, 219
Kibera 100, 111–112
Kikuyu 14
Kinshasa 66, 68–70, 72, 80, 86, 91, 95–97, 124, 159, 166
Kisangani 66, 68–69, 72, 86, 88, 91, 96
Kisumu 10–11, 27
kitchen VII, 83, 85, 158, 162–163, 172, 180
Koutaba 179, 183

la maison extensible 82, 91
– expanding house 82
labor 1, 4, 6–9, 11, 14–16, 24–25, 28, 31–32, 39–41, 51, 55–57, 65, 102, 110, 141, 149, 151, 159, 165, 183
– casual labor 14
– labor aristocracy 1
– wage labor 7–8, 15, 28
laborer. *See* worker
land grabbing 171
landlord 2, 10, 23, 36, 43, 104–105, 109–110

language V, 3, 5, 25, 46–47, 51, 100, 120, 141–142, 144, 153, 166, 207, 212, 219
– language usage V, 25, 141–142, 207
latrine. *See* toilet
Le Corbusier 24, 67, 92–96
League of Nations 171
lease 42, 59–60, 63
Lefebvre, Henri 93
Legislative Council 7, 46–47, 51, 53–56, 59, 61
liberalization 7
Limbe 34, 177–178
Livingstone 3, 13, 21, 32, 42, 45, 47, 50–51, 57, 63, 217–218
loans 31, 35, 40
local knowledge 193
loitering 179
London 4–5, 13, 18–19, 28–29, 34–35, 37, 44–45, 48, 64–65, 98, 100, 102, 114, 118–120, 167–168, 170, 183–184
low-income VIII, 24, 100–101, 113, 118, 173–174, 176, 179–182
Lubumbashi V, VII–VIII, 3, 6, 22–23, 25, 66–70, 72–76, 79–80, 84, 86, 88–89, 91, 93–97, 121–129, 131–133, 135–141, 144–147, 150, 156, 165–166, 217–218. *See also* Elisabethville
Lusaka 3, 15, 28, 34–37, 41–43, 48, 51, 57, 59–60, 62, 64–65, 102, 120, 218

maintenance 14, 168, 192, 199–200
maison à étage 80, 84
malaria 25, 72, 127
Malonda 131, 135
mapping 80, 88, 100, 119
Mau Mau 7
medical facility 76, 172
memoirs 48, 50–51, 64
meters 25, 56, 72, 110, 145
– metering 56
metropolis 2–3, 5, 15, 17, 20, 29, 144, 163
middle class. *See* class
migrant 14–15, 28, 86, 110, 118, 123, 132
migration 2, 24, 67, 110, 145, 165
military 18, 26, 176, 179, 183
mining VII, 17–18, 25, 40, 67, 70, 73, 141, 144, 146–147

mobility 3, 8–9, 20, 49, 105, 144, 159, 165, 219
modernism 18, 84, 92, 94
modernization 7, 97
Mombasa 8, 10, 13, 28
Mondoni 178
Mount Cameroon 170–171
municipal housing. *See* housing categories
Muyuka 178
Mwangi, Meja 65, 119–120

Nairobi V, 3, 6, 9–10, 12–15, 20, 24, 27, 36, 64, 98–105, 107–115, 117–120, 181, 184, 186
National Archives (Kew) 10, 19, 27, 34, 63, 204
native location 9, 42, 62
native town VII, 68–70, 72–74, 146
Native Urban Areas Act 121
neighborhood unit 69, 75–76, 89
Nigeria 170–171, 184
Northern Rhodesia V, 9, 17, 23, 28, 31–32, 34, 36, 40, 44–50, 53–54, 56–58, 62–64, 145–146

occupant 9, 14, 132–133, 173, 180, 195
Office des Cités Africaines (OCA) VII–VIII, 23–24, 66–71, 73, 75–77, 79–82, 84–91, 93, 95–97

Panopticon 168–169. *See also* Bentham, Jeremy
paternalism 39, 44, 62, 145, 152
– paternalistic 23, 82, 89, 150, 152–153, 162
periphery 68–69, 79, 201
– peripheral 72
Pessac V, 24, 66–67, 69, 71, 73, 75, 77, 79, 81, 83, 85, 87, 89, 91–95, 97
planner 2, 17–18, 38, 41, 46, 64, 69, 75–76, 79, 85, 91, 94, 142, 181–182, 190, 193, 199, 202
planning
– physical planning 173
– planning advisers 20
– planning authorities 31
– planning discourse 168
– planning ideas 5
– planning legislation 46
– planning policies 70, 169, 183
– planning principles 76
– planning process 75
– planning professions 45
– planning projects 183
– town planning 13, 18, 20, 27–28, 34, 76, 97, 167, 184
– urban planning 1, 4, 16, 18–19, 29, 46, 70, 72, 76, 81, 92, 95, 142, 146, 168–172, 176–177, 179–180, 182–184, 218
plantation 169–171, 177–178
politician 7, 13, 35, 38, 40, 46–48, 51, 65, 113, 210
polygamy 24, 105, 110, 149, 181
poverty 16, 98–99, 112, 115, 214
praxis urbaine 93
prefabrication 74
privacy 21, 26, 162
private land 205
private property 16
privatization 23
promiscuité 125, 127, 133, 136–137
property 16, 32, 36, 53–54, 61–62, 103, 108, 115, 170–171, 210
protest 7–8, 36, 147, 197
Public Works Department 12, 51, 65
Pumwani 9
Puttkamer 170

racism 44, 47, 49
– racially discriminatory legislation 44
– racist 44
railway 8, 12–13, 15, 18, 39, 41, 58, 91, 108, 178, 185–187, 190, 203, 219
rate 19, 31, 37, 42, 54, 56, 58, 68, 203
rent V, 10, 12–14, 22–23, 31–49, 51–65, 82, 104–105, 115–116, 199–201
– rent collection 43, 57, 59
– rent payment 32
– rent withholding 33, 182
– rental agreement 36
reservate 170
– locations 9, 13, 42, 62–63, 72, 144, 186
– reservations 47, 170

residence 1, 31, 37, 48, 74–75, 82
resident III, 2, 14, 16–17, 20–22, 31, 37, 53–55, 57–58, 60–61, 82, 98, 106, 112, 172–173, 178–179, 199–200
retirement 14, 39, 49
roads 16, 47, 55, 69, 76–77, 194, 203, 208
Ruashi V, VII, 23–24, 66–67, 69–73, 75–89, 91, 93–97, 123–124, 130
rural 8, 14, 16, 25, 39, 41–42, 51, 64, 68, 86, 110, 113, 198, 212–213

sanitation 16, 53, 141, 146, 166, 173, 194–195, 208
sanitation syndrome 141, 166
– syndrome sanitaire 121
satellite city 66, 69–70, 72, 212
Saxon Horf 178
security 14, 32, 57, 59, 61, 152, 179–180, 183, 199
– sécurisation 123, 133, 138
– sécuritaire 121, 123, 133–134,
– sécurité 123, 127, 134, 138
segregation 18–19, 25–26, 28, 70, 97, 108, 141–142, 169, 173, 179, 182–183
– ségrégation 70, 96, 121, 124, 128, 131, 138
– ségrégationniste 121, 123, 127–128
servants' quarters. *See* housing categories
settler 3, 7, 21, 29, 34, 38, 44–45, 54, 56–59
– settler colony 7
– settler government 3
sexual relation 4
shelter. *See* housing categories
shower 104, 107–109, 161–162, 208
sites-and-services 199. *See also* home-ownership
slum 5, 8, 16, 28, 36, 66, 99–100, 111, 119–120, 207–209
social benefit 2, 32, 41, 199
social change 4
social engineering V, 23, 25–26, 67, 85, 91, 141–143, 145, 147, 149, 152, 158–159, 163, 165, 167
social mobilization 8
social unrest 3
societal field of force V, 3, 23, 31, 33, 45, 52, 61–62

South Africa 4, 31, 34, 36, 49, 53–54, 63–64, 145, 185, 188, 191–192, 197, 200–201, 204, 206, 209, 211–214, 219
Southern Rhodesia 9, 31, 34
spatial dominance and control 18
stabilization (of labor) 16, 25, 31, 55, 123, 127, 132–133, 135–136, 141, 147, 150–151, 162
sub-economic 55
subsidization/ subsidies 46, 61
subsistence 110
supervision 26, 42, 74, 150
surveillance 3, 135, 145, 151, 162, 180, 182
Swahili 5, 105, 108, 124, 126, 135, 143–144, 151, 153–154, 165–166, 219
Système Grévisse VII, 74–75, 150

Tanzania 15, 29, 36, 64, 219
technical aspects 74, 154, 187
technical knowledge 198, 203
technician 81, 203, 210
technology 4, 28, 158, 186, 212, 216–217, 219
Ten-Year Plan for the Social and Economic Development of the Belgian Congo 68
tenant 2, 10–11, 13, 23, 36–38, 42, 45–46, 56, 59–60, 104, 107, 109–110, 112, 199–200, 210
tenant-purchase scheme 11. *See also* home-ownership
tenement housing 36
tenure 32, 35–36, 59, 61, 65, 170–172, 184
toilet VIII, 14, 26, 104–105, 107–111, 116, 161–162, 172–173, 175–176, 201, 208
– latrine 111, 172
township 1, 10, 15, 27, 35, 39, 47, 53, 55–61, 63, 118, 121, 193, 205, 209
trade union 7, 40
tribalisme 134
Tropical Building Section 19

unauthorized housing/ settlement. *See* housing categories
unemployed 13, 16, 43, 55, 121
unemployment 39, 42–43
union française 8

Union Minière du Haut-Katanga (UMHK) 19, 25–26, 123–125, 128, 130–139, 141–153, 156–165
United Nations 100, 171
unskilled worker. *See* worker
urban development. *See* development
urban life 5, 11, 24, 41, 64, 99, 202
urban novel V, 6, 98–99, 101–103, 105, 107, 109, 111, 113, 115, 117, 119
urban planning. *See* planning
urbanization 2, 5–7, 10, 19, 24, 28–29, 31, 69, 100–101, 113, 118, 178

ventilation 9, 84, 154
Vienna 3, 100, 142, 186, 191, 212, 216–219
ville blanche 123–125, 127–128, 130
ville bunkerisée (privatized environment) 89
ville européenne 72, 146
ville noire 25, 123–124, 127–128, 130, 138

wage labor. *See* labor
water 14, 26, 55–56, 60, 81, 153, 156, 161–162, 173, 189, 194–195, 198
welfare 1, 6–7, 19, 31–32, 35, 41, 43, 45, 50, 58–60, 62–63, 68, 152, 172
wife 11, 14, 34, 50, 105–106, 110–111, 114–115, 117, 142, 147–149, 154–155, 158, 163, 181
Woerman 170

women 2, 13–14, 20, 29, 37, 47, 76, 84, 86, 99–100, 106, 111, 113–114, 116–117, 120, 148, 153, 159, 161, 165, 198
worker
– contract worker 104, 109
– European worker 49
– industrial worker 10–11, 32
– laborer VIII, 1, 11, 13, 39, 42–43, 57, 69, 75, 172–173, 177, 181–182,
– low-income worker 180
– main-d'œuvre 123–124, 127–128, 130–133, 135–136,
– mine worker 6
– ouvriers 125, 128, 131–132, 137
– railway worker 13, 108
– sex worker 100, 113, 117
– travailleurs 125–126, 128, 130–140, 147, 149–151, 156–157, 165
– unskilled worker 10
– white-collar worker 13
World War I 171
World War II 151, 171, 176

Zambesi Saw Mills 39, 41
Zambia 3–4, 9, 13, 21, 31–32, 35–36, 39–41, 44, 49, 51–54, 58–59, 61–62, 64–65, 218
zone neutre 25, 123, 127–128, 145–146
zoning 45, 201